Metropolitan G‹

Canadian Cases, Comparative Lessons

THE HALBERT CENTRE FOR CANADIAN STUDIES
THE HEBREW UNIVERSITY OF JERUSALEM

THE ISRAEL ASSOCIATION FOR CANADIAN STUDIES

Metropolitan Governing:
Canadian Cases, Comparative Lessons

Edited by

Eran Razin and Patrick J. Smith

THE HEBREW UNIVERSITY MAGNES PRESS, JERUSALEM

This book is published under the auspices
of the Halbert Centre for Canadian Studies
of the Hebrew University of Jerusalem
and the Israel Association for Canadian Studies

Distributed in North America by
The University of Alberta Press
Tel +1 (780) 492-3662
Fax +1 (780) 492-0719
Email ccrooks@ualberta.ca

965–493–285–7
ISBN–13: 978–965–493–285–1

Printed in Israel

Typesetting: Ronit Goldberg

This Volume is dedicated to our colleagues who started the discussion

Professor Arie Shachar

And

Professor H. Peter Oberlander, OC

Table of contents

Acknowledgements

This book was initiated following a series of two meetings supported by a PIRL (Program for International Research Linkages) grant for a research network entitled: "The 21st Metropolitan Century" Project, Metropolitan Governance in Canada and Abroad. We thank the International Council for Canadian Studies that administered the program on behalf of Foreign Affairs Canada.

We also thank the Israel Association for Canadian Studies and the Halbert Centre for Canadian Studies – organizers of the biennial Jerusalem Conference in Canadian Studies – for supporting the second meeting of the research network that took place as part of the 8th Jerusalem Conference.

This book was long in the making – a work that took place in an extremely dynamic environment of metropolitan reforms, subsequent reforms and retreat from reforms that occurred at a much more rapid pace than anytime since the 1970s. Authors thus deserve special thanks for revising and updating their original papers – frequently more than once.

Special thanks also to Tamar Sofer for redrawing all figures and maps and to Shlomo Ketko for copy-editing all chapters. Both have contributed immensely to the quality of the outcome. Needless to say, only the co-editors are responsible for any remaining errors.

We are indebted to Professor Arie S. Shachar (Hebrew University of Jerusalem) and to Professor H. Peter Oberlander, OC (Simon Fraser University/University of British Columbia), to whom this book is dedicated. Arie S. Shachar – the founder of Israeli urban geography – has pioneered and led the study of metropolitan processes and metropolitan governance in Israel for nearly half a century. He has been central to Canadian Studies – in Israel and abroad. H. Peter Oberlander has been one of Canada's pre-eminent urbanists; he served as Canada's first Deputy-Minister of Urban Affairs. Work on Habitat I,

Vancouver 1976, and on the World Urban Forum, Vancouver 2006, are among his numerous initiatives and contributions. Shachar and Oberlander initiated the PIRL Project and have accompanied us in advice and assistance throughout the preparation of this book. Their contributions to so many who they have encouraged to follow in the study of urban matters will always serve as reminders and models of collegial academic generosity.

Part I
Introduction

ERAN RAZIN AND PATRICK J. SMITH

Metropolitan Governing: Been There, Done That, Where
Are We Now?

Objectives – been there

We have been there, many times. The metropolitan reform discourse is
not new to the public administration agenda, and confronting issues of
efficient, effective, equitable and responsive governing of expanding
urban areas has been a source of debate since cities began growing at a
rapid pace in the 19th century. It is sometimes surprising how little the
fundamental dilemmas of local government in metropolitan areas have
changed since the late 19th century, when many central cities engaged
in aggressive policies of annexation, and large-scale amalgamations
such as the formation of New York City.

Professional debates over forms of metropolitan government,
emphasizing the case against municipal fragmentation, seemed to
emerge in the 1920s and 1930s, just as the era of large-scale
annexations and consolidations was over (Paytas, 2002). The classic
work of Victor Jones (1942) is perhaps the best known early study that
suggested structural local government reform as a solution to problems
of metropolitan governance. In the post-World War II decades, the
construction of the welfare state was accompanied by such reforms in
many metropolitan areas – frequently involving the establishment of an
upper-tier level of metropolitan government rather than fully
consolidating central cities with their suburbs (Self, 1982).

Particularly in the United States, such structural reforms faced
considerable resistance, increasingly backed by notions associated with
public choice theory (Bish, 1971). Canada, however, was at the
extreme opposite. In the history of metropolitan governing, Canada has
become, since the 1950s, a forerunner in metropolitan reforms, both in
the magnitude of reforms and in the diversity of new structures
proposed and imposed on metropolitan areas (Graham et al., 1998).
Some of these structures were pioneering experiments that differed

from any experience south of the Canadian border or at the other side of the ocean. Along with the implementation of these reforms, Canadians, such as Rowat (1980), Barlow (1991) and Sancton (Rothblatt & Sancton, 1993; 1998; Sancton, 1994; 2002), also made significant contributions to the comparative study of reforms.

A wave of metropolitan reforms in Canada began in the 1950s subsided during the 1970s, and resurged in the 1990s and into the 21st century. What might be termed "remetropolitanization" has put Canada again in the forefront of metropolitan reforms, in a period when many policy analysts and policy makers assumed that large-scale public intervention focused on structural change in metropolitan government was a phenomenon of the past. New regionalism (Savitch & Vogel, 1996), becoming a mainstream approach during the 1990s, has advocated an emphasis on processes or governance – partnerships and networks – rather than on structures; thus Canadian reforms seemed to form a break from the prevailing trends and perceptions, in most instances back to solutions of past decades.

Canadian metropolitan governance can thus be regarded as a "laboratory" of metropolitan reforms, providing valuable lessons – positive and negative – for sustainable urban governance. The frequent attempts to reform local government in Canadian metropolitan areas can also gain from lessons based on studies of reforms elsewhere, including places where reforms have been successful, failed or have never been seriously considered.

Idiosyncratic policy and governance studies still predominate in this field and the need for studying metropolitan reforms from a comparative perspective is clearly evident. New publications on metropolitan governing in Canada from a comparative perspective are particularly timely given the latest round of reforms in cities such as Halifax, Toronto, Ottawa, Montreal and smaller metropolitan areas such as Hamilton, Sudbury and Kingston. This book was initiated following two meetings on metropolitan governance in Canada and Israel, held in 1999 and 2000, sponsored by the Program for International Research Linkages (PIRL) of the International Council for Canadian Studies. The years that elapsed since this book was envisioned were extremely dynamic in terms of local government reforms in metropolitan areas. Major reforms and changes took place, particularly in the Provinces of Quebec and Ontario, as well as out of

Canada – in places such as Greater London, Korea, South Africa and the United States, and, to an extent, even Israel, as the outcomes of the major reform undertaken in Canadian metropolitan areas were gradually unfolding. While it has been a challenge to keep pace with unfolding realities, including a partial retreat from reform in one case (Montreal), it has been a timely endeavor in terms of the need and interest in evaluating recent Canadian reforms from a comparative perspective.

Some of the central questions that deserved attention and guided the research in this volume include:

- What has driven the new agenda of metropolitan reform – in Canada and elsewhere?
- Given the formidable obstacles for local government reforms in most Western democracies, how have Canadians managed to implement such reforms that often involve stiff opposition and substantial political risk?
- Where opposition for reform has expressed itself, how have metropolitan reforms gone ahead?
- Have reforms in Canada fulfilled expectations and proved successful in light of criteria for the evaluation of local government reforms?
- Can experiences from elsewhere provide lessons for Canada and vice versa?
- Are there lessons, best practices and good governance indicators for processes of metropolitan reform?
- And, what does the Canadian and comparative experience with reform of metropolitan governance offer in terms on understanding shifts in multi-level governing – in particular with local/regional-metropolitan intergovernmental relations with senior provincial/state and national jurisdictions?

The major objectives of this book are thus threefold:

1. To present an account of recent local government reforms in major Canadian metropolitan areas and to evaluate metropolitan governance and reforms in these metropolitan areas. Proposed criteria for evaluation include (a) access: representation, accountability and equity; (b) service: efficiency and effectiveness; and (c) metropolitan sustainability.

2. To present an account and evaluation of metropolitan reforms or attempts for reform in several other countries – Britain, the United States, Israel and Korea – emphasizing similarities, differences and lessons for the Canadian city cases: Toronto, Montreal, Vancouver, Ottawa and Winnipeg.
3. To explain differences in the ability to implement metropolitan reforms between Canada and these other democracies. Metropolitan reforms were implemented in Canada at a scale and frequency greater than anywhere else in the democratic world. Some countries such as Israel are at the opposite end of the spectrum, consciously avoiding such mega changes. Others, such as Korea, Britain and the United States, offer a mixture of experiences and lessons. How do most – though not all – jurisdictions in Canada respond to political barriers to metropolitan reform and why are these barriers such effective impediments to reform in other countries?

Structure of the book – done that

What has been done in the recent round of reform? Following this introduction, chapters in Part II discuss Canadian cases. Golden and Slack assess the 1998 Toronto Megacity reform – the first co-author with a special angle, as she chaired the GTA Task Force, whose 1996 recommendations (the Golden Report) were not implemented by the Harris government that instead undertook the Megacity reform despite widespread local opposition in Toronto. Although reform in Halifax – Nova Scotia – was the first in this recent wave of metropolitan reforms in Canada, it was the Toronto reform – and local reactions to the process – that seemed to have the major impact on reform discourses in Canada and even elsewhere in the world.

Caroline Andrew evaluates the subsequent reforms made in Canada's capital region, in both the Ontario and Quebec parts of the metropolis. Amalgamated Ottawa was a product of the same reform policy of the Harris government in Ontario, whereas amalgamated Gatineau was indeed influenced by the reform momentum and precedent set south of the Ottawa River, but represented a somewhat different reform strategy undertaken by the province of Quebec in the context of a somewhat different political culture.

The case of Montreal, presented by Pierre Hamel, demonstrates the unique Quebec version of metropolitan reform – influenced by the Canadian inclination toward imposed local government reform, but in a more compromising, less resolute approach toward such changes by the senior provincial authority. Leo and Piel's assessment of the case of Winnipeg provides a longer term perspective on the comprehensive 1972 amalgamation reform that created Unicity, including reference to recent changes that started in 1997, and resulted in a new City of Winnipeg Charter, affecting the power of the amalgamated city.

The final Canadian case – of Greater Vancouver – is discussed by Smith and Oberlander. The authors emphasize the distinctness of this metropolis, in the Canadian context, expressed in avoiding much of the change that has visited other major and some middle-sized Canadian cities. The authors, however, come to a different conclusion than Sancton (2001) or Bish (2001) – both of whom have praised the British Columbia regional district system in Greater Vancouver as efficient and flexible. Rather than presenting Vancouver as a model for future metropolitan/regional governance, they indicate that Vancouver's regional district system, so successful over its history, is showing signs of having past its best before date.

Part III presents comparative insights from Great Britain, the United States, Korea and Israel. Stewart compares the reinstitution of an upper-tier metropolitan government for Greater London (Great Britain) by Blair's New Labour with the abolition of lower-tier governments in Toronto by the Conservatives led by Harris. He suggests an unexpected relationship between the approach toward the reform decision – "big tent" consultation and consensus seeking (London) versus "big stick" resolute and confrontational approach (Toronto) – and the subsequent levels of elite and public support for reforms.

The message from the United States, as presented by Savitch and Vogel, emphasizes the concept of new regionalism, as a response or variant of laissez faire public choice principles. The authors are skeptical about the desirability of reforms in the structure of local government, such as those imposed in some Canadian metropolitan areas.

The case of Korea (Kim and Smith), demonstrates the similarity of dilemmas and debates over metropolitan governing in diverse political cultures. Two themes stand out: city-county consolidations and metropolitan reconsiderations. Israel in Eran Razin's article presents a case of extremely high resistance to local government reforms, quite the opposite to the Canadian case, despite a centralized political legacy – more in line with Canadian and British ones than with the United States. These cross-national case studies provide a perspective on the role of different political systems and political cultures in determining the metropolitan governance agenda and the reforms undertaken, revealing considerable similarities in the agenda and diversity in responses.

In the following section we do not intend to summarize systematically the conclusions of each chapter, but rather to sketch messages that seem to emerge from the contributions and questions that still lie ahead. These generalizations and assertions solely reflect our editorial impressions and judgements, and are not necessarily fully in line with the views expressed by authors of the individual chapters.

The message – where are we now?

The lack of sufficient time perspective

A definitive appraisal of the metropolitan reforms implemented in Canada since the late 1990s still lacks a sufficient time perspective. In fact, details of implementation, including a partial retreat from reform in the case of Montreal, continue to unfold. Insights on outcomes of reforms held several decades ago, such as the amalgamation that created Unicity Winnipeg and the other reforms made in major Canadian metropolitan areas between the 1950s and 1970s, are thus much more sound than assessments of recent steps. One can, however, argue that evaluations of outcomes of reforms undertaken in the post-World War II decades of economic growth and expansion of the welfare state do not necessarily provide insights that are relevant to the circumstances of the late 1990s and 2000s, characterized by mounting pressures on the welfare state, intensified competition in globalizing markets and proliferation of neo-conservative ideologies. Here, the cases in this volume offer some basis for more contemporary reflection.

Short-term versus long-term assessments

Our impression from short-term assessments of metropolitan reforms, particularly those that involve amalgamations (Meligrana, 2005), is that these assessments tend to be extremely critical. A recent example is provided by Savitch and Vogel (2004) who assess the 2003 Louisville city-county consolidation. Much of the more critical literature on municipal amalgamations is written just before or after the change is made, when the issue is on the public agenda. Such assessments could be influenced profoundly by antagonism toward imposed changes, by protests of those opposing the steps, and by short-term difficulties and nonmaterialization of expectations. Partly, this can be attributed to the psychological tendency of people to be wary of changes that also involve losses, unless a perception of crisis conditions produces fears that inaction could result in even greater losses. Losses tend to loom larger than corresponding gains in human relations (Tversky & Kahneman, 1991), hence the resistance to major diversions from the status quo. Stewart's reflections on Toronto after the forced amalgamation are instructive here.

More specifically, promises asserted in order to promote reform are nearly always exaggerated, unrealistic, or sometimes plainly wrong. Expected savings never fully materialize, if at all; unexpected extra costs tend to emerge; administrative chaos could accompany the transition period; and major territorial reforms frequently lead to substantial unintended and unanticipated consequences (e.g. Sancton's *Merger Mania*, 2001).

According to Leo and Piel, Unicity Winnipeg did not have good public relations after its establishment, suffering from unfair criticism. This largely resulted from unrealistic expectations from the amalgamation that were based on claims made in order to secure the passage of the reform. Initial response to the 1953 Toronto reform also tended to be negative, but the reform and subsequent adjustments made in the 1960s and 1970s did prove successful in solving regional problems and having public support return. The broad opposition to the 1998 Toronto reform was associated not only with favoring the status quo, but also with the lack of implementation of the recommendations of the task force headed by Anne Golden (GTA Task Force, 1996), which was appointed by a NDP Ontario government no longer in power when the report was submitted. Short-term assessments of the

To seel idea;
unrealistic) are
promises never
made &
met

Toronto reform were indeed critical. Expected saving estimates were plainly wrong and the transition period took much longer and involved far greater spending than initially planned. In the short term, at least, as Golden and Slack found, process – in the form of a significant lack of response to negative public local reactions – mattered.

Longer perspective assessments tend to be kinder toward metropolitan reform, although there is no guarantee that the burden of mistakes would diminish, and bitterness concerning the abolition of municipalities and associated local identities could persist for decades. Partly, one can assert that as the memory of problems associated with the transition period fades and interest groups increasingly build stakes associated with the new status quo, the urge to move back to old structures diminishes. Moreover, positive effects – not necessarily those anticipated – could become more evident. These effects could refer to the political power of amalgamated local authorities, and even to longer-term savings. Perhaps, in the long-term the change in structure seems not to matter that much, and it is process – the quality of leadership and administration – that affects more efficiency, effectiveness and responsiveness of the system, as well as subsequent levels of citizen satisfaction.

In the much criticized 1998 Toronto reform, Golden and Slack also indicate ongoing adjustments made to handle some negative implications of the original move. Perhaps, as the pain of adjustment subsides, benefits of the greater economic and political power of Megacity Toronto are becoming more evident – though here Golden and Slack did identify a significant ongoing problem – the failure to "capture" the metropolitan area around Toronto in the Harris amalgamation. Some of this, in terms of planning at least, has been picked up by the newer McGuinty Ontario Liberal administration, with its various "Greater Golden Horseshoe" initiatives.

Stewart presents a clear case for the shifting attitudes toward reform in Toronto and London (UK). In the case of London, Tony Blair employed a "big tent" (insulation) strategy that involved widespread consultation to build pre-change elite consensus and popular support for a new Greater London Authority. This strategy stood in contrast to the confrontational approach of Margaret Thatcher's government that tended to view negatively tedious incrementalism and valued a resolute approach in her *streamlining the cities* removal of the Greater London

Council and the other six Metropolitan County Councils (MCCs) (O'Leary, 1987). In Toronto, Harris used a "big stick" approach that presents a clear and coherent message – less government, lower taxes, common sense revolution – for a reform largely planned in secret. With sufficient core support of the traditional right, particularly in Toronto's outer suburbs, he took a confrontational approach, using rapidity of implementation to overcome accumulating opposition.

However, despite the top-down exclusionary approach applied in the Toronto case, after implementation the once broadly opposed Megacity reform gained both elite and public acceptance – even satisfaction. Public support for Megacity was actually higher than for the Greater London Authority, hinting, according to Stewart, that prior consultation is not essential and does not necessarily determine the political price or political rewards embedded in the reform. The "Big Tent" approach was successful as an elite brokering enterprise, but the public remained rather indifferent, perhaps because of the New Labour's reluctance to devolve power. It may also be asserted that Stewart's findings provide support to psychological theories on the tendency to accept present structures unless a high threshold of problems is passed, and to the argument downplaying the significance of local government structures compared to attributes of leadership and norms of administration at all levels of government.

Objectives and the impact of political swings
Metropolitan reforms everywhere are explicitly motivated by a combination of efficiency, effectiveness, economic development, sustainable planning, social justice/equality, local democracy/ responsiveness, and good governance objectives. The weight given to each consideration depends on prevailing ideologies of political decision makers that may practically have also implicit political agendas for initiating change (Razin, 2004). Generally, it is usually assumed that the transition from the post-World War II Keynesian welfare state to the post-Keynesian competition state during the late 1970s and 1980s (Brenner, 2004; Self, 1993) was associated with a shift from an emphasis on social justice/equality and centrally directed comprehensive planning to an emphasis on efficiency, with its competitiveness, entrepreneurialism, flexibility, decentralization, privatization and fiscal responsibility aspects. This was in part reflected

by the growing influence of neo-conservative/neo-liberal ideologies that have eroded the influence of post-war social-democracy.

The substantial role of political swings in reform agendas is indeed evident in our case studies, both as major determinants of the initiation of reforms and as determinants of post implementation modifications. The UK usually provides most stark examples for the impact of political swings, as most clearly demonstrated by the abolition of the Greater London Council and the other MCCs by Thatcher's Conservatives in 1986 and the re-establishment of the Greater London Authority in 2000 by Blair's New Labour following the Greater London Authority Act of 1998. In Canada, the Winnipeg amalgamation of the early 1970s was driven by social justice left-wing ideologies, whereas the "counter-revolution" was initiated in 1997 as a cost-cutting approach, emphasizing affordable government as the Canadian version of a neo-conservative welfare state. However, the rise to power of the NDP in the province of Manitoba in the late 1990s shifted priorities again. The 1998 Toronto reform did not follow the recommendations of a task force appointed by the left-wing NDP government, and favored an alternative argued to be more in line with the ideological agenda of the right-wing Conservatives, emphasizing a smaller public sector and lower taxes. One of the key legislative bills was indeed called *The Fewer Politicians Act (1999)*. Paradoxically, the Conservatives resorted to the option of imposed amalgamation, usually associated with a welfare state social justice agenda and contradictory to public choice laissez faire principles.

The post-implementation impact of a political swing was particularly evident in Montreal, where a municipal amalgamation in the island of Montreal, imposed by a Parti Quebecois (PQ) provincial government, was partly reversed by a Liberal government. It is difficult to define motivations of the metropolitan reform inspired by the PQ as either right-wing conservative or left-wing; certainly Anglophone-Francophone relations were a factor. Although similar to Ontario in its desire to cut the budget and download responsibilities, a prime aim of imposed mergers in Quebec was equality: sharing fiscal burdens, particularly offering a solution to the perpetual fiscal crisis of the city of Montreal. The Montreal reform seemed more sensitive to central city interests, whereas in Ontario suburban influences seemed more influential (Quesnel, 2000; Trepanier, 1998). Linguistic politics perhaps also played a role – the affluent Anglophone inner suburbs of Montreal were unwillingly merged into the new amalgamated city. The Quebec government was apparently more cautious toward imposed reforms than its Ontario counterpart, introducing a less radical form of imposed amalgamations, although even the imposition of such reform seemed very contrary to prevailing political culture in that province.

Unlike in Ontario, when the opposition party came back to power in Quebec it did not see itself committed to what was already done and adopted a procedure of partial retreat from the reform. The Charest Liberals took two steps: decentralizing powers from the merged city to its boroughs; and offering an option of de-merger through referendum, subject to minimum turnout requirement. De-merged municipalities, however, were to regain more limited powers than held prior to the merger reform, and many broader metropolitan services would remain. Whereas the political pendulum seemed to have lead in the case of Montreal to a chaotic outcome, the Liberal party remained consistently committed to the redistribution principle defined by the PQ, and the minority of municipalities that chose to de-merge did not evade their tax sharing obligation or the need to harmonize their property tax rates with those of the merged city.

The impact of precedent
The Canadian case presents evidence on the impact of precedent in instigating reforms. Although Halifax was the first metropolitan area to be reformed in the 1990s, it seems that the "bold," unexpected move in Canada's premier metropolitan area – Toronto – had the prime impact, sending waves of reform initiatives elsewhere. The Ottawa amalgamation and other smaller ones in Ontario were carried out with little resistance, largely due to the sense of inevitability set by the Toronto precedent.

Moreover, it seems unlikely that imposed amalgamations in the province of Quebec – unfamiliar to the Quebecois political culture and unheard of in France – could have moved ahead if not for the Ontario precedent. The Gatineau amalgamation, previously rejected by residents at the Quebec side of the Ottawa-Hull metropolitan area, took place due to the precedent set in Ottawa. In this case, as emphasized by Andrew, it was a direct neighbor effect: the amalgamation of Gatineau was largely a no-choice decision, motivated by a fear of remaining fragmented and weak versus the amalgamated city of Ottawa at the Ontario side of the Ottawa River. Indeed, in Israel, it has been argued that the resistance of the Haifa Bay municipalities (the Qerayot) to amalgamate has left them weak versus the city of Haifa, when it comes to issues such as the location of public facilities (hospital), controlling environmental hazards and decisions over the municipal affiliation of facilities, such as the oil refineries. However, a large-scale amalgamation that could have served as a precedent and leverage for a similar reform in the Haifa metro never took place in Israel. It seems also likely that the Toronto reform made it much more feasible for Quebec to implement the reform in Montreal, partly motivated by completely different objectives, without being perceived as breaking from long held political traditions in an extreme manner.

Evaluation of outcomes
The chapters in this book provide a mixed message concerning the evaluation of outcomes of local government reforms made in Canadian metropolitan areas. The most negative assessment is provided by Golden and Slack, who argue that the 1998 Toronto reform led to negative effects in terms of service delivery, funding, capacity to plan and invest in infrastructure, accessibility, coordination of economic development and marketing. Major problems concerned the downloading of responsibility for social housing and social services, difficulties in the harmonization of services, problems in investment in infrastructure and public transportation, and lack of consideration of means to control sprawl. Their overall assessment – though limited to the Harris Megacity Toronto changes – is thus negative according to efficiency and sustainability criteria, mixed according to accountability criteria, and positive only with respect to fairness. Stewart provides a more positive view of the Toronto reform, but this concerns elite and public attitudes toward the reform rather than evaluation of its outcomes. Benefits associated with greater economic and political power of the amalgamated city of Toronto are plausible, but need to be validated empirically.

Both the chapters on Ottawa-Gatineau and Montreal find it difficult to provide a definite verdict on outcomes, due to the lack of sufficient time perspective. In the case of Ottawa, policy statements on smart growth, compact urban form, denser development and social sustainability were expressed, but impact is still unclear. Equity should have been enhanced by the amalgamation through equalizing resources across the region. However, when central city and weak cities lose power to dominant electoral power of affluent suburbs this effect could be eroded. Andrew deals also with aspects of minority representation, gender and rural representation, noting that in the amalgamated city of Ottawa suburbs are underrepresented versus central city and rural areas. As to cost savings, in the short term there is a prominent impact of amalgamated costs that are usually underestimated, including equalization of salaries and service levels. It is early to assess long-term savings due to economies of scale (relevant only to amalgamating very small municipalities) or reducing duplication. The bottom line for Ottawa seems to be that a major reorganization did take place, but its impact seems to be fairly limited. Ottawa had a fairly strong metropolitan   government   (Ottawa-Carleton)   even   before amalgamation, and its lower municipal tier was not particularly fragmented even before amalgamation. Thus, one can ask whether the reform really matters that much at one direction or another.

In Montreal it is virtually impossible to assess a reform that was never fully implemented and is still being restructured. The result, while seemingly chaotic, may end with a complex four-tier municipal structure for the metropolitan area. These include the weak top-tier metropolitan   structure   (CMM)   that   encompasses   the   whole metropolitan region, the new second-tier agglomeration of Montreal that encompasses the whole island of Montreal, including the 15 municipalities that chose to de-merge, the city of Montreal and the 15 de-merged municipalities that form a third-tier, and the relatively powerful boroughs within the city of Montreal at the bottom-tier. It is difficult to envision the end result of such a complex and major restructuring   that   aims   to   balance   considerations   of   equity, representation and efficiency. So far it seems that the provincial government has gained power, intervening more and ruling by decrees at the urban level since 2002. Moreover, despite the apparent inconsistency of the metropolitan reform agenda, there has been a clear continuity in aiming at greater fiscal equity within the metropolitan area, and even the de-merger option does not free the de-merged municipalities of sharing the fiscal burden of servicing the whole island of Montreal. A possible return of the PQ rule in Quebec by 2007/8 could either re-complicate or simplify Montreal area governing.

The overall outcome of the 1972 Unicity Winnipeg reform is assessed by Leo and Piel to be positive. Its main achievement was the equalization of general municipal revenues. It also enhanced the control of the council over a variety of municipal functions, through abolishing special-purpose bodies that led to fragmentation and blurred accountability. A problem observed in Winnipeg concerned the excessive focus on structure, neglecting function (who does what?), particularly legalistic rigidity of provincial legislation. The new City of Winnipeg Charter promises more autonomy for metropolitan Winnipeg, but, like British Columbia's similar Community Charter, its impact remains uncertain.

Perhaps the most positive assessment of metropolitan governance comes from British Columbia – a province that did not follow the approach of most of Canada's other provinces, which throughout recent decades went through substantial amalgamation and annexation reforms that kept metropolitan fragmentation low. The Greater Vancouver Regional District performs a long list of voluntary functions and a few mandatory ones, being comprehensive in territory but flexible in function. The metropolitan political culture of the Vancouver region is characterized by locally inspired development of regional institutions, employing methods of gentle imposition by the province, and avoiding the bureaucratic build-up and duplication often associated with full-blown two-tier regional governments. In recent years, the emphasis on cutting costs and red tape has taken hold also in Vancouver. If accountability and efficiency are zero sum (not necessarily true), then the pressure also in Vancouver is toward efficiency. The challenges of the 21st century in Canada's third city region are very much on the accountability side; further reform seems necessary but unlikely in the short or even medium term.

A few general messages from all these Canadian case studies seem particularly worth noting:

1. The Canadian version of metropolitan reforms tends to emphasize equality considerations – sharing fiscal burdens throughout the metropolitan regions. This emphasis is in line with the marked tendency in Canada to impose reforms that concern structures,

amalgamations, annexations and the establishment of metropolitan structures. Even in Toronto, where the Conservative party was careful not to alienate suburban interests beyond the boundaries of former metro Toronto (by leaving them out of the forced amalgamations) and was committed to a cost saving efficiency agenda, outcomes seem positive with respect to fairness.

2. Weak metropolitan upper-tier bodies seem problematic to maintain and unstable. This concerns both recent experience in Toronto with the Greater Toronto Services Board (GTSB) and in Montreal with the CMM, as well as earlier Canadian experiences. These metropolitan bodies tend to suffer from lack of accountability and popular support. They tend to be weak politically and suffer from duplication of tasks performed also at the lower municipal level, and occasionally even at the upper provincial level. The problem of accountability at the regional level is evident even in the successful Vancouver model. Left alone, such metropolitan bodies may become weaker and weaker. Thus, their continued existence and political power depends on either provincial backing or structural reform. In Toronto and Ottawa, the province indeed chose to abolish the lower-tier rather than the frequently less popular upper-tier. Thus, weak metropolitan structures are unlikely to remain stable and can be expected to either become insignificant or strengthened through provincial political backing or reform.

3. Sub-municipal neighborhood level governments – termed resident advisory committees, community boards, neighborhood councils and the like – frequently established to alleviate accountability problems associated with large scale amalgamation reforms also seem to usually become rather weak, hardly fulfilling expectations. In fact, in some cases they can even be argued to serve as a mere fig leaf to principles of local democracy and the preservation of local identities and prove to be unstable. In the case of Montreal, substantial powers have been awarded to the sub-municipal boroughs within the city of Montreal, and it is yet to be seen which of the tiers of local government in Montreal will emerge more powerful once implementation takes place in 2006. In Winnipeg, the Resident Advisory Groups (RAGs) floundered due to lack of funding and lack of any meaningful decision-making capacity.

4. Amalgamation reforms pose the risk of making access of the public to their elected councillors more difficult, increasing the ratio of population per councillor. Thus, one can expect less direct citizen participation in municipal decision making, and perhaps greater influence of developers and lobbyists. In Winnipeg, in fact, amalgamation led to the increase in power of the bureaucracy at the expense of elected politicians. However, the cost of decreased accountability could be mitigated in some cases by benefits associated with a shift from corrupt-ridden political culture to modern bureaucracy, or with greater powers awarded to more capable and better rewarded councillors. The outcomes concerning accountability and responsiveness are thus not deterministic and could vary from place to place. Elsewhere, Smith and Stewart (2006) offer recent comparisons across major Canadian cities regarding council/staff ratios/remuneration/benefits, confirming this point.

Lessons from abroad
The view from the United States, Canada's most influential neighbor, has tended to view forced consolidations and broad territorial reforms in metropolitan areas as a phenomenon of the past. Indeed, this was the belief also among Canadian scholars throughout the 1980s and early 1990s (for example: Sancton, 1991). Obviously, laissez faire public choice approaches have had far deeper roots in the United States than in Canada (Goldberg & Mercer, 1986). Responses within the United States to the neo-conservative/neo-liberal laissez faire agenda tended to focus on the concept of new regionalism. This somewhat loosely defined concept viewed metropolitan governance as an alternative to metropolitan government. Horizontal networks, public-private partnerships, a web of inter-local cooperation and tax sharing could have made formal forms of metropolitan government unneeded. Suggesting a shift from a structural or institutional focus to a problem oriented eclectic and pragmatic approach, this approach has been skeptical about adopting unproven change, thus cautious about comprehensive territorial reforms. Managerial reforms referred to notions such as new political culture – rejecting the strong and activist welfare state – and new public management (NPM), emphasizing entrepreneurialism and measuring performance. Thickening of

institutions linking public, private and non-profit actors from cities, neighborhoods, suburbs, outlying counties and state and federal government and NGOs has been viewed as the proper response to globalization.

Debating the need to reduce disparities between central cities and suburbs, advocates of new regionalism noted that consolidations do not always work in favor of weak central cities. Portland, Oregon, has frequently been given as a most progressive example for metropolitan governance engaged in containing sprawl and promoting smart growth; tax base sharing in the Minneapolis-St. Paul metropolitan region has been given as an example for a mechanism that also deals with fiscal disparities. Savitch and Vogel noted Vancouver and French metropolitan areas as examples for mechanisms of new regionalism that avoided territorial reforms but did respond to the agenda of metropolitanization, globalization, privatization and decentralization.

Throughout Western Europe, metropolitan governance has come back to the agenda, not in past forms that prevailed during the Fordist-Keynesian period, but more in what can be termed as a European variant of new regionalism. Brenner (2003) has emphasized the shifting focus from managerialism to entrepreneurialism and onward to competitive regionalism, partly being crisis-induced transformations. Reform objectives focus on economic priorities: regional economic competitiveness and cost savings rather than on the old agendas of administrative efficiency, service provision and equality. The environmental agenda is also influential in European metropolitan policies. Since the 1990s, directly elected metropolitan bodies were established in two German metropolitan areas – Stuttgart and Hanover. The one in Stuttgart has been aimed at improving the economic position of the region and the one in Hanover acting to reduce fiscal disparities, develop regional infrastructure and represent regional interests (Fürst 2005).

Policy networks and institutional thickness that encompasses a whole series of social, cultural and institutional forms have been central to the new reform agenda in Europe (MacLeod & Goodwin, 1999). Brenner (2004) describes some of the main attributes of the renaissance of regionalism in metropolitan areas in Britain, France, Italy, Germany, Denmark and the Netherlands. A complex array of organizations has been established, moving from past vertical, coordinative and redistributive relationship within a national administrative hierarchy into a horizontal relationship between urban regions competing for development. New regionalism in Europe does view excessive inter-locality competition within an urban region as undermining regional capacity to compete – thus cooperation, coordination, planning and governance are promoted as components of economic development strategies. Some argue that traditional top-down regional planning is giving way to new, flexible forms of horizontal cooperation. However, both Herrschel and Newman (2002) and Brenner (2004) emphasize that such views of new regionalism in Europe underestimate the continuing prominent involvement of national and supranational government. Indeed, "old fashioned" broad amalgamation reforms took place in Greece (in 1998) and Denmark (in 2004).

The transition from Thatcherism to New Labour in Britain (Stoker, 2004) consisted of a mix of top-down and bottom-up approaches. The Thatcherian legacy of tight financial regime, appointed bodies at the local level (quangos), new public management, regulation, centralization and privatization was modified by the New Labour to include the best value regime, with a continued emphasis on improvement in the cost and quality of services, including a comprehensive performance assessment. New policies did emphasize partnership and devolution; the reform discourse has definitely changed, but quangos were not abolished and policy shift was gradual rather than radical. Thus, the varied European experiences hint at the emergence of new regionalism in which the central state is more involved in determining the "rules of the game" and in devising metropolitan policies than is commonly the case in the United States (although some would argue that urban regime and new regionalism literature has underestimated the role of the individual states as prime actors in metropolitan affairs in the United States as well).

The Israeli case mainly provides lessons on the nature of barriers for reform and means to overcome them. Compared to the relatively calm response in Ontario toward the imposed amalgamations and to the rather broad political support for unilateral provincial decisions, Israel presents quite the opposite case. Lack of trust in the government as a fair broker, lack of tradition of consensus building and compromise, a heterogeneous and fragmented, perhaps polarized society and rather unstable coalition governments are major impediments for meaningful reforms. Nevertheless, the context of severe economic and security crisis in 2002–2003 opened a narrow window of opportunity for a limited time toward creating a sense of inevitability in relation to some unpopular local government reforms, including a few amalgamations. The moves undertaken followed neither new regionalism nor decentralization agendas. Rather, the neo-conservative move had a Thatcherian flavor of downsizing the public sector, cutting public expenditures and privatization associated with centralization and distrust in local government. Razin's paper nevertheless suggests that the lack of radical structural reform may not be the real impediment to metropolitan governance in Israel. The fundamental issues concern deficiencies in governance culture at both the local and central government levels.

Finally, the Asian case of Korea also presents a case of a different political culture, associated with a legacy of centralization and even authoritarianism. The discourse of structural municipal reform referring to issues such as fragmentation versus consolidation, efficiency versus equity, and the need for better harmony between democracy and efficiency resembles the agenda elsewhere.

The bottom line

Canadian metropolitan reforms of the late 1990s and early 2000s are setting precedents that could influence metropolitan agendas worldwide. The old welfare state metropolitan agenda declined in the 1970s, overshadowed by an emphasis on competition, entrepreneurialism and increasing pressure on public budgets. New regionalism emerged in the 1990s in the United States and Europe as a metropolitan governance agenda that suits the new economic and political agenda. But just then, unexpectedly, Canada has taken steps, seemingly preferring old regionalism over new regionalism. The step in Halifax was little noticed outside Canada, but reforms in Toronto and Montreal – prominent metropolitan areas that were considered to possess rather enlightened metropolitan government structures – sent shock waves elsewhere. The agenda was not that of old regionalism, but reflected priorities of the late 1990s and early 2000s; the pressures on big governments and the welfare state are common everywhere. However, the solutions – primarily top down imposition of amalgamations – were in line with long-standing traditions of metropolitan reforms in Canada from the days of old regionalism.

Discussing the transition from urban governance in the era of spatial Keynesianism to the era of post-Keynesianism and competition, Brenner (2004) notes three alternative future rescaling strategies: (1) rescaling further downward: neighborhood-based anti-exclusion initiatives; (2) rescaling back upward: metropolitan reform initiatives; and (3) rescaling outward: interurban networking initiatives. One can find elements of all in recent Canadian reforms, but it seems that the top-down approach that heavily relies on amalgamation practically reflects distrust in all three strategies, retreating instead to territorial solutions implemented in the post World War II decades in Canada and even in the late 19th century in places such as New York City.

The Canadian experiences do indicate that both weak metropolitan mechanisms and neighborhood-level governments tend to be unstable, often not fulfilling expectations. Moreover, it seems that only old regionalism deals effectively with sharing fiscal burdens, whereas new regionalism approaches can be effective in development. The much praised Vancouver metropolitan governance system is also not a United States type new regionalism, but reflects much more Canadian political culture, characterized by greater acceptance of senior levels of government as fair brokers, trust in a culture of negotiation, compromise and consensus building that supports notions such as "gentle imposition" (Tennant & Zirnhelt, 1973).

One could argue that the latest round of Canadian reform overemphasizes the impact of political-administrative territorial configurations on metropolitan development, whereas most metropolitan problems require reform in processes rather than in structures. One could also argue that retreating to old regionalism – providing old solutions to new problems – might prove anachronistic. Nevertheless, the fate of present Canadian reforms, particularly those undertaken in Toronto and Montreal can be expected to substantially influence the discourse on metropolitan reforms elsewhere. Territorial reforms reshuffle opportunities for civil society to revise relations with the state and could revise central/provincial government-local government relations in unexpected ways.

References

Barlow, I. M. (1991). *Metropolitan Government*. London: Routledge.

Bish, R. L. (1971). *The Public Economy of Metropolitan Areas*. Chicago: Rand McNally/Markham.

Bish, R. L. (2001). *Local Government Amalgamations: Discredited Nineteenth-Century Ideals Alive in the Twenty-First.* Commentary 150. Toronto: C. D. Howe Institute.

Brenner, N. (2003). Metropolitan institutional reform and the rescaling of state space in contemporary Western Europe. *European Urban and Regional Studies* 10: 297-324.

Brenner, N. (2004) *New State Spaces, Urban Governance and the Rescaling of Statehood.* Oxford: Oxford University Press.

Fürst, D. (2005). Metropolitan governance in Germany, In: H. Heinelt & D. Kubler (eds.). *Metropolitan Governance, Capacity, Democracy and the Dynamics of Place* (pp. 151–168). London: Routledge..

Goldberg, M. A., & Mercer, J. (1986). *The Myth of the North American City*. Vancouver: University of British Columbia Press.

Graham, K. A., Phillips, S. D., with Maslove, A. M. (1998). *Urban Governance in Canada*. Toronto: Harcourt Brace.

GTA Task Force (1996). *Greater Toronto, Report of the GTA Task Force*. Toronto: Queen's Printer for Ontario.

Herrschel, T., & Newman, P. (2002). *Governance of Europe's City Regions, Planning, Policy and Politics*. London: Routledge.

Jones, V. (1942). *Metropolitan Government*. Chicago: University of Chicago Press.

MacLeod, G., & Goodwin, M. (1999). Space, scale and state strategy: rethinking urban and regional governance. *Progress in Human Geography* 23: 503–527.

Meligrana, J. (ed.) (2005). *Redrawing Local Government Boundaries: An International Study of Politics, Procedures and Decisions*. Vancouver: University of British Columbia Press.

O'Leary, B. (1987). Why was the GLC abolished? *International Journal of Urban and Regional Research* 11: 193–217.

Paytas, J. (2002). The organization of metropolitan areas: the development of the hybrid metropolis. Pittsburgh: Carnegie Mellon Center for Economic Development.

Quesnel, L. (2000). Municipal reorganization in Quebec. *Canadian Journal of Regional Science* 23: 115–134.

Razin, E. (2004). Needs and impediments for local government reform: lessons from Israel. *Journal of Urban Affairs* 26: 623–640.

Rothblatt, D. N., & Sancton, A. (eds.) (1993). *Metropolitan Governance: American/Canadian Intergovernmental Perspectives.* Berkeley: Institute of Governmental Studies Press.

Rothblatt, D. N., & Sancton, A. (eds.) (1998). *Metropolitan Governance Revisited, American/Canadian Intergovernmental Perspectives.* Berkeley: Institute of Governmental Studies Press.

Rowat, D. C. (ed.) (1980). *International Handbook on Local Government Reorganization.* Westport, Conn.: Greenwood Press.

Sancton, A. (1991). *Local Government Reorganization in Canada Since 1975.* Toronto: ICURR Press.

Sancton, A. (1994). Governing Canada's city regions: the search for a new framework. *Policy Options* 15(4): 12–15.

Sancton, A. (2001). *Merger Mania: The Assault on Local Government.* Montreal-Kingston: McGill-Queen's University Press

Sancton, A. (2002). Metropolitan and regional governance. In: E.P. Fowler & D. Siegel (eds.). *Urban Policy Issues: Canadian Perspectives*, 2nd edition (pp. 54–68). Toronto: Oxford University Press.

Savitch, H. V., & Vogel, R. K. (eds.) (1996). *Regional Politics, America in a Post-City Age.* Thousand Oaks, Cal.: Sage.

Savitch, H. V., & Vogel, R. K. (2004). Louisville/Jefferson County, Kentucky. In: S. M. Leland & K. Thurmaier (eds.), *Case Studies of City-County Consolidation, Reshaping the Local Government Landscape* (pp. 272–290). Armonk, NY: M. E. Sharpe.

Self, P. (1982). *Planning the Urban Region: A Comparative Study of Policies and Organizations.* Tuscaloosa, Al.: The University of Alabama Press.

Self, P. (1993). *Governments by the Market: the Politics of Public Choice.* Boulder, Col.: Westview.

Smith, P. J., & Stewart, K. (2006). Policy analysis for whom? Institutional inadequacy and the potential for democratic policy-making deviation in eight Canadian cities. In: L. Dobuzinskis, M. Howlett & D. Laycock (eds.). *Policy Analysis in Canada: The State of the Art.* Toronto: University of Toronto Press.

Stoker, G. (2004). *Transforming Local Governance, From Thatcherism to New Labour*. Houndmills, UK: Palgrave Macmillan.

Tennant, P., & Zirnhelt, D. (1973). Metropolitan government in Vancouver: the strategy of gentle imposition. *Canadian Public Administration* 13: 124–138.

Trepanier, M. O. (1998). Metropolitan governance in the Montreal area. In: D.N. Rothblatt & A. Sancton (eds.). *Metropolitan Governance Revisited, American/Canadian Intergovernmental Perspectives* (pp. 57–121). Berkeley: Institute of Governmental Studies Press.

Tversky, A., & Kahneman, D. (1991). Loss aversion in riskless choice – a reference-dependent model. *Quarterly Journal of Economics* 106: 1039–1061.

Part II

Canadian Metropolitan Cases

ANNE GOLDEN AND ENID SLACK

Urban Governance Reform in Toronto:
A Preliminary Assessment of Changes
Made in the Late 1990s

Preface

Urban Governance Reform in Toronto: A Preliminary Assessment
examines local government reforms in the late 1990s and their effects
on Toronto and its ability to succeed as a healthy and competitive city-
region. The city was created through the amalgamation of a
metropolitan-level government and six lower-tier governments on
January 1, 1998. Shortly thereafter, the Province also established the
Greater Toronto Services Board to provide coordination within the
Greater Toronto Area on issues affecting the new municipality and its
neighbors. In addition, the Province realigned responsibilities for
services provided by the province and Ontario municipalities in 1998,
and introduced a new property assessment system.

The article finds that while some gains were made through these
four changes, overall they had negative effects on both the city and
city-region in terms of service delivery and funding, capacity to plan
and invest in infrastructure, accessibility, and coordination of economic
development and marketing – the very foundations of Toronto's
success. After the article was written in the spring of 2000, further
developments occurred in some of the events it describes. The authors
find that their conclusions remained valid in the fall of 2002, and
provide an epilogue to update readers on the state of affairs in Toronto
up to that year. Subsequently, there has been a multi-year delay in the
publication of this volume, with the result that a number of events have
transpired (not least of which is the proposed new City of Toronto Act)
that are not referenced in this paper. Thus the current landscape is very
different than it was six years ago when the paper was written.
However, it may still be of interest as a snapshot of the situation as it
was.

Introduction

For many years, the City of Toronto has had an enviable reputation as one of the best places in the world to live and do business. In 1996, *Fortune* magazine ranked Toronto first among international cities as the best place to live and conduct business. Among the reasons cited were low crime rates, clean streets, green space, its many theatres and ethnic restaurants, and a "veritable national park mentality." In 1997, the Geneva-based Corporate Resources Group ranked Toronto third (after Auckland and Geneva) among major world cities with the highest quality of life. Peter Ustinov's often-cited description of Toronto as "New York run by the Swiss" captures the city's unique combination of cosmopolitan dynamism and civic order.

There is, however, a growing perception that Toronto's quality of life is threatened. Increasing income polarization and the disproportionate share of low-income households situated in Toronto relative to the rest of the Greater Toronto Area (GTA),[1] have reduced the city-region's cohesiveness and seriously undermined its ability to provide needed services. Homelessness, the ultimate symbol of poverty, is on the rise. A slow recovery in transit ridership since a sharp decline from its peak in 1991 and the growth of road traffic congestion outside the city in regions under-served or hard to serve by public transit both suggest that Toronto may soon be immobilized by gridlock. Infrastructure is deteriorating, and investment in new or rehabilitated roads, bridges and other facilities is either inadequate or repeatedly deferred. The city's decreasing capacity to maintain service levels on a budget supported only by property taxes and user fees confirms the likelihood that Toronto could be entering a downward spiral – one that could ultimately undermine Toronto's quality of life.

In this article, we review the decisions and policies that have contributed to Toronto's past successes and propose five key building blocks needed to ensure the city's future competitiveness. We then

---

1   The Greater Toronto Area (GTA) comprises the City of Toronto plus the Regions of Durham, Halton, Peel, and York. The population of Toronto in 1999 was 2,385,421. The populations of the other regions in the GTA are: Durham – 452,608; Halton – 329,613; Peel – 869,219; and York – 618,497. These estimates, taken from the 1999 Ontario Municipal Directory, show that the population of Toronto represents about half of the population of the GTA.

describe four provincial initiatives – amalgamation, the downloading of provincial services onto municipalities, the formation of the Greater Toronto Services Board (GTSB), and property tax reform – and evaluate the impact of each on Toronto's future and ability to compete internationally.

We then comment on the extent to which the policy changes meet four basic criteria:

1. *Accountability*: Accountability requires that the system of government be as understandable to the average citizen as possible, so as to promote participation, access to the political decision-making process, and informed public scrutiny. The public must know who is responsible for making and carrying out decisions. A clear link between expenditure and revenue policies is also essential.
2. *Fairness*: Fairness requires that costs and benefits be shared equally among all those who live in a region. Equity also requires that all members of society have access to needed services and information, and that government programs respond to community needs.
3. *Efficiency*: Efficiency requires that service delivery achieve maximum value with available resources. Linked to efficiency is the subsidiarity principle, which states that services should be delivered by the lowest level of government with the capacity to do so effectively.
4. *Sustainability*: Sustainability is an extension of the idea of efficiency. It requires that services be delivered and planned in a way that takes into account long-term social and fiscal consequences and the fact that each generation is responsible to the next in using the world's resources.

Past success and future competitiveness

The success enjoyed by Toronto for so many years was, in part, the result of deliberate policy choices by the city and the Province of Ontario.

Policy choices that contributed to Toronto's success in the past
The creation of Metropolitan Toronto in 1954 was a bold and far-

sighted move. It established a regional body with responsibility for planning, funding, and implementing region-wide infrastructure and services. It also provided access to the city of Toronto's rich tax base to help finance infrastructure in the suburbs. At the same time, lower levels of government that provided local services ensured access and local responsiveness. In 1967, when 13 lower-tier municipalities were amalgamated into six, some services, such as social services and policing, were transferred to the metropolitan level. In the 1970s, regional governments were created around Toronto, modelled on the successful two-tier system in Toronto.

Historically, there has been a strong commitment to planning and infrastructure investment in the region. During the first eight years of its existence, Metro Toronto constructed trunk sewers and water mains, sewage treatment plants, schools, roads, and bridges. In the 1970s, the regions around Toronto followed this example. Infrastructure investment made possible the systematic outward expansion of Toronto between the 1950s and the 1970s.

There has also been a strong commitment to sharing social costs within Metro Toronto. This included distributing social housing across the metropolitan area and spreading the welfare burden more evenly between the downtown core and the suburbs. When the metropolitan level of government assumed responsibility for social services in 1967, social service costs were shared throughout the metropolitan area.[2] Social service costs are now pooled throughout the Greater Toronto Area, although this was a controversial move on the part of the provincial government.[3]

Continued investment in education by both provincial and local governments ensured the health of the public education system in

---

2   Some U.S. cities are starting tax base sharing programs throughout the city-region to share the costs and benefits of development. See, for example, Myron Orfield, *Metropolitics: A Regional Agenda for Community and Stability* (Washington, D.C.: Brookings Institution Press and Cambridge, Mass.: The Lincoln Institute of Land Policy, 1997). Tax base sharing has been a reality in Toronto since the creation of metropolitan government in 1954.

3   It is controversial because the suburban municipalities around Toronto do not want to pay for what they perceive to be Toronto's problems. Notwithstanding recent evidence that more than 47% of the homeless population in Toronto originated from outside the city, there is resistance to pooling social service costs. The more fundamental problem, however, is one of taxation without representation. All municipalities in the GTA contribute to social service and social housing costs, but no regional body oversees expenditures.

Toronto and discouraged middle-class families from moving to the suburbs to find better schools or taking their children out of the public system and sending them to private schools. Before recent, province-wide changes in education funding, school boards could raise property taxes for education, allowing the city to add to provincial dollars and ensure that the school system had sufficient resources to address the higher costs associated with the concentration of special needs in the city.

Toronto, with the assistance of the province, remained committed to public transit as the transportation mode of choice for all residents. Historically, Toronto's transportation policies have balanced the need for both roads and transit. While, in the United States, cities were becoming increasingly dependent on freeways and automobiles, capital investment in transit in Toronto remained roughly equivalent to investment in freeways and suburban roads.[4]

Toronto has also remained committed to preserving established urban neighborhoods. This has been an official planning policy since the mid-1970s. The commitment to maintaining and renewing old neighborhoods was matched by a willingness to create new neighborhoods, such as the St. Lawrence Neighborhood, which houses about 10,000 people on reclaimed industrial land in the downtown area. Suburban municipalities, such as Markham, Richmond Hill, Oakville, and Burlington, have successfully regenerated their historic downtown cores by reviving main streets and restoring villages.

Provincial interest and timely interventions were instrumental in shaping the urban region's post-war development. For example, the Province made a commitment to protecting the Niagara Escarpment and recognized the need to protect green lands and waterfront areas. The province has also supported arts and cultural institutions, which have enhanced the vitality and attractiveness of the entire region.

4   International comparisons of public transport trips per inhabitant per year for selected world cities shows Toronto with an average of 186 trips per inhabitant per year compared to 17 in San Diego and 78 in Philadelphia. However, transit use is lower in Toronto than in some European cities such as London, Paris, and Milan. See Pietro Nivola, *Laws of the Landscape: How Policies Shape Cities in Europe and America* (Washington, D.C.: Brookings Institution Press, 1999), pp. 58–60.

Making Toronto competitive: five essential building blocks

Global competition in general and the North American Free Trade Agreement (NAFTA) in particular forced businesses in the GTA, as elsewhere, to undergo massive restructuring in order to compete in the global marketplace. Increased competition has meant that businesses must continually look for ways to provide high-quality goods and services at the lowest possible cost.

Prospering in the new competitive economy requires the use of computer-based technologies, access to skilled labour, a concentration of specialized firms, and the smooth flow of goods and information. City-regions like the GTA are the best places to meet these requirements, because they alone can provide the benefits that arise when businesses are in close proximity (agglomeration economies). These benefits include the opportunity to do business face-to-face, the availability of business services, access to a large pool of skilled labour, and well-established transportation and communications networks.

To be competitive, Toronto needs policies that stimulate investment and create jobs. The City's future success will depend on its ability to position itself as "the location of choice for companies and workers who can locate anywhere."[5]

There are five essential building blocks necessary if Toronto is to attract, retain, and promote globally competitive businesses:

1. *Service funding and delivery:* Services that lead to a high quality of life at a reasonable cost must be provided. These include not only roads, transit, water, and sewers, but also parks, recreational and cultural facilities, schools, and hospitals.
2. *Capacity to plan:* Toronto must be able to plan transit, urban land use, and the environment in a way that makes the region work effectively and maintains the quality of life.
3. *Investment in infrastructure:* Investment in physical and human infrastructure is essential to attracting business. Investment is needed to build, maintain, and upgrade airports, transit facilities, roads, and telecommunications networks as well as schools and hospitals.

5   *Greater Toronto*, Report of the GTA (Golden) Task Force (Queen's Printer for Ontario, 1996), p. 68.

4. *Access and participation:* An essential element of local government is that citizens feel that they can influence local government policies.

5. *Coordinated approach to economic development:* Attracting and promoting business must be coordinated on a regional scale to ensure that common economic development interests are served.

Local government reform: an overview

Several recent provincial policy changes have affected the City and the city-region, including amalgamation, local services realignment, the formation of the Greater Toronto Services Board, and property tax reform.

The amalgamation of Toronto
On 1 January 1998, the new City of Toronto was created to replace the former metropolitan level of government and its six constituent lower-tier municipalities (Toronto, Etobicoke, North York, Scarborough, York, and East York) with a single-tier city. Restructuring was not the result of local initiative, but was imposed by the provincial government through Bill 103, the *City of Toronto Act, 1996.*[6]

The new amalgamated City of Toronto has been dubbed the "megacity." It has 2.4 million residents and covers 632 square kilometres. The City's operating budget is about $6 billion – larger than six of Canada's ten provinces. The City employs 26,000 people; an additional 18,000 work for its 214 agencies, boards, and commissions.

The new Toronto City Council was composed of 57 councillors (two elected from each ward) and the mayor. Although this was a much

---

6   Municipal restructuring in Ontario is widespread. In some cases, such as in Kingston, restructuring was initiated by the municipality itself with provincial assistance. At the request of some municipalities (for example, municipalities in Kent County and Chatham, and in Temagami), the provincial government appointed a commissioner to make recommendations on restructuring. In four regions (Ottawa-Carleton, Hamilton-Wentworth, Sudbury, and Haldimand-Norfolk), the Province appointed special advisors whose recommendations were subsequently adopted and turned into provincial legislation (the first three will be single-tier megacities; Haldimand-Norfolk will be divided into two single-tier cities). Other municipalities have initiated and implemented restructuring locally. To date, all but four counties in Ontario have undertaken some restructuring.

larger council than is the norm in Ontario,[7] Toronto councillors represented more constituents than is generally the case in GTA municipalities. For the 2000 municipal election, however, the number of councillors in Toronto was reduced to 44 under the Province's *Fewer Municipal Politicians Act, 1999*. This will result in one councillor for every 54,214 persons in Toronto.

Six standing committees and other sub-committees and task forces handle much of the work of the council. The city is also required to have community councils, in which members of Council represent particular areas of the city. Community councils correspond to the boundaries of the former lower-tier municipalities. They deal with neighborhood issues such as development applications and local recreation needs.

Local services realignment
Beginning in 1998, the provincial government increased the responsibility of municipalities for funding. Table 1 shows the division of responsibilities between the Province and municipalities in 1997 before local services realignment and compares it to the situation in 1998 and afterwards.

Local services realignment involved the province transferring many formerly provincial responsibilities to municipalities and, in return, taking over the funding of elementary and secondary education. (Before local services realignment or "downloading," the province funded about 40% of the costs of education; 60% was funded by property taxes levied by school boards.[8]) These changes meant that Ontario municipalities had to take responsibility for water, sewers, roads, transit, social housing, public health, and ambulances. The province also downloaded greater responsibility for social services onto municipal governments.[9] In 1999, the Province reassumed some responsibility for funding ambulance services and public health.

---

7   Don Stevenson, Richard Gilbert, "Restructuring Municipal Government in Greater Toronto: Amalgamation to Form the New City of Toronto and Creation of the Greater Toronto Services Board, 1996–1999" (paper prepared for the City of Montreal, 16 July 1999), p. 18.

8   The Province took over the education property tax (residential and non-residential) to pay for part of the costs of education. The Province then cut provincial residential property taxes for education in half in 1998 to leave tax room for municipal purposes. Further cuts were made in 1999.

9   Regional pooling of social service, social housing, and inter-regional transit costs in the

The formation of the Greater Toronto Services Board

The Greater Toronto Services Board (GTSB) was established after the amalgamation of the City of Toronto to promote and facilitate coordinated decision-making among municipalities within the GTA.[10] The GTSB, however, was given virtually no legislative authority, except to oversee regional transit. As it was not another level of government, it was not given direct taxing authority.

The GTSB was made up of 40 members and a chair. Membership included all 25 GTA mayors, the four regional chairs, ten additional members from Toronto's city council, and one member who sits on both the Mississauga and Peel councils. The Chair of the Regional Municipality of Hamilton-Wentworth also sits on the GTSB when it is dealing with transit issues.

The GTSB, with its narrow mandate for regional transit and transportation, faced crippling divisions among its central city, suburban, and rural members, who did not share common values. As a result, consensus on how to proceed to resolve pressing regional problems was difficult to achieve. The Board's mandate thus came under review.

Property tax reform

In January 1998, a new province-wide assessment system was introduced in Ontario, replacing the outdated approach previously used. The new system resulted in uniform assessment based on "current value" (interpreted as "market value"). As the change to a uniform province-wide assessment system by itself would have resulted in large shifts in tax burdens within and between classes of property, it was necessary to introduce tax policy changes at the same time.

Greater Toronto Area has spread the impact of these changes throughout the region. This is discussed in greater detail below.

10   The *Greater Toronto Services Board Act, 1998*, sets out the structure and responsibilities of the Greater Toronto Services Board (GTSB) and the Greater Toronto Transit Authority.

Table 1: Changes in responsibilities between provincial and municipal governments

Responsibility	1997	1998/99
General welfare assistance: Benefits Administration	 80-20 50-50	 80-20 50-50
Family benefits assistance	Provincial	80-20 benefits 50-50 admin.
Child care services	80-20	80-20
Long term care	Provincial	Provincial
Hostels	80-20	80-20
Homes for special care	Provincial	Provincial
Women's shelters	95-5	Provincial
Social housing	Provincial-Municipal	Municipal
Child welfare	80-20	Provincial
Municipal transit	33-67	Municipal
GO transit	Provincial	Municipal
Ferries	Provincial	Municipal
Airports	40-60	Municipal
Sewer and water	10-90	Municipal
Policing	10-90	Municipal
Farm Tax Rebate	Provincial	Municipal
Property assessment	Provincial	Municipal
Libraries	5-95	5-95
Public health	70-30	50-50
Ambulances	90-10	50-50
Roads*	Provincial-Municipal	More municipal
Gross receipts tax	Municipal	Provincial
Provincial offences	Provincial	Municipal
Residential education taxes	School boards	50% provincial for education; 50% municipal

* Provincial road grants to municipalities were cut back in 1996; maintenance of some provincial highways was also transferred to municipalities. Changes were made to the downloading of public health and ambulances in 1999.

Before property tax reform, municipalities were required by legislation to levy a residential tax rate equal to 85% of the non-residential rate. As a result of reform, municipalities are now allowed to levy variable tax rates for different classes of property, including residential, multi-residential, commercial, industrial, pipelines, farms, and managed forests. Optional classes that municipalities may use include new multi-residential, shopping centres, office towers, parking lots and vacant land, and large industrial.

Varying tax rates by type of property allows municipalities to shift tax burdens from one property class to another. In order to ensure that municipalities do not increase inequities among property classes, however, the province has set ranges that represent a fair proportion of the tax burden for each property class. Municipalities can move their relative tax burdens closer to the provincial ranges of fairness or maintain them as they were before property tax reform. They cannot, however, move relative tax burdens farther away from the ranges of fairness.

In addition to variable tax rates, the province legislated phase-in provisions and tax deferrals to address shifts that would occur within classes of property, especially within the residential property class. Municipalities must also establish a program to mitigate assessment-related tax increases for residential properties owned by low-income seniors and the disabled.

Even with the phase-in mechanisms, property tax reform resulted in large shifts in tax burdens. In particular, the tax burden on small retail commercial properties in Toronto increased relative to that of large office towers, because of the recession in office markets in June 1996 (the valuation date). Programs were introduced to cap the allowable increase in property taxes on multi-residential, commercial, and industrial properties.

Reforming property taxes has resulted in shifts in property tax burdens among different types of properties, but it has not reduced the differences between property tax on commercial and industrial properties in the City of Toronto and on those in the outer suburbs. Continued higher taxation of commercial and industrial properties in the city acts as a disincentive to businesses to locate in the city. Furthermore, the commitment of the City of Toronto (and other cities in the GTA) to a property tax freeze is similar in some ways to California's Proposition 13.[11] In any event, the results are likely to be

---

11   In 1978, the State of California's Proposition 13 set a ceiling on property tax increases.

the same – a decline in infrastructure investment and reduced service levels.

Observations on local government reform

The provincial governance reform initiatives were designed to make the city more competitive internationally by streamlining services, reducing costs, and lowering taxes. However, local services realignment, political restructuring, and property tax reform may have had the opposite effect. The education system, which is a key to Toronto's competitiveness, has also been weakened.

The downloading of responsibility for social housing and an increased portion of social services has created the most serious problems for municipalities. This move goes against the advice of every committee, task force, and panel commissioned in this province over the last decade to study provincial-municipal funding responsibilities.[12] Using well-established public finance principles, these reports all said the same thing: social services should be funded entirely by the province. In fact, Ontario became one of only two provinces in Canada requiring municipalities to fund social services; the other was Manitoba.

There are three main arguments against downloading an increased portion of social service costs to municipalities:

1. The property tax is not the appropriate mechanism to fund social service programs, which redistribute income to the poor.[13]

---

12   See, for example, Hopcroft Report in 1991; Fair Tax Commission Report in 1993; the Report of the Greater Toronto Area (Golden) Task Force in 1996; and the letter dated 23 December 1996 to the (Ontario) Minister of Municipal Affairs and Housing from the provincial "Who Does What" Panel.

13   In other countries in which social services are a municipal responsibility, the main source of revenue is not the property tax. See: M. McMillan, "Taxation and Expenditure Patterns in Major City-Regions: An International Perspective and Lessons for Canada," in Paul Hobson, France St. Hilaire, eds., *Urban Governance and Finance: A Question of Who Does What* (Montreal: Institute for Research on Public Policy, 1997), p. 42. In Stockholm, for example, local governments provide social assistance, education, and health care. The primary source of tax revenue is the income tax which funds almost half of local expenditures. Revenue sharing in Frankfurt means that the City benefits from a share of the income tax.

2. Municipalities are put under great financial pressure to reduce welfare payments (or increase property taxes) when needs increase.[14]

3. Social services standards should be uniformly applied across the province. Although the provincial government sets standards for service provision, it does not pay all of the costs. Municipalities must also pay a portion of the costs, but have limited flexibility in terms of how the service is provided.

Transit was downloaded to municipalities without any transfer of corresponding revenues. Formerly, transit was funded through a combination of user fees, property taxes, and provincial grants. With the realignment of local services in 1998, the provincial share of the capital and operating costs of transit was downloaded to municipalities – giving them complete funding responsibility. By contrast, in the Greater Vancouver Regional District, the transit authority has access to some provincial fuel tax revenues for local transportation. Similar sources of revenue are not available to GTA municipalities.

Realigning services between the provincial government and municipalities has meant that the city has been forced to take on new municipal responsibilities, without receiving sufficient revenue to pay for them. The downloading of social services to the municipal level and the transfer of responsibility for elementary and secondary education to the province has created two problems. First, the funding of social service costs was placed upon an inelastic revenue source (the property tax) and, second, local governments lost their ability to enhance the quality of education by increasing local property taxes.

In the long run, the reforms are unlikely to improve, and may seriously undermine, the city's competitiveness. They are cause for concern not only because of their individual impact on the City, but also because all of these changes have taken effect simultaneously. This has resulted in turbulence at the City level and left the public unable to evaluate which changes are positive and which are negative.

---

14   The swap of services also has implications for the future. The provincial takeover of education funding at a time when the population is aging means that education expenditures will decrease, while the social service demands on municipalities will increase.

In the following sections we examine the effects of local government reform on the five building blocks required to make Toronto a healthy and competitive city-region.

Service funding and delivery

Toronto is responsible for providing a wide range of services. Table 2 shows the categories of services provided, and summarizes operating and capital expenditures per household. In 1998, total operating expenditures in the new City of Toronto were more than $5.6 billion, or $6,013 per household. The three largest expenditures were:

- general welfare assistance (19.5%);
- transit (14.3%);
- policing (9.5%).

The largest capital expenditures are generally for transit and roads, followed by sewers and water. Transit expenditures increased significantly in 1998, mainly because of the downloading of capital and operating costs of transit to municipalities that year.

As municipalities are prohibited from incurring operating deficits, operating revenues are roughly equal to operating expenditures. Table 3 summarizes the distribution of operating revenues by source for the new City of Toronto in 1998.

Table 2: Operating and capital expenditures per household, new City of Toronto, 1998

	Operating ($)	Capital ($)
General government	660	46
Fire	242	11
Police	569	33
Conservation authority	8	5
Protective inspection and control	57	0
Subtotal: Protection to persons & property	877	48
Roadways	258	138

Winter control	42	0
Transit	860	611
Parking	63	0
Street lighting	17	0
Other	0	7
Subtotal: Transportation services	1,239	757
Sanitary sewer system	228	81
Storm sewer system	3	22
Waterworks system	192	39
Garbage collection	66	9
Garbage disposal	77	8
Pollution control	6	0
Other	0	1
Subtotal: Environmental services	572	159
Public health services	86	
Public inspections and control	9	
Hospitals	0	
Ambulance services	73	
Subtotal: Health services	167	2
General assistance	1,175	5
Assistance to aged persons	149	14
Assistance to children	0	0
Day nurseries	214	1
Subtotal: Social and family services	1,539	20
Parks and recreation	342	65
Libraries	131	23
Other cultural	49	6
Subtotal: Recreation and cultural services	522	94
Planning and development*	436	41
Total	6,013	1,167

* Includes social housing

Source: Calculated from MARS data, Ministry of Municipal Affairs and Housing.

The property tax is the main source of revenue, followed by user fees for services such as transit, parks and recreation, parking, garbage disposal, and assistance to the aged. Provincial grants come third; most grants are conditional and must be spent on functions designated by the provincial government. Other revenues include fees from licenses and permits, contributions from reserve funds, investments, and other income.

In terms of capital financing, the main source of revenues are: current revenues, contributions from reserves and reserve funds (which are composed of some property taxes and user fees set aside for capital purposes), development charges, provincial grants and loan forgiveness, and municipal borrowing.

Table 3: Distribution of Operating Revenues, New City of Toronto, 1998

	1998 (%)
Property taxes	45.2
Water and sewer billings	6.9
Total taxation	52.1
Payments in lieu of taxes	3.6
Provincial unconditional grants	0.9
Provincial conditional grants	14.2
Total provincial grants	15.1
User fees	16.6
Other municipalities grants and fees	3.8
Other revenues	8.9
Total	100.0

Source: Calculated from MARS data, Ministry of Municipal Affairs and Housing.

Impact of amalgamation[15]

Amalgamation has resulted in the harmonization of lower-tier services.

---

15   This section draws largely from Enid Slack, "A Preliminary Assessment of the Toronto Amalgamation," *Canadian Journal of Regional Science* (2000) vol. 23, no. 1.

Service harmonization applied to only 30% of the new city's total expenditures, because 70% of total expenditures (social services, transit, and policing) had already been amalgamated at the metropolitan level of government. The areas targeted for harmonization were solid waste collection and recycling, winter control (snow and ice removal), public health, and library services.

Service harmonization has been difficult to achieve, mainly because of differences in per-household expenditures among the former lower-tier municipalities. In some cases, higher expenditures meant higher service levels; in other cases, they reflected the need for specialized services. For example, in central Toronto, the former City of Toronto, fire expenditures per household have been considerably higher than in the other former municipalities, because of the higher density of the downtown area. Similarly, garbage collection costs are higher in the former City of Toronto, for two reasons. First, there is a greater proportion of commercial properties requiring pickup in Toronto and, second, the former municipalities had stricter criteria governing commercial garbage collection than Toronto. Public health expenditures are higher in the former City of Toronto because of the diversity of the population living downtown. Expenditures on winter control were higher in the former City of North York because it was the only municipality that cleared sidewalks in addition to roads.

An initial review of service harmonization in the new city shows an overall increase in annual expenditures for winter control and public health and some reductions in expenditures for solid waste management.[16] This initial review of service harmonization excluded fire protection. Subsequent analysis has revealed the need for increased expenditure for fire services.[17]

The primary opportunities for user fee harmonization are recreation centres, water and commercial garbage collection. Surprisingly, the harmonization of user fees has led to a reduction in user fee revenues in the new City of Toronto compared to the combined revenues of the former municipalities before amalgamation. In particular, fees for parks and recreation have fallen. Overall, service and user fee

16   City of Toronto, "Building the New City of Toronto – Status Report on Amalgamation" (January 1998 – June 1999).

17   City of Toronto, "2000 Preliminary Operating Budget" (Presentation to Budget Advisory Committee and Policy and Finance Committee, February 2000), p. 23.

harmonization is expected to result in increased costs to the new City of Toronto in 2000 and beyond.[18]

One-time transition costs in Toronto included the acquisition of new technology for financial, human resources, and payroll systems; the renovation of existing facilities such as the Toronto City Hall; and hiring technical and professional experts in areas such as telecommunications.[19] In addition to these one-time costs, there were also costs associated with downloading and staff severance packages.[20]

It was estimated that the expenditure for one-time transitional costs in Toronto would be approximately $153 million for the period 1998 to 2001. Costs associated with staff severance packages and downloading add a further $56 million for 1998 and 1999.[21] The City received a $50 million grant from the province and an interest-free loan of $50 million in 1998. The province granted an additional $63 million interest-free loan in 1999. This provincial assistance was intended to help with the transition costs of downloading. The loan arrangements call for the repayment of the loan from savings achieved once amalgamation is complete.

Amalgamation has not resulted in cost savings
Although the City claims to be on target in achieving cost savings, this claim fails to compare savings to the increased costs of service and user fee harmonization or to other budget increases. For example, the City's estimates of cost savings do not include increased costs from amalgamation, such as salaries for 62 new fire-fighters, recommended following a review of fire services. Nor do they factor in the cost of administrative restructuring, service expansion for solid waste disposal, increased litter cleaning services, and other changes in service delivery. Furthermore, new collective agreements negotiated by inside and outside workers had not at that point been incorporated into the budget.

18   See note 17 above, p. 38.

19   Ibid., p. 70–71.

20   Municipal amalgamations generally result in transitional costs that are often higher than anticipated. See Igor Vojnovic, *Municipal Consolidation in the 1990s: An Analysis of Five Canadian Municipalities* (Toronto: Intergovernmental Committee on Urban and Regional Research, 1997).

21   See note 17 above, p. 70–71.

One advantage of amalgamation is that the former City of York and the former Borough of East York, both of which were experiencing declining levels of assessment and inadequate levels of service, now enjoy higher levels of service. Although amalgamation may have improved service levels in some parts of the new municipality, it does so at an increased cost. Furthermore, amalgamation reduces competition between municipalities, because there is less incentive to be efficient and responsive to local needs in a single, large municipality compared to several smaller municipalities.

Amalgamation has not improved Toronto's ability to provide services
Based on *actual* revenues and expenditures, Toronto is not financially self-sufficient. Fiscal imbalances occur when revenues fall short of expenditures. When own-source operating revenues (total revenues minus federal and provincial grants) are compared to operating expenditures, it is clear that Toronto cannot meet its expenditures from its own revenue sources. Expenditures are about $5.6 billion and own-source revenues are about $4.8 billion. The local fiscal imbalance is about $0.8 billion or about $354 per capita. With increased responsibilities at the local level combined with the wave of property tax freezes across the province, this fiscal imbalance could worsen.

On the capital side, the city's net debt load is expected to increase from $1.1 billion in 1999 to $2.3 billion in 2004. Although Toronto is well within provincial borrowing guidelines,[22] an increased debt load means less money available to meet future operating needs, possible reductions in service levels, higher property taxes, or all three. In short, amalgamation has not reduced the fiscal imbalance.

Amalgamation has done little to address key social service needs
Research prepared for the Mayor's Tax Force on Homelessness showed that the incidence of poverty and homelessness is increasing in Toronto. In 1996, almost 26,000 different people used the city's emergency shelter system. Furthermore, there is a growing disparity in incomes between Toronto and the rest of the GTA. According to the most recent census data, the incidence of poverty for families in Toronto was 24.4%, compared to 11.5% for the rest of the GTA and

22   The guidelines state that debt charges may not exceed 20 percent of operating expenditures.

12.2% for Ontario outside of Toronto. Toronto has a disproportionate share of poor households.

Toronto is also over-represented relative to the rest of the GTA in terms of households at greater risk of poverty. Toronto has roughly half of the GTA population but more than 70% of its new immigrants, tenant households, and single-person households, 63% of the region's seniors, and 61% of its single-parent families.[23]

The City of Toronto, with the largest share of low-income households in the city-region, faces greater demands for social services and has fewer resources to pay for them. The downloading of social services to municipalities in 1998 has exacerbated this problem. To some extent, the pooling of social service and social housing costs across the GTA has cushioned the impact on Toronto, but this policy is contentious within GTA municipalities. Indeed, some regions have expressed interest in withdrawing from pooling and York Region sought a cap on the funds made available for pooling. Poverty and homelessness have not been ameliorated by amalgamation.

The capacity to plan

The ability to manage the city-region's future socio-economic prosperity depends, in part, on a healthy infrastructure. Studies prepared for the GTA Task Force confirmed that compact urban form is a critical competitive advantage, as it lowers the cost of infrastructure and raises the quality of life for residents. This section explores the impact of governance reform on the capacity to plan in the city-region.

Barriers to efficient development patterns
The Report of the GTA Task Force, tabled in 1996, concluded that the biggest barrier to a more efficient development pattern in the Greater Toronto Area was the absence of integrated planning across the city-region. Numerous submissions to the Task Force confirmed that the GTA needed a development plan that integrated urban growth patterns

---

23   United Way of Greater Toronto, *Toronto at a Turning Point: Demographic, Economic and Social Trends in Toronto* (Toronto: United Way of Greater Toronto, November 1999).

with efficient, region-wide infrastructure investment. As the Canadian Institute of Public Real Estate Companies noted in its submission to the Task Force, planning within the GTA had become "fragmented, compartmentalized, and complex."

The Task Force identified three ways in which urban planning and management within the GTA are fragmented:

1. *functionally* by urban element;[24]
2. *geographically* by regional and local municipal boundaries;[25]
3. *hierarchically* by provincial, regional, and local municipal jurisdiction.[26]

Urban sprawl in the city-region is the most visible – and negative – consequence of fragmented planning and inefficient development patterns. Indeed, few issues are of more urgent and direct concern to the City of Toronto and to the regions beyond its borders than unconstrained growth.

Benefits of a more efficient development pattern
The economic costs of unrestrained growth radiating out from the City of Toronto should be contrasted with the benefits of a more strategic approach to development and planning. According to a study prepared for the GTA Task Force,[27] a more compact and efficient development pattern could save the city-region an estimated $12.2 billion in hard

---

24   Division by *function* refers to administrative fragmentation by city department. Transit, roads, and traffic are overseen by transportation planners; buildings by city planners; municipal infrastructure by public works, and so forth. Functional division means that the interrelationships among administrative areas are not adequately recognized, leading to inadequate coordination and poor decision-making.

25   Division by *geography* also creates coordination problems. In the GTA before amalgamation, there were 35 planning departments employing more than 850 people at the local level and about 200 people at the regional level. In the absence of a region-wide coordinating body, these geographical divisions along municipal and regional lines result in uncoordinated planning and, even worse, competitive planning between municipalities.

26   The Task Force estimated that, in 1996, the Province of Ontario alone employed an estimated 130 planning and review staff in various ministries.

27   See note 6 above, p. 111. This is based on revised IBI Group estimates, presented in "The Economics of Urban Form" (prepared for the GTA Task Force by Pamela Blais of Berridge Lewinberg Greenberg Dark Gabor Limited, September 1995).

infrastructure capital costs over the next 25 years – or roughly 22% of the projected $55 billion capital investment required to sustain current development patterns.[28] This translates into annual savings of approximately $500 million in capital and maintenance expenses alone. An additional $200 million could be saved in costs related to air pollution, health care, and policing associated with automobile accidents. When lower congestion, parking, and land acquisition costs are factored in, the total cost savings to be realized by containing urban sprawl could average $1 billion a year over 25 years.

Compact development patterns make economic sense. They can also foster a higher quality of life. Urban neighborhoods that are considered to be attractive and safe places are generally characterized by mixed land use patterns. The opportunity to walk to a corner market, cycle to work, or enjoy a variety of entertainment and cultural activities within a few blocks of home are among the benefits that could be lost if development patterns continue to radiate outward without form or boundaries.

Solutions – A regional planning capability
Recognizing the need for improvement to both economic and quality of life measures, the Task Force recommended, among other things, that planning for most of the current regional municipal functions should be undertaken at the Greater Toronto regional level. As conceived by the Task Force, a GTA planning council (the antecedent of the GTSB) would have responsibility for directing infrastructure investment and responding to economic imperatives, such as sponsoring and funding initiatives to revitalize particular areas of the city-region.

A regional planning capability would eliminate the existing fragmentation and duplication of functions between regional municipalities and allow for coordination at the city-region level. In an era of limited resources and intense competition between city and

---

28   The Task Force's estimates of savings from alternative development patterns were based on a review of the literature, analyses of comparative costs in the GTA, and updated cost estimates from the 1990 "GTA Urban Structure Concepts Study." This research confirms that the basic physical structure (or urban form) of the city-region significantly affects the level of capital and operating costs of municipal infrastructure, as well as external costs related to pollution, traffic congestion, and land acquisition.

regions, important infrastructure and development investments must be strategic. They need to be coordinated and ranked in order of importance to ensure that investment decisions are cost-effective.

As the Task Force concluded, coordination will only be possible at the Greater Toronto regional level if a comprehensive perspective on urban structure, transportation, transit, economic competitiveness, and environmental quality can be ensured and regional objectives integrated and achieved.

Evaluating the Greater Toronto Services Board
The GTSB proved to be a poor substitute for the integrated planning body recommended by the Task Force. The GTSB's mandate was confined to transportation management. In spite of the efforts of the Task Force and the compelling expert evidence presented in its report, the GTA was still divided in its approach to planning, the GTSB remained an embryonic institution in search of a mission, and the GTA continued to grow and sprawl across the landscape at an unprecedented rate.[29]

The GTA is expected to grow by approximately 110,000 new residents a year over the next 20 years. By 2021, the city-region would be home to more than 7 million people and account for 19% of Canada's population.[30]

The high levels of prosperity currently enjoyed across the GTA can be attributed to several factors:[31]

• The GTA has a diversified economic base, with a concentration in the fast-growing sectors of manufacturing, finance, and tourism.

---

29 On 1 May 2000, Alan Tonks announced that he would resign as Chair of the GTSB, at the end of his first term, on the grounds that he was unable to make progress. Royson James, "Tonks' exit shows GTA hasn't jelled" (*Toronto Star*, 1 May 2000).

30 Greater Toronto Services Board, *Why the Greater Toronto Area is Important to Ontario and Canada* (background Paper prepared for the GTSB by Strategic Projections Inc., undated). See also Toronto Board of Trade/World Trade Centre Toronto, *Grappling with Gridlock – Bringing the GTA's Infrastructure Up to Speed*, Feb/Mar/Apr. 2000. A recent report in the *Toronto Star* cites new, and as yet unreleased, projections: by 2028, the GTA's population will explode to 7.3 million – a 46 percent increase over 30 years. See Rosemary Speirs, "Toronto is the big magnet" (*Toronto Star*, 9 April 2000).

31 Greater Toronto Services Board, *The State of the GTA in 1999* (prepared for the GTSB by Strategic Projections Inc., November 1999).

- Its job creation rate outpaces that of the rest of the province.[32]
- New jobs, requiring a wide range of skills and providing diverse rates of pay, are being created and attract more and more people.[33]
- It has a relatively young and well-educated population.
- The rate of labour force participation (68.4%) is among the highest in the country.

At the same time, the first *State of the GTA* report prepared by the GTSB,[34] pointed out some worrying trends:

interesting!
- Even though the GTA enjoys the highest standard of living in Canada, it is still significantly lower than that of the wealthiest metropolitan areas in the United States, as well as that offered by most American metropolitan areas of a similar size.
- Although the GTA has the highest standard of living in Canada – by a margin of 30 percent – one out of five GTA families spends more than half of its income to pay for accommodation and food.
- Poverty levels are increasing and becoming concentrated in the City of Toronto. While the incidence of low-income families in the GTA is higher than the national average and most other metropolitan areas in Canada, within the City of Toronto, one in every 3.5 people is poor.[35]
- Resolving the paradox of worsening social conditions in the midst of an improving economy requires an integrated policy-making

---

32   Ibid., p. 9. The GTA created more jobs in absolute terms (240,000 between 1988 and 1998) than any other metropolitan area in Canada.

33   Ibid. "The share of the GTA's total employment accounted for by the business service sector – the fastest growing job creator on an industrial basis in Canada – at 11.7 percent, is among the highest in the country."

34   Ibid., p. 28.

35   This finding is contained in a report prepared by the Canadian Council on Social Development ("CCSD") entitled, *Urban Poverty in Canada* (released 17 April 2000). See Elaine Carey, "Toronto tops the 905 poverty list" (*Toronto Star*, 17 April 2000), p. A1. According to the CCSD, every part of Toronto has a higher percentage of people living in poverty than the provincial average of 17.7%, ranging from a high of 32% in the old City to a low of 23% in Etobicoke. These new statistics will further fuel the debate over the pooling or apportioning of social costs across the GTA. In York Region, for example, municipal councillors recently passed a motion asking for an immediate cap on all funds pooled for social services in the GTA. See Gail Swainson, "York wants cap on social service pooling," (*Toronto Star*, 28 April 2000).

capacity. Unfortunately, increasing levels of prosperity and growth in the city-region have not been accompanied by the development of an appropriate planning framework.

The Oak Ridges Moraine: A case study
The battle fought over development on the Oak Ridges Moraine illustrates the weaknesses in the city-region's existing planning arrangements.

The moraine is a 160-kilometer ridge formed by glacial deposits. It runs north of Toronto from the Niagara Escarpment east to the Trent River, passing through the regions of Peel, York, and Durham. It has been described as the "rain barrel" of the GTA because its deposits of sand and gravel act as reservoirs for the headwaters of 65 rivers and streams – waterways that recharge Lakes Ontario and Simcoe and Georgian Bay, the main sources of water for GTA residents.

At issue is a development proposal before the Town of Richmond Hill, which has been asked to amend its official plan by re-designating 3,250 hectares of ecologically sensitive land on the moraine to accommodate 17,000 new homes over the next 20 years. The proposal raises serious environmental and planning issues. Is it environmentally sound to permit large-scale housing projects on the moraine? How much housing is really needed? How will sprawl affect the water supply? Who has the power to preserve the moraine and control development?

The resolution of this issue will have ramifications far beyond the borders of Richmond Hill and will determine whether and how ecological values in the city-region are protected.

By virtue of its importance, the moraine has received repeated consideration in planning documents and reports. In July 1990, the provincial government of the day announced a "provincial interest" in the Moraine, followed by guidelines for development within the moraine. A technical working committee and a citizens' advisory committee were formed and charged with the task of creating a strategy for the moraine's long term management and protection. Fifteen studies were conducted between 1991 and 1994 to improve understanding of the hydrologic and ecological functions of the moraine. In 1994, a strategy to protect the moraine was proposed, recommending modifications to the provincial *Planning Act*, and the development of a specific plan and legislation to protect the moraine.

Unfortunately, the recommendations were never fully implemented by the Province,[36] even though the Province is in the best position to develop a comprehensive plan for the management of the Moraine, which crosses more than a dozen municipal boundaries. The provincial government took the position that municipalities already have the tools they require (that is, zoning bylaws and official plan amendments) to manage the moraine in an environmentally responsible manner – despite the fact that these tools are difficult to apply across municipal boundaries.

In Ontario, no overriding policy establishes which planning values should have precedence. Provincial planning policies themselves are inherently contradictory: for example, they require municipalities to protect wetlands and woodlots and at the same time designate enough space for housing for the next 20 years. Ontario's *Planning Act* requires developers to "have regard" for the environment – but nothing more.

In February 2000, Richmond Hill tried to force the province's hand. It reversed its initial decision to allow development and asked the provincial government to come up with a plan to protect the moraine. Richmond Hill argued that, as an individual municipality, it lacked the capacity to deal with an issue that extended beyond its boundaries.

As a result of the planning vacuum, it has fallen to the Ontario Municipal Board (OMB) – a body of government appointees with the authority to override local planning and zoning decisions – to determine the future of the moraine. Since OMB decisions are based on provincial development policies, the absence of appropriate policies may advantage to the pro-development side. Even the best result at the OMB would provide only piecemeal protection of the moraine and would do nothing to help establish a provincial anti-sprawl policy.

Interestingly, the impasse over the moraine has caused the formation of new alliances in the GTA between inner and outer cities. Although the Moraine does not run through Toronto, the city asked for standing before the OMB, because of fears that large-scale development on the

---

36   Professor Robert M. Wright, *The Evolving Physical Condition of the Greater Toronto Area: Space, Form, Change* (University of Toronto: The Neptis Foundation Study, February 2000), p. 49.

moraine would pollute city water supplies. However, the OMB decided that Toronto, as well as the Region of Peel, did not have a "unique interest" sufficient to allow them to make submissions to the Board. Toronto intended to appeal this decision to the Ontario Divisional Court, arguing that the City should have standing, because the OMB's decision would have a permanent effect on the entire city-region.

On 4 May 2000, the Province filed a report with the OMB, setting out its official position on the matter. The report said it would be "inappropriate" to urbanize the Richmond Hill portion of the moraine, and provided a map detailing exactly how the public interest and ecological features of the moraine would best be protected. The Province also indicated that a plan for the entire moraine would be forthcoming. Although the Province's plan weakens the position of development proponents, the protection of the moraine has still not been enshrined as either a provincial policy statement or as legislation that would override the OMB's deliberations.[37] Moreover, the plan deals only with the lands affected by the Richmond Hill proposal – about 1% of the entire Moraine.

Municipalities, environmentalists, and the public agree that there is an urgent need for a provincial policy to protect the moraine. Despite its intervention before the OMB, the province was still leaving this crucial planning decision to an arm's-length body.

Investment in infrastructure and urban sprawl

Nowhere has the absence of integrated planning in the GTA been felt more acutely than in the area of urban transportation. Rapid population growth, urban sprawl, and free trade are colliding in the city-region, revealing a transportation system ill-equipped to keep pace with demand and woefully unprepared to meet future needs.

Causes of congestion in the GTA
No matter how one measures the problem, congestion in the GTA is

---

37 One report suggested that recent polling showed that 60% of voters committed to the current government would consider changing their loyalties if Queen's Park allowed development on the Moraine. See David Lewis Stein, "Tory turnabout could save the Moraine" (*Toronto Star*, 4 May 2000).

severe and shows no sign of abating. Every day more than 2 million auto trips take place in the GTA. A recent report from Statistics Canada found that commuting by car takes longer in the GTA than almost anywhere else in the country.[38] Travel time is up, as are vehicle counts and the duration of rush hours on major roads. Not only is moving people within the GTA a problem, moving goods in and out is getting harder and harder. Retail businesses suffer because congestion and scarce parking means that customers and deliveries cannot reach their destinations.

The stress on the transportation network caused by general population growth is exacerbated by two additional factors:

1. Transborder trade has more than doubled since the North American Free Trade Agreement was signed in 1989, expected to double again within the following three years. Most of that is trade carried by trucks travelling on the traffic corridor between Windsor and Oshawa – right through the GTA.
2. Suburban sprawl has increased demand for transit services across vast but lightly populated areas. Transit systems work best when they are moving large numbers of people to a few main destinations. Low-density sprawl makes it difficult to provide transit cost-effectively and threatens environmental sustainability.[39]

Economic costs of congestion
Traffic congestion costs the GTA approximately $2 billion every year and may have even greater long-term costs because of the area's economic significance. The city-region generates nearly a third of Canada's gross domestic product, but traffic congestion could damage the GTA's long-term productivity and competitive advantages. If people and goods cannot move freely within the GTA, and if links to external markets are constrained, the area's attractiveness as a place to live and invest is diminished.

---

38   Statistics Canada, *Traffic Report: Weekday Commuting Patterns.*
39   For a detailed discussion of environmental constraints on city-region growth, see: Richard Gilbert, "Environmental and Resource Aspects of Self-sufficiency for the Toronto Region" in *Toronto: Considering Self-Government*, M.W. Rowe, ed. (Toronto, The Ginger Press, 2000), p. 21–32.

Under-investment in infrastructure

While congestion is increasing, the GTA is lagging behind American and European cities in making much-needed investments in rehabilitating and renewing roads and transit facilities.[40] The pressure on the GTA's transportation system is increasing much faster than the system's capacity.[41]

Toronto was the envy of large American cities in the 1970s. The situation is now reversed. American policy makers seem to understand that city-regions will define economic prosperity in the 21st century, and that every dollar spent on infrastructure – whether on roads, public housing or social services – will be more than paid back with higher productivity.

A study prepared for the Canadian Urban Institute found that while major American cities are undergoing a remarkable renaissance, Toronto is in relative decline.[42] Toronto is investing in new infrastructure at about one-fifth the rate of equivalent American cities, according to the report. Drawing on generous capital grants made available by the U.S. federal government, as well as a broad range of corporate and philanthropic funds, American cities are repairing themselves. All three levels of government in the United States recognize that cities are engines that can drive regional and national economies and are funding them accordingly.

As part of local services realignment, the Province of Ontario transferred responsibility for transit to municipalities and increased local responsibility for highways. Toronto now pays for the entire transit system with money from fares and property tax revenues, without any provincial grants. Although this is one service that is financially self-sufficient, it is strapped for funds.

In Vancouver, by comparison, responsibility for the transit system and regional transportation functions were transferred from the

40 Greater Toronto Services Board, *Transportation, Congestion and Economic Competitiveness in the GTA: Local, Provincial and National Implications* (background paper prepared for the GTSB by Richard Di Francesco, undated). In typical Canadian understatement, the background paper describes a GTA transportation network that has become "less predictable."

41 Ibid.

42 Urban Strategies Inc., *Reinvesting in Toronto: What the Competition is Doing* (Toronto, report prepared for the Canadian Urban Institute, 1999). See also the editorial, "The Road Too Heavily Travelled" (*Globe and Mail*, 27 October 1999).

provincial government to the Greater Vancouver Transportation Authority (TransLink).[43] TransLink receives a share of provincial fuel taxes collected in the Greater Vancouver Area.

A tax on motor fuels earmarked for transportation, construction, and improvement makes good economic sense, and is similar to a user fee that charges road drivers for the costs of providing road-related services. Receiving a share of the fuel tax (and possibly vehicle license fees and other transportation-related charges) to fund road or transit improvements, as recommended by the GTA Task Force, would increase Toronto's financial self-sufficiency and its ability to pay for transit and transportation in the region.[44]

Access and participation

The report prepared by the Toronto Transition Team, the group that oversaw the amalgamation of the city, observed that "this is a city where people get involved."[45] In this section we evaluate whether the traditions of citizen involvement that defined Toronto in the past have been lost in the transition to the new city and examine the criticism of some observers that, one of the "main failures of amalgamation" has been the decline in active citizen participation.[46]

Citizen participation defined
The term "citizen participation" can be defined in many ways. Some definitions have extreme expectations of radical structural changes in the existing system; others consider participation at the ballot box alone. Our definition begins with the assumption that there are degrees

---

43   This was accomplished in July 1998 by an Act of the provincial legislature of British Columbia.

44   See note 6 above, pp. 129–131. The Task Force recommended that the Province should allow the proposed Greater Toronto Council to introduce user fees on private vehicles, including a region-wide user fee on gasoline, up to a stipulated maximum. Revenues generated from these user fees would be dedicated to transportation and transit infrastructure in Greater Toronto.

45   Toronto Transition Team, *New City, New Opportunities – Interim Report* (Toronto: October 1997), p. 82.

46   Interview with Toronto City Councillor Jack Layton, 24 March 2000.

of meaningful participation within the present system. For the purpose of this paper, we will define citizen participation as:

> A component of the democratic system which permits non-elected members of the community to exercise some control over decision-making which goes beyond elections.[47]

Principles of citizen participation

A high level of meaningful participation by city residents in decision-making, policy development, and the monitoring and evaluation of services and programs is a fundamental requirement of local government. Measuring citizen participation, however, is a difficult proposition.

In 1999, Toronto City Council adopted four principles of civic participation, designed to guide the city in developing a broader framework for citizen participation.[48] The city made a commitment to foster:

- *Collaborative Decision-Making*: governing in partnership with the citizens of Toronto;
- *Accessibility*: continuously working to remove barriers to effective citizen participation;
- *Continuous Improvement in Citizen Participation*: using innovative and creative ways to foster citizen participation in other jurisdictions;
- *Community Capacity Building*: supporting Toronto's citizens in cooperative problem-solving.

Common approaches to citizen participation

At the time of amalgamation, the City of Toronto provided many opportunities for and approaches to citizen participation:[49]

47 Bureau of Municipal Research, *Citizen Participation in Metro Toronto: Climate for Cooperation?* (Toronto: Bureau of Municipal Research Bulletin, January 1975), p. 11–12.

48 The four principles are set out in a memorandum prepared by the city's Chief Administrative Officer to the Special Committee to Review the Final Report of the Toronto Transition Team, 1 February 1999.

49 See note 45 above, p. 82–83.

- *direct contact* with individual ward councillors in person, by phone, in writing, or through neighborhood meetings;
- *deputations* by individuals and organizations to committees of council and participation in formal public consultations on specific issues;
- *opportunities for involvement* in council sub-committees, task forces, and program management and advisory committees;
- *membership on municipal agencies, boards and commissions* responsible for city services such as recreation and community centres, civic theatres, the Metro Zoo, and the Board of Health;
- *involvement in partnerships, coalitions, and joint working groups* among citizens, business groups, elected representatives, and municipal staff to address challenging problems over time;
- *community development initiatives* to overcome barriers to participation for groups of citizens or neighborhoods that might not otherwise be involved in civic or community affairs.

In the next three sections we look at direct citizen contact with local government in Toronto, as measured by electoral representation ratios, opportunities for deputations to council and committees of council and participation on task forces.

Electoral representation
The most important local government contact for citizens is their councillor or ward representative. Under the old system, each ward in the city had one councillor at City Hall and another at Metro Hall. Under the new, post-amalgamation system, each ward still has two representatives, both sitting as ward councillors.

However, representation levels were fundamentally altered by amalgamation. Initially, there was one councillor for every 41,850 Toronto citizens. For the November 2000 municipal elections, the province, through the *Fewer Municipal Politicians Act, 1999*, has further reduced the number of councillors in Toronto to 44. Ward boundaries were matched to the electoral boundaries used for the 22 federal and provincial ridings in the City.[50] This results in a ratio of one councillor for every 54,214 Toronto citizens.

50   The *Fewer Municipal Politicians Act, 1999*, gave the Province authority to reduce the size of

This ratio should be contrasted with representation levels across the city-region, shown in Table 4, which are universally better than in Toronto.

Table 4: Summary of representation, Greater Toronto Area, 1997[51]

	Population	Number of representatives	Representation by population
Toronto	2,385,421	57	1:41,850[52]
Durham	452,606	62	1:7,300
Halton	329,613	43	1:7,665
Peel	869,219	38	1:22,874
York	618,497	75	1:8,247

To justify the reduction in the number of wards in Toronto, the province made comparisons with the City of Chicago, which has similar representation levels and with Los Angeles, Houston, and Dallas, which have poorer representation levels.[53]

Due to amalgamation, the obvious answer to high ratios – smaller, more manageable wards – is impractical because it would make the council too large.

In January 2000, in response to the province's request for advice on the implementation of the *Fewer Municipal Politicians Act, 1999*, Toronto City Council adopted a model for 44 single-member wards by bisecting each of the 22 federal-provincial ridings into two.[54] The

---

Toronto's Council to 44 plus the mayor. The government then sought the City's direct advice to determine how the 22 federal and provincial ridings would be divided through regulation.

51 Enid Slack, *Municipal Finance and Governance in the Greater Toronto Area: Can the GTA Meet the Challenges of the 21ˢᵗ Century?* (Toronto: The Neptis Foundation, January 2000), p. 32–33

52 The number of representatives was reduced to 44 for the 2000 municipal election. This means representation of 1:54,214.

53 Ministry of Municipal Affairs and Housing, "The case for fewer politicians in the City of Toronto" (fact sheet, released 2 December 1999). Within Canada, Calgary has a ratio of 1:52,700; Edmonton's ratio is 1:51,340; Vancouver's ratio is 1:49,430.

54 The Province gave the city little time to undertake public consultations on the new ward boundaries. Peter Clutterbuck, co-director of Toronto's Social Planning Council, criticized the process in his deputation to the Administration Committee on Ward Boundaries (11 January 2000) as follows: "As commendable as [the] attempt at establishing acceptable

council's decision has been widely criticized, because the 22 individual boundary decisions were taken in isolation and without regard to maintaining overall local neighborhood coherence, thereby potentially splitting or diluting the voice of communities at City Hall.[55]

Councillors have an office budget for their constituencies and other ward-related work. Although constituency budgets have been increased to reflect the larger size of wards, many councillors report that they have less time to deal with ward-level issues than ever before.[56]

Some observers have suggested that the reduction in the number of city councillors in Toronto has already fundamentally altered decision-making dynamics at the city council.[57] For example, developers may now have more influence at city council because councillors are reportedly taking a "hands-off" approach to zoning decisions outside their own wards. In other words, if a ward councillor supports a local development proposal, there is little likelihood that an application to rezone will be challenged by other members of Council.

Deputations to city council

Before amalgamation, citizens' deputations to city council were the most visible measure of citizen participation.

City officials and councillors alike suggest that there is frustration with the inefficiencies associated with this traditional form of public consultation. Deputations use up staff energy and resources that could, for example, be more effectively spent delivering programs and

---

objective criteria [for the ward boundaries] might be, 57 incumbent Councillors, faced with 13 fewer available seats, are naturally lobbying with each other for ward boundaries that give themselves the best chance for re-election. The primary defining criterion for the long-term ward map may well be the short-term political prospects of the current City Councillors."

55   Ibid. It is important to emphasize the provincial role in this move: the province unilaterally decided to reduce the number of wards and, in doing so, eliminated municipal boundaries that were familiar to all, while retaining for itself the authority to determine final ward boundaries.

56   Councillor Anne Johnston explains that she is overextended because of several new board and committee responsibilities. The alternative to sitting on boards and committees, she explains, is to have municipal "bureaucrats do it," which would be less acceptable. (Interview with Toronto City Councillor, Anne Johnston, 27 April 2000). Similarly, Councillor Brad Duguid states that he lacks the time to be as proactive on community-level issues as he would like to be. (Interview with Toronto City Councillor, Brad Duguid, 28 April 2000.)

57   Interview with Jack Layton.

services.[58] Some argue that the volume of deputations is irrelevant to council's final decision.

At the same time, lobbyists are becoming more powerful and central to the council's deliberations than ever before. Although it is impossible to determine the effect that a larger city size has had on this new dynamic, the curtailing of evening hours for the council and standing committee meetings has certainly made a difference. Before amalgamation, full meetings of the council would often continue into the evening. Now, a procedural bylaw prevents (in most circumstances) council meetings from continuing past 7:30 p.m., severely limiting the ability of citizens who work during the day to attend or make deputations before council or standing committees.[59] Lobbyists have moved in to fill the vacuum, and councillors have come to rely increasingly on informal conversations with them rather than on direct citizen participation.

Issue-specific task forces

Post-amalgamation Toronto has seen a proliferation of Task Forces appointed to address specific issues crossing program and departmental lines. The City's website lists some 18 Task Forces and Special Committees,[60] ranging from the Mayor's Homelessness Task Force to a Task Force to Review the Taxi Industry.

Some observers argue that, given the limitations and frustrations with the traditional methods of citizen participation that have dominated the business of the council, task forces are more effective because they:[61]

- create energy around an issue that might otherwise not emanate from the City's bureaucracy;
- integrate the public into the process at the "ground level";

58   Interview with Sean Goetz-Gadon, Executive Assistant for Council Liason - Mayor's Office, 14 April 2000. According to Goetz-Gadon, the "less we see (of social service organizations), the better."

59   Although there is flexibility to schedule evening meetings, this has never been done under the amalgamated City. Standing committees are open to citizen deputations.

60   See http://www.city.toronto.on.ca/council/committees.htm.

61   Interview with Sean Goetz-Gadon.

- make it possible to advance a specific policy agenda outside the constraints of the regular process;
- allow for a less formal procedure than deputations, making it easier to engage in informal discussions and to brainstorm around solutions.[62]

Moreover, once the council decides to create a task force on a particular issue, staff become more involved and the councillors on the task force develop a level of expertise that exists long after the task force has disbanded. Also, arguably, because a task force report is published, the council will be held accountable to its research, findings, and recommendations.

Community councils
Community councils were created by the new *City of Toronto Act, 1997*, and were, to some extent, a political response to those who opposed amalgamation. They were designed to be "accessible civic forums" where citizens could bring local concerns.[63] Each of the six municipalities that make up the new city had a community council with a mandate designed to enable a better focus on local matters of common interest than could be achieved by a city-wide standing committee. The tasks of these community councils included:[64]

- holding public meetings on proposed official plans and amendments, zoning by-laws and amendments that relate to land lying within the community council area;
- hearing deputations and making recommendations to the council on matters such as business improvement areas, area streetscape improvement plans, traffic and parking regulations, and exemptions to fence, sign, ravine, and tree by-laws;
- hearing deputations on staff decisions about building permits, encroachments on municipal property, requests to remove trees, damage caused by trees on municipal property, and bills related to snow removal, cleaning and clearing debris, and cutting weeds or long grass;

---

62   Interview with Councillor Brad Duguid.
63   See note 45 above, p. 85.
64   City of Toronto website, http://www.city.toronto.on.ca/council/comm_council_cttees.htm.

- involving citizens in neighborhood issues such as identifying recreational needs or safety concerns, monitoring the well-being of local neighbourhoods, and reporting to city council on how well community needs are being met.

The community council approach has the potential to involve citizens earlier in the decision-making process than deputations and public hearings. Whether community councils have, in practice, become an important venue for community participation and outreach is difficult to assess. However, anecdotal evidence suggests that:

- Community councils are operating mostly as local planning committees rather than forums in which broader issues relating to community well-being can be addressed.
- The councils generally address individual interests, not city-wide issues. With no venue for collective community participation in city-wide matters, these issues become more distant for people.[65]
- They have occasionally been used to generate momentum, particularly around issues that will ultimately be decided at council.[66] However, councillors have been known to reverse a position taken at community council when the matter comes before city council.
- Community councils participated actively in the 1999 budget process, hearing deputations from local citizens. In 2000, however, the city's desire to control the fiscal agenda resulted in a truncated process. With community councils excluded from the process, opportunities for citizen participation were limited.

The *Fewer Municipal Politicians Act, 1999* dissolves the existing community councils (as of 1 December 2000) and allows the city to establish new community councils. The city has the option not to

---

65   Interview with Peter Clutterbuck.

66   By way of example, Peter Clutterbuck described the efforts of the York Community Alliance, a coalition of ethnocultural groups that had no community meeting space. They started their advocacy at the York Community Council and obtained a resolution giving them rights to space at the local civic centre as well as a right to participate in the determination of future uses of the centre. The resolution was ultimately approved by city council.

re-establish community councils (although this course of action has not been recommended). On 11 April 2000, Toronto City Council approved a process to determine the boundaries and appropriate size for community councils.

The city also debated the appropriate size for the communities represented by councils. The Toronto Social Planning Council favored dividing the city into smaller "civic districts" – areas based on historic associations among neighborhoods that could balance the size and workload of community councils.[67] The argument is that smaller-scale community councils would reinforce residents' identification with their local communities and help them recognize their connection to the larger city. Some city councillors, however, favored larger community councils, arguing that smaller groups tend to become "cliquish" and parochial, and that the opportunity for a community-wide perspective and decision-making would be lost by creating smaller councils.[68]

Recommendations to resolve this issue were to be presented in a larger report on ways to encourage residents to participate in neighborhood and city-wide issues, expected to go before city council in September 2000. The hope was that the process would result in outcomes that are "enduring" and "permanent" so that citizens can help set the city's agenda and ... gain an appreciation for the challenges now faced by municipal government."[69]

Coordination of marketing efforts

While the city-region is experiencing unprecedented levels of population and employment growth, competition from other city-regions is fierce. This section examines the impact of changes to local government in the GTA on its ability to attract and maintain new investment.

---

67   This recommendation of the Toronto Transition Team is supported by the Toronto Best Practices Group in their "Response to the Interim Report of the Toronto Transition Team" (31 October 1997).

68   Interview with Councillor Brad Duguid.

69   Councillor David Miller, quoted in Jennifer Lewington, "Megacity raises questions of citizenship, professor says" (*Globe and Mail*, 20 April 2000), p. A17.

The building blocks of economic growth
A coordinated approach to economic development is essential to attracting, retaining, and promoting globally competitive business activity. An effective economic development strategy for the GTA should build on regional and local efforts coordinate the spectrum of tools already available to promote growth.[70]

GTA's levers for local economic growth
Admittedly, the extent to which any local government can create a competitive environment for business or leverage local economic growth is limited. For example, it is largely beyond a city-region's power to alter general economic trends or influence the global rationalization of firms. City-regions also have little control over areas that are regulated and taxed by other levels of government.

However, the city-region can affect economic growth by:

- *investing in infrastructure*, including building, maintaining, and upgrading airports, transit facilities, arterial roads, and telecommunications networks;
- *investing in human capital*, which is necessary to support knowledge-intensive businesses;
- *sustaining the quality of life of the City's residents*, which is critical to attracting and supporting business and financial services, as well as tourism;
- *attracting and retaining investment effectively*, with policies that target growth sectors;
- *organizing economic development for competitiveness*, by coordinating regional and local efforts.

The situation before amalgamation: fragmentation and lack of coordination
The report of the Task Force on the GTA concluded that economic development activities should be coordinated across the city-region. At the municipal level, the GTA's profile was being diminished by

---

70   These tools range from the broad (general infrastructure, promotion) to the very specific (customized training, procurement programs, job creation incentives). It is important to focus on growth opportunities that offer the highest leverage – that is, those goods and services that drive the economic well-being of the city-region.

fragmented regional economic development. Research carried out for the Task Force revealed that, of the 30 local municipalities in the GTA, 25 had economic development budgets covering a full spectrum of activities – from small business incubators to international marketing campaigns.

Unfortunately, by trying to offer a complete package of economic development programs, municipalities were spreading themselves too thin and achieving, at best, marginal results. For example, the lack of coordination in business attraction resulted in subscale operations that provided little opportunity to develop specialized marketing expertise.

The Task Force also found that the absence of strategic focus and coordination across the city-region was costing the GTA: at the local level, municipalities were paying about $17 million for what was, at best, disjointed and fragmented economic development activities. Development efforts were being duplicated, opportunities to collaborate across local boundaries were lost, and there was no single, identifiable voice for the GTA in economic development.

The local role

This is not to say that local government has no role to play in economic development. Because local economic development staff are close to their clients, they are well positioned to collect company data and sectoral information for analysis at the regional level. They can also pay regular visits to companies and attend to local business needs through, for example, business retention efforts. It is important, however, to distinguish these functions from business attraction and promotion efforts, which are best pursued at a regional level, where common economic development interests can be served.

The response: The Greater Toronto Marketing Alliance

The Greater Toronto Marketing Alliance (GTMA) is a public-private sector cooperative, established in 1997 to attract jobs and international investment to the GTA. The partners are the 29 municipal and regional economic development agencies and the 27 Boards of Trade and Chambers of Commerce in the GTA. The GTMA's goal is to pursue new business investments by speaking with one voice for the entire city-region. Its stated services include many of those identified by the

Task Force as most appropriately provided at a city-region level, including:

- identifying key markets and sectors;
- aggressively promoting the advantages of relocation to the GTA to these key markets and sectors;
- providing relocation services, information, and assistance to business; and,
- acting as a liaison between investors and civic leaders.

Measuring the GTMA's success
The GTMA has established strategic goals to be achieved over five years:

- *job growth* of 20,000 new primary jobs;
- *economic impact* of $22 billion on the GTA's economy;
- *increased non-resident capital investment* of $1.7 billion a year (measured by additions to the real estate tax rolls);
- *increased collective personal income* of approximately $4.5 billion over five years;
- *a balanced industry mix*, targeting specifically the high technology, automotive, medical/bio-tech, financial services, pharmaceuticals, arts and entertainment, and aerospace industries;
- *enhanced international reputation* for the GTA as measured by major magazines influencing opinion makers worldwide.

It is still too early to evaluate the success of the GTMA. The $3 million now invested in marketing the GTA to a global audience is consistent with expenditures made by similar city-regions in Canada and the United States.[71] Ten new businesses have located in the GTA as a result of the GTMA's efforts. (Most are in the industry, trade, and technology field and will be locating in Toronto.) The development of a marketing alliance agreement and a protocol for handling investment "leads" should provide a foundation for strategic cooperation across

71 The GTMA website (www.greater.toronto.on.ca/mission/htm) compares Toronto GTMA investment with Halifax ($0.5 million) and Montreal ($3 million) as well as the American cities of St. Louis ($4.05 million), Philadelphia ($2.25 million), Cleveland ($5.5 million), Dallas ($4.8 million) and Atlanta ($4.3 million). All figures are in Canadian dollars.

the city-region. However, the GTMA's situation is similar to that of the GTSB – the struggle to define its mission and to obtain buy-in from the political level is hampering its success.[72]

The GTMA's problems (and those of the GTSB) can be linked to the lack of a broader vision for the city-region. Without this vision, both the GTMA and GTSB are essentially adrift. Leaders from the municipalities within the GTMA continue to market their particular cities abroad and the City of Toronto is formally reviewing its participation in the GTMA.

The challenge now facing the GTMA is to find a way to work collectively with its municipal partners, rather than at cross-purposes. The organization will act on the recommendations of an internal performance review and focus on securing stronger public-sector participation.[73] The outlook, however, is not promising in the short-term, given the current political climate.

Conclusion

It has been more than two years (in 2000) since the Province of Ontario implemented some of the most dramatic changes in local government that municipalities have seen for decades: the amalgamation of Toronto, the transfer of many services to the local level, the formation of the Greater Toronto Services Board, and property tax reform. Although it is too soon to grasp the full impact of these changes, we can make the following preliminary observations:

- Amalgamation has not resulted in the cost savings that were predicted, nor has it improved Toronto's ability to provide services or address key social service needs. There is one constructive change: the agreement on the pooling of social service, social housing and inter-regional transit costs continues the tradition of sharing costs throughout the city-region.
- Local government reforms have not improved Toronto's capacity to plan. The GTSB was not given a mandate to do regional planning,

---

72   Interview with Ken Copeland, (former) president and CEO, Greater Toronto Marketing Alliance, 28 April 2000. Copeland's departure from the GTMA was announced 2 May 2000.

73   Interview with Ken Copeland.

and the provincial government insists that local development tools are sufficient to address planning matters, even those that cross municipal boundaries.

- Problems created by under-investment in infrastructure and congestion have intensified. The necessary funding to address these problems is not forthcoming.
- Amalgamation has resulted in larger wards relative to population without establishing compensating mechanisms for access and participation.
- The coordination of marketing activity has not been achieved. Clearly, each city wants to compete on its own and is providing minimal support for a united marketing effort on behalf of the region.

In evaluating these conclusions using our four criteria, we can make the following observations:

- *Accountability*: Amalgamation has increased accountability to the extent that there is now only one level of government in Toronto. On the other hand, the implementation of local government reforms at the same time has confused citizens and reduced accountability.
- *Fairness*: Local government reforms have improved fairness in a number of ways. Pooling social service costs throughout the GTA has resulted in a fairer sharing of these costs. Fairness has also increased as a result of specific decisions made by the new city, such as permitting second suites (basement apartments) throughout the new city. Before amalgamation, only the former City of Toronto permitted second suites. Municipalities in Toronto with a smaller assessment base and lower service levels in the past have benefited from improved service delivery.
- *Efficiency*: The cost of services has increased as a result of amalgamation. Furthermore, Toronto's financial stability is being threatened as a result of the amalgamation and the downloading of social services, social housing, and transit.
- *Sustainability*: Current policies are not sustainable. They do not take account of the long-term social and fiscal consequences of urban sprawl. Unrestrained growth in the GTA will mean significant costs

in the future for infrastructure, parking, land acquisition, air pollution, policing, and health care.

Toronto is at a turning point. Amalgamation, combined with other local government reforms, have reduced its ability to compete in the new global economy and are threatening its enviable reputation as one of the best places in the world to live and do business.

Epilogue

The process of change has continued in Toronto since this paper was written in the spring of 2000. The authors find their conclusions remain valid in the fall of 2002, especially the findings that the Toronto amalgamation has not resulted in the promised cost savings and has not improved the city's ability to provide services. The authors offer the following notes to update readers on changes which occurred since 2000.

Perhaps most striking change is the dissolution of the Greater Toronto Services Board (GTSB). The primary responsibility of the GTSB – operating GO Transit, which provides service and links municipal transit systems within Hamilton and the Greater Toronto Area – was resumed by the province. A Crown agency to run the system was appointed by the province as of January 1, 2002.

In addition, the province announced its intention to establish five Smart Growth Management Councils throughout the province to advise the province on coordinated planning, infrastructure, and service delivery across municipal boundaries. Waste management and traffic gridlock were set as priorities for the Central Ontario Council, which includes the Greater Toronto Area, when it was formed in February 2002. It is too early to tell whether the panel, which released interim advice on gridlock in August 2002, will be effective. However, it functions only in an advisory capacity.

The future of the Oak Ridges Moraine, a case study in the need for planning across municipal boundaries, hung in the balance before the Ontario Municipal Board at the time this paper was written. Following almost a year of hearings, the province put an end to the OMB proceedings with the announcement of a development freeze in

November 2001 pending release of a conservation plan for the moraine in April 2002. The plan protects most of the moraine from development; a foundation was also established to monitor the area and fund public education. The plan allows development on a portion of the land that had been subject to the appeal to the OMB, and the province is arranging a land exchange with developers who own other lands now protected in the plan.

Other institutions established during the amalgamation period continue. The six Community Councils were re-established in 2000 and report to Toronto City Council primarily on local planning and transportation matters.

The quality of life in Toronto continues to be uncertain. Roads are congested, major infrastructure upgrades are required, and homelessness and poverty continue in deep pockets throughout the inner city and older suburbs. A study by the United Way of Greater Toronto and the Canadian Council on Social Development[74] found that even during the economic recovery of the late 1990s, the poverty rate among Toronto residents actually increased.

Notwithstanding these concerns about the deterioration of the quality of life in Toronto, the Toronto community is rising to meet the challenges ahead. A City Summit co-sponsored by the Toronto Board of Trade, the United Way of Greater Toronto, the Canadian Urban Institute, and Rogers Cable was held in 2002 to set an agenda for the next five to 10 years. New plans for the city and its waterfront are coming forward. As the producer of nearly one-fifth of the nation's GDP, the GTA was profiled in a paper released by the TD Bank Financial Group in 2002, as part of its challenge to Canadians to meet or surpass the U.S. standard of living in the next 15 years.[75]

The future of Toronto is also being debated, in part at the national level, as the importance of cities in the nation's economy and social fabric receives increasing recognition. The Prime Minister's Caucus

---

74 United Way of Greater Toronto and The Canadian Council on Social Development, *A Decade of Decline- Poverty and Income Inequality in the City of Toronto in the 1990s* (Toronto: United Way of Greater Toronto, n.d.)

75 TD Bank Financial Group, "The Greater Toronto Area (GTA): Canada's Primary Economic Locomotive in Need of Repairs". TD Economics Special Report, May 22, 2002.

Task Force on Urban Issues released an interim report in April 2002,[76] calling for a new approach to Canada's urban regions. The Federation of Canadian Municipalities has widely publicized the shortfall between the responsibilities that cities must carry and the revenues at their command. Business and political leaders alike are looking for a new deal for Canadian cities. The future of Toronto – its quality of life and economic competitiveness – may be looking brighter. At the very least, interest in Canadian cities has increased significantly since this paper was written in 2000.

---

76   Prime Minister's Caucus Task Force on Urban Issues, *Canada's Urban Strategy, A Vision for the 21st Century*, Interim Report, April 2002.

CAROLINE ANDREW

Evaluating Municipal Reform in Ottawa-Gatineau:
Building for a More Metropolitan Future?

Preface

On January 1, 2001, the amalgamated City of Ottawa was created, covering the urbanized (and urbanizing) territory on the Ontario side of Canada's National Capital Region. One year later, January 1, 2002, the Quebec side of the Region also created a single municipality, named Gatineau. The objective of this chapter is to provide an evaluation of these reforms and attempt to understand how it was that such major reorganizations came about. Three criteria were used to evaluate the reforms: access (including accountability and equity), service (both efficiency and effectiveness), and sustainability. In addition I will evaluate the intergovernmental processes involved.

It is, however, clear that it is still too early to fully evaluate these reforms. This is particularly true in the case of Gatineau, which, at the time of writing this chapter, has just succeeded in avoiding de-amalgamation. This aspect will be examined in greater detail below, but suffice it to say that this context has slowed down the development of the amalgamated city. Even in the case of Ottawa, three years later the municipal government is still in the throes of post-amalgamation organization and not yet in a position to evaluate the results of the reorganized structure. However, this makes it an appropriate moment for a preliminary evaluation, at least in the case of Ottawa. The city itself has been evaluating some of the new structures and, even more importantly, being close to the creation of these structures allows an analysis of the transition, of the initial model for the reforms and of the directions being taken. Thus, it is a good moment to evaluate both the process and the product of reform, including the intergovernmental aspects of this reform.

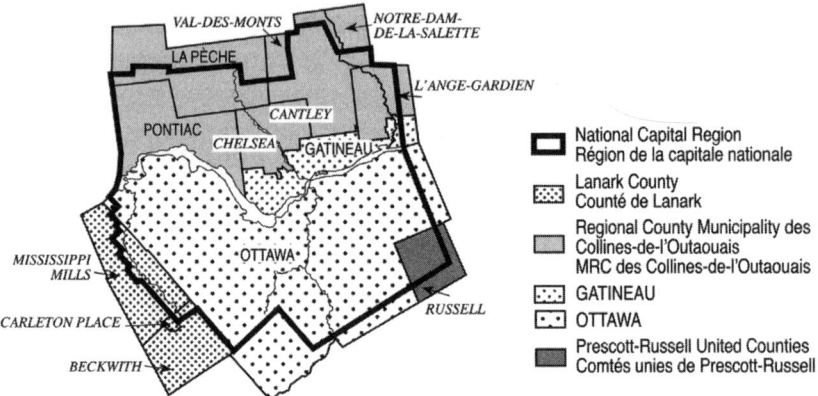

Figure 1: The Ottawa-Gatineau metropolitan area

Before starting the evaluation, it is important to give some initial description of the regional structures in the national capital region (Figure 1). On the Ontario side, the amalgamation reduced a two-tier system of local government to a single structure. The former regional municipality of Ottawa-Carleton (territory 2,757 square kilometers, 1999 population 747,650) included eleven municipalities, from the City of Ottawa with 45% of the population to the village of Rockcliffe Park with a population of 2,010. The territory includes four essentially rural municipalities, which at the time of amalgamation had 9% of the population and 61% of the area. The new City of Ottawa has a population of 774,072 (2001 census).

Ottawa: The historical context

Ottawa was the second area in Ontario to have regional government structures, after the creation of Metro Toronto. The regional municipality of Ottawa-Carleton was created on January 1, 1969, bringing together 16 lower-tier municipalities. In 1973 the 16 municipalities were reduced to 11. Throughout the lifetime of the regional municipality of Ottawa-Carleton, a number of commissions were created (Mayo Commission Report 1976, Bartlett Commission Report 1988, Graham Commission Report 1990, Kirby Commission Report 1992) and these gradually led to increased responsibilities and powers at the regional level (Gervais, 2001). In 1991, the direct election of the Regional Chair was adopted and in 1994 the direct election of the regional councillors.

Despite, or because of, the constant increase in regional responsibilities, there was ongoing dissatisfaction in the Ottawa area about duplication, lack of planning and lack of consultation. This dissatisfaction led to the creation, in August 1997, of a Citizen's Panel on Local Governance in Ottawa-Carleton with a mandate to recommend, in consultation with the citizens of Ottawa-Carleton, a new structure for local government. The Citizen's Panel disbanded in March 1998, arguing that "the opportunity for an objective and open-minded process has been lost due to the promotion by others of entrenched positions and particular governance models" (Gervais, 2001: 5). The failure of the local community to devise a governance model led to the feeling of inevitability about a provincially imposed decision. This seemed all the more inevitable, given the insistence with which the provincial government had imposed amalgamation on an unwilling Toronto. Therefore Ottawa area residents were relatively resigned to the provincial decision in September 1999 to appoint an Advisor to report on reforms in the Ottawa-Carleton region and then in December 1999 to adopt legislation in order to amalgamate the municipalities constituting the regional municipality of Ottawa-Carleton.

When the Ottawa Transition Board was appointed in January 2000 there was some criticism of the composition of the Board, on the grounds that it was very partisan politically, with close links to the Ontario Conservative Party. This was particularly true of the Chair, Claude Bennett, seen to be a close political ally of Premier Mike Harris and therefore aligned ideologically to a right-wing privatization agenda.

Although amalgamation represented a major restructuring, in terms of responsibilities there was a great deal of continuity between the former regional government and the new city of Ottawa. At the time of amalgamation, at least 80% of public spending locally in the region was being done by the regional municipality of Ottawa-Carleton. The two major areas that were affected by amalgamation and that moved from a local level to a more regional level were recreation and local planning (Andrew, 2005).

Gatineau: The historical context

The Quebec side of the region has a double reality; linked in part to the more populous Ontario part of the metropolitan region, it is also linked in part to the rest of Quebec. This system of dual links has defined the Outaouais for much of its history (Gaffield, 1994) and is an essential part of understanding the history of Gatineau. The region has tried to attract the interest of the Quebec government to support its development, attempts that have been intermittently successful. At the same time the region has also tried to gain federal government support for its development. Federal government support came in the 1970s under the Trudeau government, as part of a federal strategy to counter the independence movement in Quebec.

At the time of the municipal amalgamations in Quebec there was some anti-amalgamation organization in Aylmer, the most Anglophone of the municipalities in the Outaouais. But even here the anti-amalgamation movement was relatively weak because of the regional context. The fact that Ottawa was to be amalgamated made many people in the Outaouais feel that this would only strengthen the Ontario role in the governing of the region and that Quebec's interests and presence would be even weaker if the Quebec municipalities were not to speak with a single voice.

However, more recently the anti-amalgamation movement has come back on the scene, following the victory of the Quebec Liberal Party in the Quebec elections of April 2003. The Liberal Party platform included the possibility of voting on de-amalgamation and, since the election, the government has adopted a timetable for referenda. In the Outaouais, this has led to organization both in the former municipalities of Aylmer, and in Buckingham and Angers, more rural and the furthest removed from the urban core. This has led to debates in the new city as to whether infra-municipal structures should be created, in the hopes of appeasing anti-amalgamation forces by some recognition of local identities. It has also led to enormous uncertainty as to whether the integration of services should proceed.

This is a major question, as the regional level of government had been less active and where, therefore, amalgamation involved a major reorganization of activity and service delivery. On the other hand, Quebec municipalities have none of the social welfare or public health responsibilities that exist in Ontario, and therefore services are more concentrated in the "hard services" sector. On the Quebec side, amalgamation brought together five municipalities (Aylmer, Buckingham, Gatineau, Hull and Masson-Angers) with a total population of 228,052 in 2001. One of the most controversial elements of the amalgamation was the name given to the new city. Instead of keeping the name of the central municipality, Hull, Gatineau was the name chosen by the transition team and approved by the Quebec government, reflecting both the fact that Gatineau was a French word and that Gatineau, although not the traditional center, had the larger population (Gatineau had 104,542 residents at the time of amalgamation, as compared to Hull's 65,248).

Evaluation of the amalgamations

It is important to recognize that, despite some grass-roots reactions, the amalgamation processes were relatively calm both in Ottawa and in the Outaouais. The sense of inevitability was very strong on both sides of the river. We will come back to this point in interpreting the reforms, but it is important to keep it in mind as it distinguished the processes of amalgamation in Ottawa and Gatineau from those, better known, in Toronto and Montreal.

   Although this chapter is about the governance of the Ottawa-Gatineau region in the post-amalgamation era, the detailed analysis will principally focus on the city of Ottawa. The reason for this is simple; amalgamated Gatineau has not yet had the chance for results to emerge. The more regional focus will come into play in looking toward the future. For, indeed, the governance of the National Capital Region will, in the medium and long run, be greatly influenced by the amalgamations; there are now three major regional players (the City of Ottawa, the City of Gatineau and the National Capital Commission) instead of some 30. The impact of this is speculative at the moment, but this change will clearly have significant results over the next 20 years.

   We have chosen to analyze the amalgamations in terms of three criteria: access, service and sustainability, as well as an evaluation of the intergovernmental dimensions. These were chosen in order to comprehend the fundamental aspects of the quality of the governance system that was established. The access and service dimensions correspond to classic dimensions of evaluating local governments (Tindal & Tindal, 1990) and the sustainability dimension was added to better permit the analysis of long-run strategic directions of the new cities and of the overall metropolitan region. This last dimension necessitates an understanding of the intergovernmental relations that have evolved through the amalgamation processes. Our fundamental interest is in the governance capacity of the Ottawa-Gatineau metropolitan region and, in this regard, intergovernmental relations are fundamental.

Access

The criteria of access raise a series of questions relating to the relationship between citizens and their local governments. It relates to contacts with municipal officials, both elected and civil servants, and also to the structures for citizen participation.

The Ontario government process for amalgamation was a transition board to manage the creation of the new municipality. It was the transition team that established the overall framework for the political structure of the new City of Ottawa. The explicit intentions of the provincial government were clear: amalgamations were to reduce the number of elected officials and to cut costs. Whether or not the provincial government truly believed this to be possible is not clear, but what was very clear is that this was the way it was presented to the public. Although municipal amalgamations had not been a part of the "Common Sense Revolution," the platform of the Ontario Conservative Party when Mike Harris took power, the amalgamations were presented by the Conservative government in the same light as their general policies– a smaller public sector that would result in lower taxes. The act was entitled the Fewer Politicians Act 1999, and the mandate of the transition board for Ottawa was laid out in this Act:

> The primary function of the transition board is to facilitate the transition from the old municipalities and their local boards to the city and its local boards:

- By controlling the decisions of the old municipalities and their local boards that could have significant financial consequences for the city and its local boards; and

- by developing business plans for the city and its local boards in order to maximize the efficiency and cost savings of this new municipal structure. (Gervais, 2001: 10)

The Ottawa transition team was headed by Claude Bennett, ex-municipal councillor in Ottawa and provincial politician and close ideological ally to Mike Harris. Bennett began his work with the intention of creating a new model of municipal government, paring it down to the essential services and installing a more entrepreneurial spirit (Gervais, 2001: 10). At a widely attended public meeting Bennett stated that if a service could be found in the yellow pages, municipal government should not be doing it. However, Bennett was not entirely successful in installing the kind of model he had argued for, in part because of the decision-making processes that the transition team established. Bennett's ambition to rethink and restructure the City of Ottawa led to looking at areas that then involved wider consultation and therefore the expression of a broader set of opinions. For example, it created a Political Infrastructure Project team to look at the political structures, a group made up entirely of volunteer members not on the transition team. Bennett's suggestion that the City should perhaps think in terms of part-time councillors was universally denounced and disappeared rapidly from public debate. It was seen as a political tactic to allow wealthy business sector representatives to continue their business activity while serving on the council, something that was considered to be contrary to the Ottawa tradition where, since the 1970s, many of the municipal councillors had been full-time politicians. Indeed, the final recommendations of the transition team in regard to the political infrastructure proposals were seen as enhancing the role of the councillors, they were to be paid more and have more staff support than before. The transition team did recommend, at its June 12, 2000 meeting, that the council members have offices only in the community and not in City Hall, a recommendation that was simply ignored by the members of the first post-amalgamation council, most of whom had been elected previously, either at the regional or municipal level. The councillors simply stayed in City Hall and, indeed, had their office space renovated and enlarged.

Despite the significant role described for the municipal councillors, amalgamation has led to more limited access to municipal elected representatives, because of the great reduction in the number of elected representatives. This, of course, was one of the major objectives that the Ontario government had set for the amalgamations and, indeed, the reduction was important: Instead of 84 elected representatives, there were to be 21 councillors and one mayor.

The increasing work load, and resulting problem of access, stems not only from the increased number of electors for each councillor but also from the increased policy role. The transition team (August 28, 2000 meeting) described the councillor's fundamental role as that of legislation, with a task of developing policy, and indeed the new city council has placed an increasing role of policy development on the elected councillors. However, at the same time, the political logic of re-election is still based on satisfying specific, and very local, requests from residents. The councillors are therefore torn between policy development and satisfying constituents, and the combination of the two creates an almost impossible workload.

This increased workload for the councillors has resulted in more difficult access for the public. Access to officials within the municipal bureaucracy has also been more difficult but this is, at least in part, transitional. The reorganization and resulting processes of fitting people into jobs has meant that it is often very difficult to find out who is responsible for which program and, even harder, to contact them.

The transition team also established the initial framework for advisory committees, trying to create a more standard and formalized system. The Political Infrastructure Project Team had made recommendations about the role of advisory committees and so too had the Volunteer Sector Project Team. In addition, the new council increased the number of advisory committees. Despite these recommendations there was not a very clear general policy at the beginning of the new city. Ottawa created a process for applications, and councillors then reviewed the applications and chose initial members of the committees. Criteria would appear to have been experience and a desire to have representatives from across the city. Once the new city began operating, it became obvious that the organization of the advisory committees, their mandates and their links to one another and to the council were not clear. Meetings were called with the chairs and vice-chairs of all the advisory committees as the city attempted to determine what should be the role, and resources, of these committees.

The minutes of one of these meetings clearly indicate the dissatisfaction of the members of the advisory committees and the lack of clear direction by the city.

> Ken Clavette, Chair, Heritage Advisory Committee, expressed concern over the apparent lack of recognition or awareness of the advisory committees, as was evidenced during the work plan debates when advisory committees appeared before their standing committees requesting funding.
>
> The Mayor indicated it was unfortunate that advisory committees were set up without budgets and that although it may not have appeared so to many members, Council members do appreciate what advisory committees do and that the best decisions are the results of consultation. (City of Ottawa Minutes, 2002, iv)

A staff review, made after one year of operation, was then discussed with the chairs and vice-chairs and some clarifications recommended. An amount of $150,000 was made available to be divided annually among the eligible committees, on the basis of work plans that were to be drawn up for the coming year and were to be approved by the relevant standing committee and the city council. There was an attempt to clarify the roles of the committee coordinators, the Lead Department Representatives and the councillor-liaison, but there was little clarification neither of the relations between the committees nor of those between advisory committees and the standing committees of the city council (City of Ottawa, 2002, Annual Review). The committees were to "provide expertise and input" and to "act as a forum for community involvement and public participation" (Annual Review, 3), but in fact with very little organizational capacity for initiating research or policy formulation. It is clear that the role of the advisory committees will evolve. It may be that the Chairs and Vice-Chairs Committee will take on a coordinating role, or that this might evolve to a bureaucratic level with the council and Committee Service Division.

At the present time, the advisory committees are not seen as central to the city's decision-making. One example of this relates to the development of a city-wide policy for citizen participation. City council staff were developing this policy and the initial work was done without any input from, or even information to, the advisory committees. Somewhat belatedly in the process, members of the advisory committees were invited to a meeting to give input to the development of the participation policy. To say the least, this reflects the fact that the advisory committees are seen as peripheral to decision-making.

It should be noted that Ottawa did not set up sublocal entities, based on neighborhood or other territorial definitions. The advisory committees are all content or constituency oriented; they are not spatially defined. This is different from most of the other amalgamations, such as Montreal, Toronto, Halifax or Quebec (Quesnel, 2002). It will be interesting to observe the evolution of sublocal units and whether neighborhood interests will seek ways of influencing municipal policy, particularly if access through the elected officials continues to appear more difficult than before amalgamation.

Over all, it would appear that access has become more institutionalized and more formalized since amalgamation. The advisory committee system may become a significant channel of citizen access, but certainly at the moment it is not clear whether the system will work, both in terms of relations between the different committees and relations between the advisory committees, city staff, neighborhood interests, council committees and the council.

Another of the principal objectives of amalgamation was to create a more accountable political system. Much of the criticism of the two-tier system had been that it was difficult for citizens to understand and assign responsibility and therefore did not meet the criteria of accountability. Even after 1994 when regional councillors began to be elected directly, it was obvious that large numbers of voters were unclear about who was responsible for what. The non-party municipal political system only adds to this confusion, as there is no clear way of holding any individual elected member accountable for decisions taken.

Amalgamation does increase the possibility of accountability. There is one council that is responsible for all local questions in the region.

However, the benefits of this simpler system will take some time to be seen and this because of the confusion between amalgamation and provincial down-loading. As amalgamation took place at the same time as the provincial government decentralized responsibilities for public housing, public transit and increased activities in public health and social welfare, this has led to confusion about what is local, what should be local, what is provincial and what should be provincial (Graham & Phillips, 1998). At the moment the system does not necessarily appear more understandable from the citizen point of view but this may be because of the recency of the political down-loading.

It is on this question of accountability that the Ottawa amalgamation is clearly different from that of Toronto or Montreal. The new City of Ottawa covers basically all the urbanized and urbanizing area and therefore, at least for the foreseeable future, the council can be held responsible for decisions concerning the development of the urban region (at least for the Ontario part – more about this below). In the case of much larger areas such as Toronto and Montreal, the amalgamated cities do not in any way cover the whole urbanized area and the question of how responsibility for urban development can be exercised has not been solved through the amalgamations. In the case of Ottawa, accountability is at least theoretically possible. And, indeed, since the new council has been functioning, the mayor and some of the councillors do appear to be interested in addressing the broader issues of urban development. This was not apparent during the initial election campaign for the new city, but more recently there are signs of interest in the larger questions.

After an initial Smart Growth summit where the broad issues of the policy dilemmas around urban growth models were debated, the City of Ottawa embarked on an ambitious planning process involving the creation of five plans: an Official Plan, a Human Services Plan, an Arts and Heritage Plan, an Economic Strategy and a Corporative Strategic Plan. These were collectively called Ottawa 20/20 and their preparation involved a very active public information and consultation process. By the summer of 2003 the plans had been adopted, calling for denser development in the urban core and a more compact urban form. The recommendations call for a more pro-active public policy if they are to succeed in redirecting present growth trends in Ottawa. They therefore do reflect policy innovation on the part of the municipal council.

The question of access also relates to questions of equity. Has municipal amalgamation in Ottawa led to more equitable local government? Two rather different arguments developed about the likely impact of amalgamation: one was that through equalizing resources across the region greater equity could be achieved, and the second, that by diminishing the political weight of the inner-city and increasing that of the suburbs, it would be more difficult to create and/or maintain the political support for policies and programs aimed at increasing equity. Toronto seemed to illustrate the second. In Quebec, there had been discussion and organization around the question of the impact of amalgamation on women, but it is too soon to know the concrete results.

The question of equity can be examined in the Ottawa case around four dimensions: policies with regard to the Francophone population, women, the multicultural population and the rural areas. The question of bilingualism was the most controversial political question of the entire transition period. The Report of the Special Advisor on Local Government Reform (Shortliffe, 1999) that was the precursor to amalgamation in Ottawa had recommended that the City of Ottawa be legislatively designated bilingual, but the Ontario government did not accept this at the time and has continued to refuse to grant it bilingual status. The transition team formed a Language Services Working Group early in the transition period in order to determine a policy "so as not to interfere with the municipal election campaign" (Gervais, 2001: 53). Its policy did not recommend a bilingual status, preferring to propose the provision of services in French. It was a continuation of the policy framework of the Regional Municipality of Ottawa-Carleton with the addition, from the old City of Ottawa, of the designation of certain positions as bilingual. The senior management team "preferably will either be bilingual or become bilingual" (Gervais, 2001: 54). Neither of the major candidates for mayor of the new city campaigned for a bilingual status, both arguing that services in French were more important than an official status (neither being clear on what services were to be included). The result was that the amalgamation process missed the opportunity of creating a city more equitable to the Francophone population or more symbolically attuned to being the capital of a bilingual country. The debate continues on this question, and in the spring of 2003 the leader of the Ontario Liberal Party announced that, if elected, the Liberal Party would designate Ottawa with bilingual status. Following the election victory of the Liberals, they did not adopt a full bilingual status for the City of Ottawa but rather adopted legislation endorsing the existing policy of the City of Ottawa.

The advisory committee system of the new city does not explicitly deal with the question of gender equity, although the Diversity Advisory Committee appears, by its membership, to cover not only issues of multiculturalism and sexual orientation but possibly gender equity. However, a Working Group on Women's Access to Municipal Services,[1] created prior to amalgamation, following the endorsement by the regional council of the Declaration by the International Union of Local Authorities (IULA) on Women and Local Government reported after the amalgamation, and this context increased the interest of the city in having a bench-mark evaluation of the experiences of marginalized groups within the population with municipal services (Andrew, 2002; 2005; Working Group, 2001). As the Working Group had focused very clearly on doubly-disadvantaged women, the interest of the city was as much, if not more, related to its interest in issues of ethno-cultural diversity, than to its preoccupation with gender equity. The city accepted the report and agreed to study the detailed recommendations by the fall of 2002 in order to indicate what they had implemented, what they would implement and what they did not feel should or could be influenced. The Working Group has not led to specific changes so far, but it has somewhat increased the saliency of gender in terms of service delivery. For example, the Human Services plan quotes the Working Group's report in underscoring the need for greater awareness of gender. This report has led to a second phase of the project, entitled the City for All Women Initiative.

Ottawa is currently becoming more diverse in ethno-linguistic terms. Although not the third urban center in terms of overall population not born in Canada, it is presently the third Canadian urban area in terms of recently arrived immigrant population, behind Toronto and Vancouver (Rose, 2002). Amalgamation could have been an opportunity to rethink city services, but this has not happened up to the present. As has been

---

1   The author was one of the members of the Working Group, and therefore this account should be understood as that of a participant observer.

previously stated, the general political context of amalgamation was that of budget restraints and service restrictions, not one of service expansion.

Toward the very end of the transition period, some grass-roots organization began in favor of a more pro-active local government, including youth groups and multicultural groups (Gervais, 2001: 30-31). These groups made recommendations consistent with the Ottawa tradition of a fairly open municipal system, in reaction to the early excesses of the transition team's entrepreneurial vision. The more recent Human Services Plan does give major consideration to the question of ethnocultural diversity and to the importance of integrating this dimension into service delivery, but this remains, at present, largely at the level of recommendations.

Finally, the issue of rural representation which was examined by the transition team has exploded as a political issue. The rural areas were initially given two representatives for each area so as to increase the rural voice. The new council set up an external committee that recommended new boundaries and when the city council voted to implement the new boundaries, the provincial government blocked the municipal action, arguing that it was unfair to the rural areas. The municipal council was furious, arguing that it had the power to take the decision and that the under representation of the rapidly growing suburban areas was a denial of democracy. This issue is still unresolved. Clearly, from a strictly numerical point of view, it is the suburban wards that are the most under represented. But the rural areas are those most closely linked to the Ontario Conservative government and therefore the areas with the greatest political weight at the provincial level. The November 2003 elections took place under the old boundaries.

In conclusion, access seems both to have suffered and improved with municipal reform. The link between citizens and their elected representatives is more distant, inevitably because of the reduced number of elected officials. On the other hand, the system is simpler and, in that way, the potential for improved accountability has increased. The City did not take advantage of amalgamation to rethink service delivery in a more equitable fashion, but given the overall ideological context of amalgamation, it is perhaps more significant to indicate that services were not reduced.

Service

Improved service delivery was certainly one of the explicit aims of the municipal reform. However, the aspect of improved service that was most often discussed by the provincial government was that of reducing duplication, but this discussion was rarely supported by specific examples or concrete figures. Both Ottawa and Gatineau were supposed to have reduced costs with service levels being maintained. In both, financial shortfalls have been indicated, with the inevitable link to discussions about cuts to services. This serves as a reminder of the complexity of judging the efficiency of service delivery and the limits of simply making expenditure comparisons or staff comparisons without knowing exactly what was being done before and after. For instance, recreation policies varied across municipalities– some municipalities charged higher fees, either because they made more use of professional staff and less use of community volunteers or because they wanted fee-for-service programs. The two largest suburban municipalities had had very different philosophies in regard to recreation policies. Nepean had developed highly professional services and charged in consequence. Gloucester, on the other hand, had developed extensive use of volunteers and charged less. But when judging both efficiency and effectiveness, these differing models are not easy to evaluate. Should municipal recreation programs be judged in terms of the total cost divided by the numbers of users, or should equity factors be included – what is the use made by the poor? by ethnic minorities? by women? by the handicapped?

Perhaps the most interesting innovation in terms of service effectiveness was Ottawa's decision to create a Department of People's Services bringing together social services, housing, public health, library and recreation services. Potentially this has the capacity to provide integrated policy across a broad social policy perspective. On the other hand, this creates a large bureaucratic structure with enormous challenges in establishing the kind of horizontal coordination that would lead to coordinated policy. Politically there are also huge challenges with the new department, as the constituencies linked to the social welfare programs were most concerned that the political popularity of recreation programs would dominate the budget process of People's Services and that, as a consequence, if cuts had to be made, they would be made to the social welfare activities rather than to recreation. The constituencies linked to recreation have the same fears for their programs.

Indeed, People's Services was reorganized in 2004 to become the base of Community and Protective Services, a less encompassing service. Even with this smaller unit, it is still a debate as to whether Ottawa can end up with a pro-active population health vision of municipal social policy. If it works, it would be a major improvement to service effectiveness.

Sustainability

Does amalgamation increase the likelihood of having municipal structures capable of planning for the long run and therefore more able to consider long-term goals of environmental sustainability? Or, another possibility, does it create a political structure even more influenced by the short-term or by political pressure favorable to the continuation of low-density sprawl development. Certainly there is sufficient literature to suggest that current municipal policies relating to land-use and to the built form are not sustainable when one considers the pollution caused by the private automobile, the costs in commuting time, the expenses of low density infrastructures, etc. But how does amalgamation affect this?

It depends very much on the way the political scene evolves. Are larger structures more conducive to taking a bigger picture – or are they more under the control of existing suburban interests? Certainly the first municipal election campaigns for the new cities, both in Ottawa in 2000 and in Gatineau, in 2001, gave no indication of a larger picture – almost all the candidates were politicians already in municipal politics with very low-key and pragmatic positions and seemingly with little desire to take a larger perspective or to argue in favor of an enlarged role for the new city government. However, following the Ottawa election, Mayor Bob Chiarelli has taken some initiatives that are indicative of a broader vision, with longer-term objectives that give greater weight to sustainability. The June 2001 "Smart Growth" Summit was an attempt to get a public discussion going about the consequences of the present system of low-density development. By encouraging citizen input into the Summit, the mayor was hoping to build political support for denser development and better public transit.

Not a lot of specific policy developments came out of the Smart Growth Summit, but this was not unexpected. The City then moved on to the planning process and the elaboration of recommendations connected to the five plans. By the summer of 2003 the overall recommendations, as described above, called for a more compact urban form with a denser urban core based on mixed commercial-residential development on the main commercial streets. One of the principal elements of the plan is better public transportation, and the mayor has been a strong advocate for a major investment in a light rail system. The mayor has been strongly lobbying the federal government to invest in the Ottawa transit project, and some federal support has materialized. Indeed, private development interests have indicated that they will object to the city council's recommendations for denser development. The results of these objections are as yet unknown, and so is the degree of political will of the Ottawa Council to stand fast behind the principles of a more compact form of urban development.

Another dimension of sustainability is that of social sustainability and the extent to which amalgamation facilitates policies that act to reduce income and spatial polarization. Present-day urban development across the world is increasing social polarization and even in Canadian cities these processes are taking place. One very concrete example of this are the growing numbers of the homeless in Canadian urban centers, a complex phenomenon but at least in part linked to the federal government's abandonment of public housing and to federal and provincial programs of de-institutionalization without increasing community resources (Bourne, 2000; Harris, 2000; Peressini & McDonald, 2000). Ottawa has been quite active at the municipal level in putting resources into initiatives aimed at reducing homelessness and in pressuring senior government officials to act. This activity can be related to the strong community mobilization on this question and to the links between the community mobilizing and the city structure, both in terms of city staff and elected officials. However, the politics of the council are not all that supportive of major municipal initiatives; there is some support (and an Ottawa tradition) for looking after the unfortunate, but much less support for a structural analysis of exclusion, and policies consequent with the analysis.

The criteria of sustainable development bring us back to the broader region of the National Capital and the impact of the two amalgamations on the sustainable governance of the region. Coordination should be more likely with only three major actors and, indeed, the National Capital Commission seems already to be consulting more closely with the mayors of Ottawa and Gatineau.

Conclusion

This overview of the impact of municipal amalgamation comes to a somewhat paradoxical conclusion as to the importance, but also the limits, of amalgamation. It is a major reorganization of municipal services, but the structural reform alone has had a relatively limited impact. The more important impact will stem from the political dynamic emerging from municipal amalgamations. Will the major political actors be interested in the potential for broader policies and for a coordinated vision of urban development? If so, the amalgamated structures may provide opportunities but, if not, the amalgamated structures can coexist with very conservative municipal politics.

Why did amalgamations take place? The most immediate answer is that Gatineau happened because of Ottawa, and Ottawa because of Toronto – if the Ontario government had succeeded in pushing through the Toronto amalgamation despite the very strong opposition, it was felt that amalgamation in Ottawa was inevitable. And, as stated above, once Ottawa was to be one city, the amalgamation of Gatineau became inevitable.

There are, of course, more long-term factors that lie behind these explanations. The Canadian tradition of strong provincial governments provides a base of political support for unilateral provincial decisions. This in turn can be linked to questions of Canadian political culture, to the mixture of conservation and radicalism, or of authority and equality, that mark Canadian development. Authority implies that political initiatives can come from above, that provinces are seen as legitimate actors in areas of municipal development and equality, that provincial policies have often created reformed structures to equalize resources on a regional basis.

This is certainly not to suggest that amalgamations are inevitable and, indeed, the Gatineau example illustrates this clearly. De-amalgamation was a possibility and the Quebec context, particularly in Montreal, remains uncertain. Not only are amalgamations subject to political strategies and decisions, this also implies that their impact cannot be determined in advance. The politics of amalgamation are vital and this involves the analysis of the patterns of governance with a multiplicity of actors – the governments, organized civil society, the media, the population, individual staff and individual politicians. The evaluation of the impact of amalgamation involves an understanding of these governance patterns. We hope to have at least demonstrated the interest of such an analysis.

For the case that interests us here, the Ottawa-Gatineau metropolitan area, the major factors that will play out for the overall governance capacity are intergovernmental. Will Ottawa and Gatineau establish effective mechanisms to plan and direct development of the whole metropolitan area? Will these mechanisms include the federal government and, if so, will it be through the National Capital Commission? The amalgamations have created the potential for a governance system for the metropolitan area, but only time will tell if this potential will be translated into reality.

References

Andrew, C. (2002). Municipal restructuring, urban services and the potential for the creation of transformative political spaces. In: W. Clement & L. Vosko (eds.), *Changing Canada.* Montreal: McGill – Queens University Press, pp. 311–334.

Andrew, C. (2005). Diversité des femmes, services municipaux et la construction d'un espace public dans la nouvelle ville d'Ottawa. In Louis Guay, Pierre Hamel, Dominique Masson & Jean-Guy Vaillancourt, *Mouvements sociaux et changements institutionnels: L'action collective à l'ère de la mondialisation.* Québec: Presses de l'Université du Québec, pp. 157-170.

Bourne, L. (2000). Urban Canada in transition to twenty-first century: Trends, issues and visions. In T. Bunting and P. Filion (eds.), *Canadian cities in transition*. Don Mills: Oxford University Press, 2nd edn., pp 26–52.

City of Ottawa (2002). Annual Review of Advisory Committees.

City of Ottawa (2002). Minutes of City Council.

Gaffield, C. (1994). *Histoire de l'Outaouais*. Québec: Institut québecois de recherche sur la culture.

Harris, R. (2000). Housing . In: Trudi Bunting & Pierre Filion (eds.) *Canadian cities in transition*. Don Mills: Oxford University Press, 2nd edn., pp. 380–403.

Gervais, M. (2001). *Public record of the Ottawa Transition Board*. Ottawa: Transition Board.

Graham, K.A., & Phillips, S.D. (1998). Who does what in Ontario: The process of provincial – municipal disentanglement. *Canadian Public Administration* 41: 175-209.

Peressini, T., & McDonald, L. (2000). Urban homelessness in Canada. In: T. Bunting & P. Filion (eds.), *Canadian cities in transition*. Don Mills: Oxford University Press, 2nd edn., pp. 525–543.

Quesnel, L. (2002). Large cities: An opportunity for innovation in sublocal units. Presentation at the Urban Affairs Association Conference, Boston, April.

Rose, D. (2002). Making space for ethnocultural diversity issues in the 'Smart Cities' Discourse. Presentation at the Thinking Smart Cities Conference, Carleton University, Ottawa, October.

Shortliffe, G. (1999). *Report of the Special Advisor: Local government reform in the regional municipality of Ottawa-Carleton*.

Tindal, C.R., & Tindal, S.N. (1990). *Local Government in Canada*. Toronto: McGraw-Hill Ryerson.

Working Group on Women's Access to Municipal Services in Ottawa (2001). *Making the new city of Ottawa work for women*. http:/aix1.uottawa.ca~candrew/womenhome.html.

PIERRE HAMEL

Institutional Changes and Metropolitan Governance:
Can De-amalgamation be Amalgamation?
The Case of Montréal

Since the late 1980s, there has been a renewed interest, both among public-sector decision makers and urban-studies researchers, in metropolitan issues and management of large urban areas (Lefevre, 1998). The transformation of these areas – by multiple interrelated processes, such as urban sprawl, the breaking up of the traditional center, and the appearance of new types of fragmentation associated with a redefinition of social and spatial inequalities – testifies to a change in modes of regulation and of social relationships with the urban space (Balme et al., 1998; Savitch, 1998; Soja, 2000). This is what certain researchers are trying to convey when they speak of passing from the era of the "city of urbanization" to that of "metropolitanization" (Kaufmann et al., 2001).

In many respects, the metropolitan question is becoming a major political issue. This is reflected in particular in reforms undertaken in recent years – aimed, among other things, at setting up supra-municipal institutions (Petitet, 1998) – in order to adapt territorial-management structures and mechanisms to the new economic, social, cultural and urban realities that characterize large urban areas. From this point of view, what has taken place in Montréal in the last six years, which we will examine in detail below, is not remarkable for its originality. Nevertheless, the issues involved in this metropolitan reform, undertaken by the government of Quebec, make it a particular case – in the White Paper announcing the project, the Minister of State for Municipal Affairs and the Metropolis spoke of the "unique status" of the metropolis (Gouvernement du Québec, 2000a: 37) – which merits our attention.

The economic and social difficulties facing the Montréal region are similar to those encountered by other urban areas in northeastern North America. Since the 1970s, economic and industrial changes have required wholesale modernization and conversion of production systems, including their Fordist structure, to respond to a new wave of tertiarization of the economy and to adjust to transformations in economic and social demand. However, given its geographic position, the past advantages of which have dwindled, and its particular history, notably linguistic – considering its bilingual character (Levine, 1990) – Montréal must deal with irritants that other large cities in North America do not have to be concerned with. In addition, even though the costs of moving to the Montréal region are very favorable for new companies, the city nevertheless has a low degree of attraction.

Leaving aside for the moment the challenges that the Montréal region must face in coming years in order to increase, or at least maintain, its competitiveness on a continental scale and then within the constellation of world-class cities (Fossaert, 2001), it must be recognized that in the context of strongly tertiarized economies, the organization of the territory is a differentiating factor (Jouve & Lefevre, 1998). Although Montréal's city center is very dynamic, the form of the urban area has obeyed the principle of the spread city that prevails throughout North America, testifying to the same failure of government policies to control urban sprawl (Stephens & Wikstrom, 2000: 5). Patterns of land development comprise only one problem confronting metropolitan governance, but, given the ineffectiveness of past solutions to this problem alone, it is prudent to raise crucial questions about the effectiveness of recent reforms proposed by governments.

From this point of view, what does the metropolitan reform drawn up for Montréal in the past years change? Above all, how effective will it be on the institutional level with regard to metropolitan governance? To what extent will it contribute to resolving problems such as urban sprawl and the other economic and social problems currently associated with globalization? These include, notably, competitiveness and capacity to innovate in terms of research and development, social integration of new immigrants, and protection of the environment, but also the prevention of the emergence of new forms of poverty and the multiplication of social inequalities (Dubet, 2000). In relation to these factors, will the metropolitan reform add coherence on the city-region scale?

I advance the following hypothesis regarding the present metropolitan reform. Even if this reform has revealed an unprecedented determination on the part of the leaders of the government of Quebec with regard to the municipal level – in light of the numerous and vigorous protests made by mayors of the suburbs on the Island of Montréal and of the cities on the North Shore – its range in terms of institutional innovation is weak. Thus, it seems above all to reflect a number of economic, political, cultural and governance-related changes that had already occurred, rather than being the harbinger of major transformations to come, which might be impelled by the new bodies set up by the reform. One must be careful, however, in advancing this hypothesis, because the political uncertainty created by the installation of new cooperation, coordination and planning structures on the metropolitan scale must be taken into account.

In light of this hypothesis and to respond to the questions raised above, I have organized this essay in three sections. First, I present an outline of the main components of the metropolitan reform that was adopted for Montréal over the last years. Then, from a theoretical point of view, I discuss the main institutional issues that metropolitan reforms raise in the present political and urban context. Then I will return to the case of Montréal to evaluate the road taken and consider some of the new challenges that the metropolis will have to face in the future.

The recent metropolitan reform in Montréal

The debate over the place, the role, and the issues of development in Montréal as a Quebec and Canadian metropolis is not a new one. We will not review the entire history of the municipal administration, though it should be noted that the first institutional concerns with regard to management of large public organizations go back to the beginning of the 20th century (Dagenais, 2000: 9). In 1970, the H. M. R. report (Higgins, Martin& Raynauld, 1970), commissioned by the Federal Department of Regional Economic Expansion, suggested that government policies with regard to revival of the development pole that Montréal represented at the time, at least within Quebec, be reviewed. The preceding year, the government of Quebec had created an intermunicipal layer on the Island of Montréal – the Montréal Urban Community (MUC) – in order to solve the problem of funding urban services, in particular the constantly growing costs of public security, which the city center was no longer able to finance (Boisvert & Hamel, 1998). The idea was to refer to a principle of distributive justice to spread the fiscal burden more evenly among all the municipalities on the island of Montréal, gaining a larger contribution from the wealthier municipalities in the western part of the island (Benjamin, 1975).

With the adoption of the new intermunicipal structure came the integration of policing services, creation of a roll for collection of municipal taxes, and the establishment of an area development plan, to name just three of the ten domains that became the prerogative of the MUC. Over the ensuing 30 years, Montréal has been examined under a microscope: reports, commissions and summits have succeeded each other without any reversal in trends in the existing governance model.

Nevertheless, the Montréal administration did not exist in a vacuum. The same influences that had marked the issue of urban governance in all Western cities since the 1980s were at work in Montréal. Experiments with public-private partnerships proliferated, especially for urban development. Public debates and deliberations were used to improve the functioning of local democracy. In 1988, the City of Montréal adopted a framework policy for public consultation in an attempt to change the relations that had prevailed between the municipal administration and the population. Under this policy, three key mechanisms were instituted by the municipal administration to broaden decision-making processes. The first was recognition of the permanent commissions of the council set up the previous year. Second, consultative committees were created in each of the nine boroughs of the old City of Montréal. The representatives to these committees were local elected officials from the territories concerned. Their role was to transmit notices and recommendations to the city's executive committee on a series of statutory subjects, including modifications to zoning regulations. Finally, the policy framework created the Bureau de Consultation de Montréal, which had the mandate to consult the public on questions or projects assigned to it by the executive committee (Hamel, 2006).

In spite of these changes, the Montréal administration remained embroiled in problems specific to large urban areas, for which the existing management structures seemed ineffective. These included the damaging effects of urban sprawl in terms of social costs and negative impacts on the dynamism of the city center, financing of regional-scale facilities, environmental problems and international promotion of the metropolis.

These problems are neither recent nor new. They can be associated with the image of the spread city or the emergent city (Chalas, 2000) or with that of the "technoburb" or "techno-city" (Fishman, 1987). According to Fishman, in the United States technoburbs appear on the periphery of city centers. They can be as large as a county and constitute viable economic zones. They develop along highways and give rise to corridors of growth, punctuated with commercial centers, functional public spaces – businesses, hospitals, schools – and various types of housing. In technoburbs, the residents find employment and fulfill their needs in the immediate vicinity. This is a new form of urban diversity, without the type of concentration that existed in city centers. The proliferation of technoburbs on the scale of an entire metropolitan region leads to creation of a techno-city – a more or less integrated network, over a vast territory of functional poles that ends up causing in-depth changes to the role of the city center.

Fishman's description of technoburbs and techno-cities, of which the Los Angeles region constitutes the most complete example, corresponds to a model of the metropolis that draws on a variety of trajectories but whose form follows a general trend: metropolitanization (Bassand, 2001). The decentralization of functions and activities, urban sprawl, and increased mobility that characterize contemporary metropolises reveal a fundamental movement to which are added political dimensions arising from fragmentation and greater competition between territorial units in a single metropolitan space (Dreier *et al.*, 2001).

Even though some features characteristic of metropolitanization are less pronounced in Montréal than they are in other North American metropolises, they are nonetheless present. In fact, it is largely on the basis of the political and institutional consequences of metropolitanization on urban fabric and urban life that the government of Quebec has justified its recent interventions with regard to metropolitan reform.

Without delving into all aspects of the reform's administrative labyrinth, it is useful to recall its main components. According to the promoters of the reform, starting with the Minister of State for Municipal Affairs and the Metropolis, Montréal, in spite of certain assets in terms of quality of life, culture, higher education – including the dynamism of many private and public research centers – the diversity of its economy, and the variety and quality of its public services, is mired in major structural problems. Among the problems of greatest concern is urban sprawl – in spite of the fact that Montréal, along with New York, is one of the most compact urban areas in North America – because it wastes resources, puts a strain on public funds, and has damaging effects on the environment.

In addition, the city is witnessing the impoverishment of a growing part of its population: "Within the city of Montréal [in 1996], one person in ten lives under the Statistics Canada low-income threshold" (Gouvernement du Québec, 2000a: 39). The result is increased expenditures on social housing and on programs related to income security. At the same time as they sometimes require supplementary disbursements by the state, these disadvantaged populations possess fewer resources to contribute to financing of infrastructure in the central city, management of major metropolitan facilities, and the international function that the city center must assume, which also requires additional resources. As a consequence, Montréal is facing growing administrative costs for its facilities and services. This is why the public authorities chose to set their sights on a "development vision on the scale of the urban area" (Gouvernement du Québec, 2000a: 40), rather than confine themselves to the central city, the hypothesis being to have the costs of operating and developing the metropolis shared by those who profit from them. This explains why the metropolitan reform was undertaken in two complementary areas.

The first step aimed to increase resources and powers for the City of Montréal by creating a mega-city through forced mergers of the twenty-eight municipalities that existed on the Island of Montréal. The new city came into being on January 1, 2002, following municipal elections held in November 2001 (Figure 1). In parallel, the government started on a second step, which was implemented before the first one. This consisted of elaborating a process of cooperation with representatives of the municipalities throughout the region, with the objective of setting up a region-wide structure for management, coordination and planning. For this purpose, the government of Quebec created the Communauté métropolitaine de Montréal (CMM), covering the territory of the census metropolitan region as defined by Statistics Canada (1996 census), with representation from all municipalities in the metropolitan region. The CMM came into existence on January 1, 2001 (Figure 2).

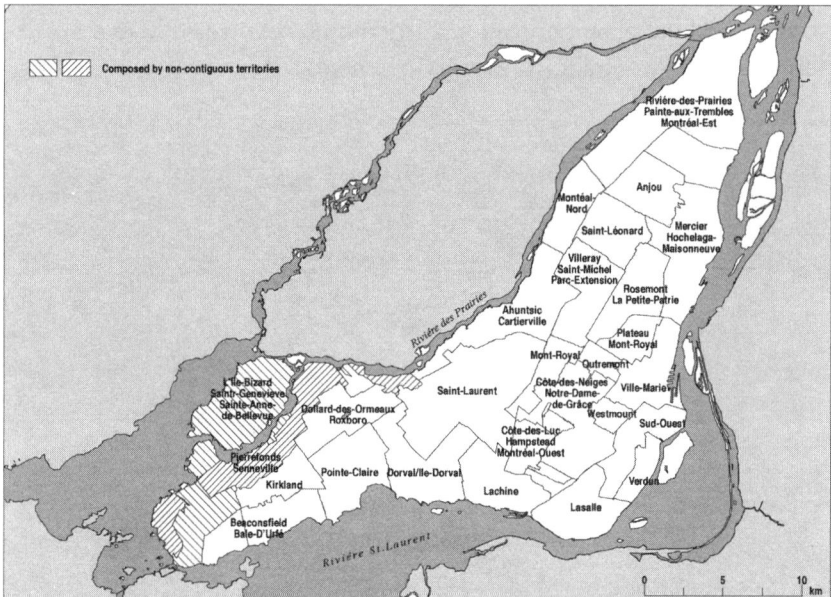

Figure 1: The new City of Montréal and its Boroughs, 2002

The creation of the mega-city of Montréal, with a population of 1.8 million, and of the CMM, which encompasses more than 3.4 million inhabitants, raised numerous controversies. On the Island of Montréal, opposition to the forced mergers came mainly from elected officials who mobilized their fellow citizens in an effort to stop the reform plan. Opposition was manifested mainly in English-speaking cities, but not exclusively: the city of Anjou, a French-speaking suburb and an enclave in the old City of Montréal, was clearly in the camp of those opposed to the government's project.

Opponents saw in the forced mergers a blow to the integrity of their communities, their culture, and the principles of local democracy (Sancton, 2000). Although opposition to the mergers on the Island of Montréal was virulent before the elections of November 2001, it was nevertheless quickly quelled following the elections, and many of the opponents joined the ranks of the Union des citoyens et citoyennes de l'île de Montréal – a new municipal political party – which had won the majority of seats in the election, taking control of the new city's municipal council. This party, led by an ex-minister of the Quebec Liberal Party, was based on a coalition formed of ex-mayors of the suburbs and the main opposition party on the council of the old City of Montréal, the Montréal Citizens' Movement.

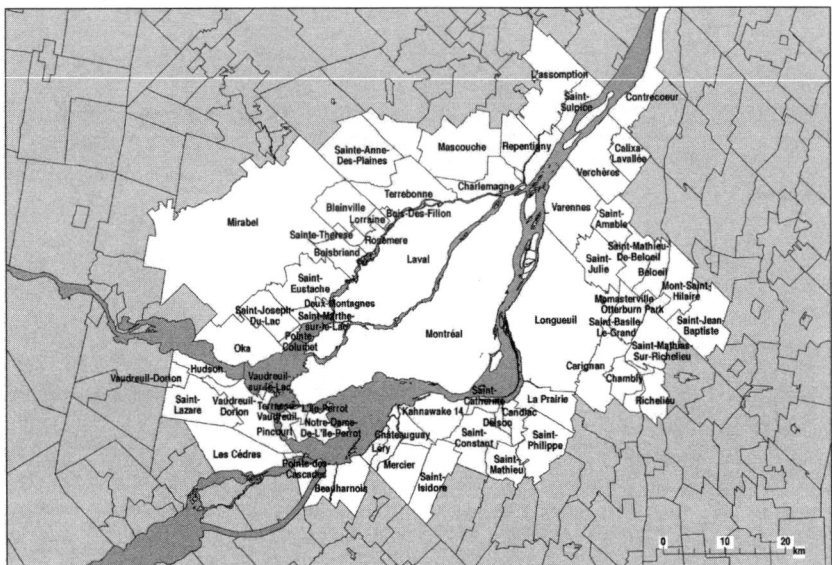

Figure 2: The Communauté métropolitaine de Montréal

If there was a calm spell after the municipal election of November 2001 concerning opposition to the forced merger of municipalities on the Island of Montréal, the coming to power of the Liberal government in Spring 2003 started again the debate and the opposition to the mergers more than ever. This can be explained by the fact that during the electoral campaign the Liberals had declared that if they won the election, it would be possible for citizens, through referendums to be consulted on a de-amalgamation process, giving them the possibility to get back their previous municipality.

Opposition to the metropolitan reform did not come exclusively from suburbs on the Island of Montréal. Elected officials on the North Shore – the suburbs off the Island of Montréal located north of Rivière des Prairies – repeatedly expressed their reservations. In this case, as far back as 1996, the provincial government had reopened the debate on the future of Montréal and its region through public consultation with all decision makers in the urban area with a view to creating a real region-wide planning and management body. But it finally set this project aside until a new strategy was engaged in by the government's political leaders.

The government of Quebec's objectives with the forced mergers on the island of Montréal – forced mergers also took place among the municipalities of the North Shore and South Shore with the same objectives – were to improve the quality of services offered to citizens, to reduce the costs of these services, and to increase the efficiency and accountability of municipal management. The government's intention was to spread the fiscal burden more evenly among all citizens in the new City in a perspective of greater equity. Thus, Bill 170 (Gouvernement du Québec, 2000b), which created the new City of Montréal, established an updated territorial-management structure. This structure is based on 27 boroughs, which respected, on the whole, the borders of the old suburbs and the main urban neighborhoods of the old City of Montréal. The new city council is composed of one mayor and 72 councillors.

The new boroughs are responsible mainly for local services (urban planning, infringements on the ban on converting a building into condominiums, fire prevention, waste removal, local economic, community, and social development, culture, recreation, borough parks and local roadwork). However, many of these responsibilities have to be shared with the city of Montréal administration. In fact, the boroughs have only two exclusive areas of power: fire prevention and infringements on the ban on converting a building into condominiums (Bruneault & Collin, 2001). In addition, the borough councils have no power of taxation. The city council supplies them with an operating budget, although they may, with approval from the city council, levy a special tax on their territory in order to improve the local services offered to the population.

Coming back to the election of the Liberal Party in spring 2003 regarding the municipal reform issue, the Quebec government made haste. A strategy in two steps was adopted. The first decision, through Bill 33 (Gouvernement du Québec, 2003a) consisted of amending the Montréal's city charter in order to increase decentralization in favor of the 27 boroughs of the new mega-city. It means, for example, that from now on the boroughs have the capacity to amend the land use plan or to levy certain taxes for nearby services. In addition, Bill 33 is also a symbolic gesture. The name of the borough's president has been replaced by the one of mayor of the borough.

The second step of the strategy was more delicate. Launched in December 2003 it consisted in a process of "consulting residents of municipalities where the merger process (that has been held by the previous government) was not voluntary," which was the case for all the suburb municipalities on the Island of Montréal. Without getting into the mechanics of the consulting process – which is rather complex – Bill 9 (Gouvernement du Québec, 2003b) will not give back to the residents exactly the same municipality they knew before the forced merger occurred. More than before the merger, they will have to share an important part of their activities and services with the City of Montréal. For that matter, Bill 9 creates an agglomeration council (conseil d'agglomération) that will take decisions over the whole territory for collective matters. It is as though Bill 9 is increasing the decentralization process initiated by Bill 33, while reiterating the necessity to maintain an overall management structure over the island controlled by the City of Montréal.

Of the 28 old suburban municipalities on the Island of Montréal, twenty-two decided to hold a referendum on June 20, 2004 in order to take action (or not) regarding de-merger (that the government presented in terms of "démembrement"). The referendum took place on June 20. Fifteen of the 22 municipalities which had decided to go for the referendum succeeded in obtaining the possibility to recover – at least partly – the previous situation of their local municipality. However, the impact on the management of the City of Montréal should not be seen as catastrophic as predicted by many observers of the local scene. For example, before the de-merger process took place, the population of the City of Montréal counted 1.8 million with a property value of $127 billion. After the de-merger Montréal still has a population of 1.6 million inhabitants with a property value of $103 billion. This can be explained by the fact that most the citizens of the 15 boroughs who decided to go for re-composing their municipality reside in municipalities of the West Island and these are small municipalities. Without any doubt however, in the mind of those who opposed the creation of the mega-city of Montréal, winning the referendum is part of an "étapiste" strategy. Their strategy is to put pressure on government once they have the power granted to their boroughs at first through Bill 33 and more recently through Bill 9. Their idea is to recover the situation that exists ex ante.

Two aspects are worth mentioning regarding the last events of this reform saga. The first is related to the management of urban services on the Island of Montréal. The second has to do with the metropolitan scale. If the impact of de-merger is not catastrophic for the management of urban services as predicted by many, there will be an impact. In different ways the de-merger process is introducing some uncertainty for the future. Further tensions to those that already exist between the boroughs and the City of Montréal are added. When the Liberal Party government launched the de-merger process, the harmonization of service management between the boroughs and the city of Montréal was still to be completed. Supplementary adjustments will be required for civil servants and managers – at least in the fifteen boroughs where the vote for de-merger was positive – opening the door to new administrative adjustments and bargaining.

On the metropolitan scale, the impact should be of less importance. The City of Montréal remains strong at this level. This said, there might be a reconfiguration of power between the three main actors at the council of the CMM (Montréal, Laval and Longueil), because Longueil lost almost 40% of the citizens – four boroughs (Saint-Lambert, Brossard, Boucherville and Saint-Bruno) of the current merged municipality.

In creating the CMM through Bill 134 (Gouvernement du Québec, 2000c), the provincial government wanted to institute a strategic authority for regional planning, the environment, transport, economic development and international promotion. The law calls for the CMM to develop a "metropolitan plan for land use and economic development" covering the entire metropolitan region. The goal of this plan is to set, for the future, "a strategic vision of economic, social, and environmental development aiming to facilitate the coherent exercise of the Community's powers" (Gouvernement du Québec, 2000c, art. 127, parag. 1). According to the law, the metropolitan plan must be adopted before December 31, 2005.

The CMM is not really a regional government. Representatives are not directly elected, but are chosen from among the elected officials of the 63 municipalities within the five administrative regions that constitute the metropolitan region. These representatives assume responsibility for the operations of the CMM through two bodies – the council and the executive committee.

The council includes 28 municipal elected officials: 14 from Montréal, three from Longueuil, three from Laval, four from the North Shore, and four from the South Shore. Under Bill 134, the chairperson of the CMM is the mayor of Montréal. During sessions of the council, if a vote is tied, the vote of the chairperson of the CMM is the tiebreaker (Gouvernement du Québec 2000c: art. 30, p. 11). In addition, the CMM is responsible for agencies with a metropolitan vocation and for special commissions. Aside from the Metropolitan Transport Agency, the Agricultural Consultative Committee, and Montréal International, which has the mandate for international promotion of Montréal, in May 2001, in conformity with the law, five commissions composed of eight elected officials were created in the following areas: transport, land-use planning, economic planning and metropolitan facilities, environment and social housing.

The CMM can intervene in a number of areas, including urban planning, economic development, and the environment, in which it must share its powers with both the City of Montréal and the city's boroughs. However, with regard to metropolitan-level facilities, infrastructure, services and activities, as well as international promotion of the region, it has exclusive powers, although it may delegate its powers relating to international promotion to a third party. This is precisely what it did in granting Montréal International – a consortium representing business interests and public agencies concerned with economic promotion of the city-region – the mandate to assume this function for the moment. For facilities, infrastructure, and metropolitan-level services, the CMM must define the mode of financing by calling upon metropolitan solidarity.

However, the CMM has few powers and resources with which to convince the 63 municipalities and the economic actors on its territory to develop and share a common vision. Its capacity to define a true development strategy for the entire metropolis also seems limited at the moment. The question that arises is that of cooperation and collective action with regard to new metropolitan issues. To what extent will the changes introduced by an institutional reform of the type that created the CMM enable a common vision and a substantial intervention strategy for the metropolitan region to be elaborated?

Metropolitan reforms and institutional issues

Associated with new trends toward globalization, metropolitanization – defined as "the process that shapes metropolises" (Bassand, 2001: 3) – is unprecedented. It goes hand in hand with the spatial and social restructurings that have profoundly changed the face of modern metropolises. Formed in the late 19th century and influenced by a quickly expanding industrial society, metropolises resulted from the specialization and fragmentation characteristic of modern societies. They were articulated around criteria of size and centralization, and they were organized in networks.

Although contemporary metropolises retain many of the distinctive features of modern metropolises, over the last 25 years they have been swept by major changes: tertiarization of the economy and gradual segmentation of the labor market (Corade & Lacour, 1995). The result has been a redefinition of the functions of the city center toward a new geography of centrality (Sassen, 1999: 141), characterized mainly by urban sprawl and the redeployment of economic and cultural activities within city-regions whose borders are constantly being pushed outward (Chalas, 2000). Due to this fact, it seems necessary to review the priorities of urban planning (Ascher, 1998).

Contemporary metropolises have more extensive and more dispersed territories – discontinuous and less dense – than did those of modern metropolises (Bourdin, 2000). Increased mobility, which has contributed to in-depth transformations to the location and organization of economic and social activities (Ascher, 1998) explains a large part of this phenomenon. New dimensions quickly emerged. One can think of economic issues, with regard to increased competition between municipalities. But environmental problems are also at stake, with regard to protection of natural resources. Finally, social dimensions in their connection to space and territory are articulated to new forms of segregation and exclusion. The latter is no doubt what has drawn the most attention from researchers in recent years.

The new social relations within the spaces that characterize contemporary metropolises have engendered not only new urban hierarchies, but also new forms of social inequality. A number of researchers (Altshuler et al., 1999; Clarke & Gaile, 1998; Donzelot, 1999; Dreier et al., 2001) have discussed widening social inequalities in contemporary metropolises between, on the one hand, the middle classes fleeing to the periphery of city centers or barricading themselves in gated communities and, on the other, the working classes, often formed of recent immigrants, for whom social recognition and integration have become almost impossible and whose living conditions are deteriorating. What flows from this is a social dualization of social relationships within the city, the repercussions of which on the metropolitan space threaten its dynamism – and even its viability.

For many researchers (Bauman, 1998; Préteceille, 1998; Sassen, 1999), these social inequalities are articulated in various ways around modes of economic restructuring provoked by globalization and are forcing local public actors to rethink the framework within which they act. As Albert Malibeau notes, "With the emergence of new local problems, flexibility in territorial public-sector action has arisen" (Malibeau, 1998: 437; our translation). It is these new forms of management that the framework of urban governance has been trying to highlight since the 1990s.

By relying on a principle of flexibility and by bringing a large number of actors into political management or the formulation of projects, governance attempts to increase the institutional capacity of local communities (Le Galès, 1995). At stake is improved performance in the light of new economic, social and political challenges that result from globalization.

The theme of governance is the reflection, within both public-sector management and civil society, of a new awareness of the limitations of traditional interventionism and of the need for increased cooperation between public and private sector actors to overcome the problems noted above. However, governance is proving to be a porous notion with poorly defined contours (Hamel, 2002). Even though it accords importance to public debate (Blondiaux, 2001), its relationship with representative democracy poses problems (Lafaye, 2001). It is not self-evident that the actors involved in governance are concerned about those who do not have the resources to participate in these cooperation activities. In addition, common use of the notion sometimes goes hand in hand with a definition of social relations that is non-conflictive. In this respect, such a definition underestimates what is at the root of these relations, namely conflict, which is precisely what the notion of governance is trying to remove. We can think in particular of the mediation processes that accompany the institution of any governance framework and engage the subjectivity of actors (Khorsokhavar, 2001).

In spite of these limitations, since the mid-1990s, the notion has seen great success, which is not due solely to effects of sociological marketing. It conveys the public sector's growing difficulty in dealing with the uncertainties that result from globalization. On the other hand, it is leading to learning and decision-making processes that throw into question the bureaucratic model and the value system that underlies it (Paquet, 2001).

One can also see governance as an intermediate solution between communitarianism and liberalism (Barraqué, 2000). In this perspective, governance encourages local communities to participate in the management of a common good. It is a matter not of proscribing the defense or pursuit of private interests but of tempering their expansion in favor of community solutions when defense of the common good requires it. In this sense, governance goes hand in hand with institutional innovations favorable to resolution of conflicts between private interests. This would appear feasible, on condition that the steps undertaken remain under the "control of institutions making use of democratic sovereignty" (Barraqué, 2000: 132).

The fact remains that in the context of advanced modernity, institutions, including those of governance, are still very fragile (Hamel et al., 1999). This fragility has even grown in recent years, such that institutions are less and less able to guarantee their ability to contribute to the renewal of solidarity. This is explained by the questioning by the middle classes of the old socio-political compromises, associated by social-sciences researchers either with the welfare state or with social democracy that supplied certain guarantees to the working class. Since the 1980s, on both sides of the Atlantic, these compromises have crumbled, with negative repercussions for the poorest people in terms of impoverishment and deterioration in living conditions – in short, some researchers describe this situation as a true process of urban secession by the middle classes from the working classes (Donzelot, 1999).

To what degree has the response to the disintegration of old models of solidarity been implemented through the setting up of new forms of metropolitan governance? Can the old conflicts between the suburbs and the city center – when the flight of the middle classes to the suburbs corresponded to a preference, in conformity with the American liberal tradition, for the values of individual freedom to the detriment of those who promote political equality (Swanstrom, 2001) – be overcome as the result of new institutional arrangements that redraw the lines of management responsibility on the metropolitan scale? Can this solution be imposed on local actors without engendering other forms of withdrawal or disaffection?

These questions, though they were not initially on the minds of the metropolitan reformers, deserve our attention. This is what we will now consider, returning to the example of Montréal.

Assessment and new challenges

Like other North American metropolises, Montréal is engaged in a process of transformation from modernity toward a cosmopolitanism open to the challenges and new opportunities offered by globalization (Soja, 2000: 231). In this context, the question of competitiveness is posed both internally, between municipalities within the urban area, and externally, in terms of the place of the urban area in the constellation of mega-cities. Although it is rife with paradoxes, if not contradictions, the question seems difficult to avoid. To be competitive, both local communities and large urban areas must improve living conditions for all their residents, but they must also be capable of supplying companies with educated and skilled labor (Clarke & Gaile, 1998). Urban sprawl, environmental deterioration, the funding and quality of public services, concentration of urban poverty – to name just a few of the challenges that face local managers – although not recent or new concerns, suddenly are seen in a fresh light. How can the performance of local communities and the urban center be improved on the whole? Could regionalization be a valid solution (Foster, 1997)? And what kind of regionalization should it be?

Proponents of the new regionalism claim that it is necessary to establish coordination mechanisms between municipalities in a single region in order to ensure the economic viability of the entire region, one of the hypotheses being that the dynamism of the suburbs goes hand in hand with that of the city center (Rusk, 1995). This position, which counts above all on governance, must be seen in relation to the solutions of traditional institutionalism, which counted more directly on taking direct charge of regional problems. The new regionalism must also be contrasted against the "public choice" approach, which emphasizes enlightened choices of the citizens and increased competition, rather than cooperation, between the public and private sectors to improve the quality of urban services (Bish & Ostrom, 1973).

In the United States, the thesis of the new regionalism was recently thrown into question. It has not been proved that fragmentation of regional governance threatens economic growth, or that the quality of life in the suburbs depends on the performance and quality of life in city centers (Swanstrom, 2001). In Canada, provincial governments have preferred to set up coordination structures that are related more to the old regionalism, even though the justifications put forward by political leaders resemble the values that the new regionalism defends (Sancton, 2001).

This is also true for the CMM. By setting up a formal region-wide coordination structure, the government of Quebec has imposed a solution from the top down. It has justified its decision by noting the specificity of the area planning problems, which often overflow the boundaries of the municipalities. Interpreting these problems from the perspective of urban governance, the government has concluded that there is a need to create a regional cooperation body (Gouvernement du Québec, 2001: 76–77).

It must be remembered that this solution is the outcome of a public debate that goes back to the 1960s, when the authors of a provincial urban planning commission complained that there were too many decision-making centers and no framework for planning and area development for the region (Commission provinciale d'urbanisme, 1968). In the early 1990s, the Groupe de travail sur Montréal et sa Région (Working group on Montréal and its region, 1993) proposed that a regional government be created, to be elected by universal suffrage. More recently, in 1996, the government of Quebec decided to appoint a new Minister of State for Municipal Affairs and the Metropolis, and the minister undertook a vast public consultation with all "decision makers" in the urban area. At the end of this process, he proposed a flexible cooperation structure in which elected officials and representatives of civil society would participate. But this was never implemented, even though the law was passed.

The CMM has proved to be an institutional response following several decades of equivocation. As with all institutional changes, there is a choice to be made by the government between the flexibility and openness that characterize, for example, approaches using governance, and the coherence and stability that increase the legitimacy of coordination bodies and reduce uncertainty. The government of Quebec has resolutely opted for the second option. What it gains in direct control of the structures and processes that it sets up, it risks losing when it comes to anticipated results (Lundqvist, 2001). This may be explained by the fact that the approval of socio-political actors will be difficult to guarantee, given their low degree of mobilization.

At first glance, the solution proposed by the government of Quebec has few of the requirements that metropolitan governance approaches lay claim to. For the moment, the leaders of the CMM have chosen to consolidate a traditional position. In 2003, they hired a consultant to elaborate the strategic vision that has been used to define the first metropolitan area and development plans. In doing this – in simply fulfilling the letter of the law rather than taking advantage of this challenge by starting a public debate open to all social, economic and political actors in the region – they have reinforced the initial choice made by the government of Quebec with regard to the CMM.

However, as Clyde Mitchell-Weaver and his colleagues (2000) have emphasized, directive approaches to metropolitan management are not without their merits. For one thing, they allow objectives of fiscal equity to be pursued on the scale of a city-region, but are they effective for attaining an objective such as "meeting the challenge of world competition" (Gouvernement du Québec, 2000a: 33; our translation), which remains one of the main goals of the metropolitan reform in the case of Montréal? How will they be able to establish a common vision among all metropolitan actors, given that the new cooperation body offers few constraints and has limited resources and few exclusive areas of power compared to the powers of the City of Montréal and the boroughs? Above all, how will it convince the old opponents to regional cooperation, in particular the municipalities of the North Shore,[1] to abandon their past recriminations against the city center and its managers and agree to participate in a collective approach that would go beyond formal support of the administrative obligations required by the law?

Finally, in the CMM's relations with the central city, three concerns arise. First, in amalgamating the suburbs of the Island of Montréal and the old City of Montréal, the government of Quebec changed the representations of the social composition of Montréal. Over all, although the poor have not disappeared, Montréal appears to be a wealthier city. The community groups and urban movements that previously succeeded in introducing debates and issues at city hall must now turn to the boroughs. Suddenly, their importance in the city and in the municipal administration has decreased. As a consequence, if they want to be able to have an impact on urban problems on the scale of the island and the metropolitan region, they will have to review their past alliances. Second, within the city-region, the question of the balance of power between the central city center and the suburbs

---

1   In the memorandum they submitted to the public hearings on Bill 134, the law creating the metropolitan community of Montréal, a body representing the prefects and mayors of the North Shore took an unequivocal position defending the rural nature and the socio-communitarian nature of their communities, reiterating their independence from the City of Montréal, and criticizing the arguments advanced by the government of Quebec. "Recognizing that the City of Montréal is having financial difficulties and that the bill has been tabled with the goal of helping to improve the finances of the city center, the municipalities of the North Shore deem it unacceptable and irresponsible to participate in the institution of the Communauté métropolitaine de Montréal, the outcome of which will lead ineluctably to the destruction of the peripheral communities of Montréal" (Table des préfets et des maires de la Couronne Nord, 2000: 4–5).

remains an unknown. How much will the city center choose to defend the interests of the old urban neighborhoods? Will a similar scenario play out in Montréal as it did in Toronto, where the amalgamation helped to strengthen an anti-urban sentiment, at least during the first months of the reform's implementation (Keil, 2000)? What forces can speak on behalf of the metropolitan region when the responsible authority, the CMM, was created to play a supportive role toward the central city while its leaders have chosen a low-profile strategy?

Conclusion

The Montréal metropolitan reform raises more questions than it answers. However, I must emphasize that the first months of the new city of Montréal have come and gone in an atmosphere of good relations between unions and the municipal administration, and between the new mayor and the citizens. From January 1, 2002 up to the coming to power of the Liberal government following the provincial election of Spring 2003, optimism has been the watchword and has helped to heal old wounds, in particular the fierce opposition to forced mergers on the island by elected officials and populations in the suburbs. Nevertheless, it is too early to judge whether the new political-administrative framework, seen from the angle of a body governing a large urban area, will become "a motivating element in the transformation of public policies" (Faure, 2003; our translation), especially if we take into account the uncertainty created by the public consultation process initiated by the government with its bylaw on territorial reorganization (Bylaw no. 9).

Since the reform was instituted, observers of the local Montréal scene have been concerned mainly with what would happen on the scale of the city of Montréal itself: the new mayor's degree of popularity; problems that might be caused by integration of certain municipal services; union demands; and action priorities for the new administration. What has taken place on the metropolitan regional scale and concerning the CMM – its operations, its ability to elicit a true sense of belonging and to meet the old and new challenges of the city region – has not drawn their attention.

Up to now, the CMM has had very limited resources and a limited mandate. In most fields, it must share its powers with those of the city of Montréal and the boroughs, not to mention the other cities in its territory, the Municipalités régionales de comté (regional county municipalities), and the five administrative regions that have not been abolished. In addition, as we have seen, many doubts remain with regard to its scope in terms of urban governance at the metropolitan scale.

In this regard, the government of Quebec has chosen an extremely conservative path. It has opted for an institutional reform that hardly modifies the prerogatives and powers of the existing actors. On the metropolitan scale, the reform seems to offer few constraints to the main partners. It does not oblige local actors engaged in an approach of regional cooperation to review their values and old modes of action – at least, not substantially. Nevertheless, we cannot conclude that over the medium term the CMM's operations will not lead to major changes with regard to the management of metropolitan space. Everything will depend on the willingness of CMM authorities to become involved in a true political debate concerning metropolitan issues and to invite civil-society actors to participate in this debate.

However, it remains true that there are also external forces to the immediate local scene that could count. For example, in the near future, will the Federal government decide to bring back urban affairs on the policy agenda, to paraphrase the title of a recent book (Andrew, Graham & Phillips, 2002)? And what about the market forces? What will be the amount and relative importance of re-investment in the Montréal city-region? The future of Montréal will certainly remain in the hands of its main economic and political leaders as long they are able to deal skillfully, on the one hand, with ongoing or upcoming global trends and, on the other hand, with local social forces. In this respect, the creation of Montréal as a viable city-region remains an issue that should be defined in terms of metropolitan governance.

References

Andrew, C., Graham, K.A., & Phillips, S.D. (eds.) (2002). *Urban Affairs Back on the Policy Agenda*. Montréal and Kingston: McGill-Queens University Press.

Altshuler, A., Morrill, W. Wolman, H., & Mitchell, F. (1999). *Governance and Opportunity in Metropolitan America*. Washington, D.C.: National Academy Press.

Ascher, F. (1998). *La République contre la ville*. Paris: L'Aube.

Balme, R., Faure, A., & Malibeau, A. (eds.) (1998). *Politiques locales et transformations de l'action publique en Europe*. Grenoble: CERAT.

Barraqué, B. (2000). Environnement, communautés et sociétés : l'influence américaine, *Espaces et Sociétés*, 101–102: 113–136.

Bassand, M. (2001). Métropoles et métropolisation. In : M. Bassand, V. Kaufmann& D. Joye (eds.). *Enjeux de la sociologie urbaine* (1 – 16). Lausanne: Presses polytechniques et universitaires romandes.

Bauman, Z. (1998). *Globalization: The Human Consequences*. London: Polity Press and Blackwell Publishers.

Benjamin, J. (1975). *La communauté urbaine de Montréal, une réforme ratée*. Montréal: L'Aurore.

Bish, R. L., & Ostrom, V. (1973). *Understanding Urban Governance: Metropolitan Reform Reconsidered*. Washington, D.C.: American Enterprise Institute for Public Policy Research.

Blondiaux, L. (2001). La déliberation, norme de l'action publique contemporaine? *Projet* 268.

Boisvert, M., & Hamel, P. (1998). CUM: 1970–2000, des jeux nouveaux et des enjeux renouvelés. In : Y. Bélanger, R. Comeau, F. Desrochers & C. Metivier (eds.). *La CUM et la région métropolitaine. L'avenir d'une communauté*, (pp. 76–82). Sainte-Foy: Presses de l'Université du Québec.

Bourdin, A. (2000). Pourquoi on s'encombre ou: la ville de la gouvernance, *Espaces et Sociétés,* 101–102: 75–89.

Bruneault, F., & Collin, J.-P. (2001). *Le partage des compétences*. Montréal: UQAM.

Chalas, Y. (2000). *L'invention de la ville*. Paris: Anthropos.

Clarke, S. E., & Gaile, G.L. (1998). *The Work of Cities*. Minneapolis: University of Minnesota Press.

Commission provinciale d'urbanisme (1968). *Rapport de la Commission provinciale d'urbanisme*. Quebec City: Gouvernement du Québec.

Corade, N., & Lacour, C. (1995). *La métropolisation: les commandements*. Cahier no. 95.04, Bordeaux: Institut d''économie Régionale du Sud-Ouest.

Dagenais, M. (2000). *Des pouvoirs et des hommes. L'administration municipale de Montréal, 1900–1950*.Montréal and Kingston: McGill-Queen's University Press.

Donzelot, J. (1999). La nouvelle question urbaine, *Esprit*. 258: 96–114.

Dreier, P., Mollenkopf, J., & Swanstrom, T. (2001). *Place Matters. Metropolitics for the Twenty-first Century*. Lawrence: University of Kansas Press.

Dubet, F. (2000). *Les inégalités multipliées*. La Tour d'Aigues: Editions de l'Aube.

Faure, A. (2003). Une île, une ville, un laboratoire politique? *Possibles*, 27(1-2): 15-27.

Fishman, R. (1987). *Bourgeois Utopias. The Rise and Fall of Suburbia*. New York: Basic Books.

Fossaert, R. (2001). Les villes mondiales, villes du système mondial. *Hérodote*, 101: 10–25.

Foster, K. A. (1997). The civilization of regionalism. *The Regionalist*, 2(2): 1–12.

Gouvernement du Québec. (2000a). *La réorganisation municipale*. Livre blanc, Ministère des Affaires municipales et de la Métropole.

Gouvernement du Québec (2000b). *Projet de Loi no 170. Loi portant réforme de l'organisation territoriale municipale des régions métropolitaines de Montréal, de Québec et de l'Outaouais*. Quebec City: Editeur officiel du Québec.

Gouvernement du Québec (2000c). *Projet de Loi no 134. Loi sur la Communauté métropolitaine de Montréal* . Quebec City: Editeur officiel du Québec.

Gouvernement du Québec (2001). *Cadre d'aménagement et orientations gouvernementales. Une vision d'action commune*. Quebec City: Ministère des Affaires municipales et de la Métropole.

Groupe de travail sur Montréal et sa Région (Working group on Montréal and its region) (1993). *Rapport final*. Montréal: Groupe de travail sur Montréal et sa région, Ministère des Affaires municipales.

Hamel, P. (2006). Participation, consultation et enjeux urbains. Le cadre du débat public à Montréal et son évolution in J.-M. Fourniau, L. Lepage, L. Simard, M. Gariépy and M. Gauthier (eds.)

Aménagement et Environnement. Le débat public en apprentissage. Regards croisés sur les expérience française et québécoise, Paris, L'Harmattan, (forthcoming).

Hamel, P. (2002). La gouvernance à l'heure de la globalisation ou la nécessité de reconsidérer les enjeux institutionnels et les défis politiques. In : C. Gendron & J.-G. Vaillancourt (eds.) *Développement durable et participation démocratique* (pp. 395–410). Montréal: Presses de l'Université de Montréal.

Hamel, P., Lustiger-Thaler, H., & Maheu, L. (1999). Is there a role for social movements? In: J. L. Abu-Lughod (ed.). *Sociology for the Twenty-first Century* (pp. 165–180). Chicago: University of Chicago Press.

Higgins, B., Martin, F., & Raynauld A. (1970). *Les orientations du développement économique régional dans la Province de Québec*. Ottawa: Department of Regional Economic Expansion.

Jouve, B., & Lefevre, C. (1998). Les institutions d'agglomération en Europe. In : R. Baulme, A. Faure, & A. Malibeau (eds.), *Politiques locales et transformations de l'action publique en Europe* (pp. 259–265). Grenoble: CERAT.

Kaufmann, V., Bassand, M., & Joye, D. (2001). Introduction. In : M. Bassans, V. Kaufmann, & D. Joye (eds.). *Enjeux de la sociologie urbaine*, pp.xi–xvii. Lausanne: Presses polytechniques et universitaires romandes.

Keil, R. (2000). Governance restructuring in Los Angeles and Toronto: Amalgamation or secession? *International Journal of Urban and Regional Research,* 24(4): 758–781.

Khorsokhavar, F. (2001). La gouvernance et la place du politique. Gouvernance, Etat et société civile. In : L. Cardinal & C. Andrew (eds.). *La démocratie à l'épreuve de la gouvernance* (pp. 117–127). Ottawa: Les Presses de l'Université d'Ottawa.

Lafaye, C. (2001). Gouvernance et démocratie: quelles configurations? In: L. Cardinal & C. Andrew (eds.). *La démocratie à l'épreuve de la gouvernance* (pp. 57–85). Ottawa: Les Presses de l'Université d'Ottawa.

Lefevre, C. (1998). Metropolitan government and governance in Western countries: A critical review. *International Journal of Urban and Regional Research*, 22: 9–25.

Le Galès, P. (1995). Du gouvernement des villes à la gouvernance urbaine, *Revue française de science politique*, 45 (1), 57–95.

Levine, M.V. (1990). *The Reconquest of Montréal*. Philadelphia: Temple University Press.

Lundqvist, L. J. (2001). Implementation from above: The ecology of power in Sweden's environmental governance, *Governance: An International Journal of Policy and Administration,* 14 (3): 319–337.

Malibeau, A. (1998). Les perspectives d'action publique autour d'un local reconsidéré. In: R. Baulme, A. Faure, & A. Malibeau (eds.). *Politiques locales et transformations de l'action publique en Europe* (pp. 433–438). Grenoble: CERAT.

Mitchell-Weaver, C., Miller, D., & Deal Jr., R. (2000). Multilevel governance and metropolitan regionalism in the USA. *Urban Studies,* 37(5–6): 851–876.

Paquet, G. (2001). La gouvernance en tant que manière de voir: le paradigme de l'apprentissage collectif. In: L. Cardinal & C. Andrew (eds.). *La démocratie à l'épreuve de la gouvernance* (pp. 9–41). Ottawa: Les Presses de l'Université d'Ottawa.

Petitet, S. (1998). *Histoire des institutions municipales*. Paris: PUF.

Préteceille, E. 1998. Inégalités urbaines, gouvernance, domination ? In: R. Baulme, A. Faure, & A. Malibeau (eds.). *Politiques locales et transformations de l'action publique en Europe* (pp. 175–184). Grenoble: CERAT.

Rusk, D. (1995). *Cities Without Suburbs*. Washington, D.C.: Woodrow Wilson Center Press.

Sancton, A. (2000). *Merger Mania: The Assault on Local Government*. Westmount: Price-Patterson.

Sancton, A. (2001). Canadian cities and the new regionalism. *Journal of Urban Affairs,* 23(4): 543–555.

Sassen, S.(1999). Cracked casings: Notes toward an analytics forstudying transnational processes. In: J. L. Abu-Lughod (ed.). *Sociology for the Twenty-first Century* (pp. 134–145). Chicago: University of Chicago Press.

Savitch, H. (1998). Les défis du gouvernement urbain pour le siècle prochain. In R. Baulme, A. Faure, and A. Malibeau (eds.) *Politiques locales et transformations de l'action publique en Europe* (pp. 41–56). Grenoble: CERAT.

Soja, E. W. (2000). *Postmetropolis. Critical Studies of Cities and Regions*, Oxford: Blackwell.

Stephens, G. Ross & Wikstrom, N. (2000). *Metropolitan Government and Governance*. New York, Oxford: Oxford University Press.

Swanstrom, T. (2001). What we argue about when we argue about regionalism, *Journal of Urban Affairs,* 23(5): 479–496.

Table des préfets et des maires de la Couronne Nord (2000). *Mémoire de la Table des préfets et des maires de la Couronne Nord déposé à Madame Louise Harel, ministre d'État aux Affaires municipales et à la Métropole*, Couronne Nord de Montréal.

CHRISTOPHER LEO AND MARK PIEL

Winnipeg:
UNICITY Superannuated at 35

Winnipeg's Unicity began in 1972, in the flush of enthusiasm over the accession to power of the Manitoba New Democratic Party. This was the first turn at the helm for a party that, in those days, would not have hesitated to style itself social-democratic. In its first term in office, the new provincial government launched an ambitious amalgamation of the 13 municipalities in metropolitan Winnipeg, under what conservative local politicians fearfully referred to as One Big Government, together with a panoply of other organizational innovations.

The original concept of Unicity was the brainchild of Meyer Brownstone, a veteran of the top ranks of the civil service in the leftist Co-operative Commonwealth Federation (later NDP) government of Saskatchewan from the 1940s until its defeat in 1964 (Gutkin & Gutkin, 1987; Lipset, 1950). Brownstone, a strong believer in social justice and a grassroots version of parliamentary democracy, sought to design a local government structure that reflected his beliefs.

Yet, even in the process of passage, the original concept was compromised and over the next 26 years a series of subsequent revisions of the City of Winnipeg Act constituted a gradual chipping-away at it. Then, in 1998, in a much more conservative era than the early 1970s, the counter-revolution struck full force in the form of a complete revamping of the remaining vestiges of Unicity under the auspicies of a Progressive Conservative provincial government.

Finally, in 2002, another NDP government, substantially more centrist than the earlier one, introduced the City of Winnipeg Charter Act, a revision of the former City of Winnipeg Act that retained the 1998 reforms, but added an ambitious devolution of power from provincial to municipal government. In these pages, we trace the main lines of this story, and consider its significance at the middle of the first decade of the 21st century.

UNICITY

The launching of Unicity in 1972 was a thoroughgoing reform of municipal government, aimed at banishing fragmentation of authority and segmentation of financial capacity, while greatly increasing citizen participation in municipal decision-making (Manitoba: Urban Affairs, 1971). In the years since then, Unicity has been subjected to a great deal of criticism, while praise has generally been muted at best. In part, this preponderance of unfavorable commentary was a response to the extraordinary ambitions of Unicity's creators, and a reaction to the unrealistic expectations raised by their promises.

To a considerable degree, too, it was motivated by partisan politics. It was not, however, fully justified by the actual performance of Unicity, which – although it fell well short of its creators' expectations – registered some achievements, and functioned tolerably on the whole. In order to draw up a balance sheet of its achievements and its shortcomings, it is necessary to begin by looking at what was being attempted in this first era of metropolitan governance reform in Winnipeg.

The task Unicity's creators set themselves was that of reversing a long-standing trend in Canadian municipal politics, which combined a progressive weakening of political control over municipal government with a steady improvement in administrative capacity. This trend, which paralleled a similar one in the American municipal reform movement of the late 19th and early 20th century, was based on the idea that municipal government should focus on effective service delivery and, insofar as possible, eschew politics.

Such institutional features as small councils, at-large elections of council, non-partisanship, and city manager or council-commissioner systems of administration were designed to ensure that the political role in local government would be limited to oversight at the level of broad policy, while municipal administrations developed a powerful capacity to formulate and implement policy (Smith & Stewart, 2005a). This is in keeping with the American separation-of-powers model of government, but at variance with the parliamentary tradition of a partisan legislative body headed by and fused with a powerful political executive (Anderson, 1979: 73–111; Leo, 1986; Weaver, 1977).

The power of municipal administrations was bolstered indirectly through a reduction of the effectiveness of political supervision, and directly through professionalization of municipal officialdom and introduction of more and more sophisticated administrative techniques. In itself, the value of improved municipal administration is beyond dispute. Indeed, the transformation of municipal administrations from the casual, bumbling, corruption-ridden organizations of last century to the modern bureaucracies we have today is a major, and largely unsung, achievement of government in the 20th century.

The trend toward weakened political control is a very different matter: the question of whether it was appropriate, and of whether it was a necessary concomitant of the administrative achievements remains controversial. The important point for us is that Unicity was a determined attempt to revamp municipal political and administrative structures in such a way as to restore political control over municipal government, by restoring parliamentary principles and leavening them with measures designed to strengthen the grassroots.

Reforming structures, ignoring functions
Both the idea and the manner of its implementation had flaws, including some rather obvious ones. The most glaring, at least in retrospect, is the fact that they addressed structures without seriously considering functions. One of the main reasons for municipal governments' loss of political strength, it is clear, is the fact that, with the passage of time, they became less and less involved in the making of important decisions.

In the last century, most of the decision-making which is now covered by the medicare, welfare and unemployment insurance programs was being made, either by municipal governments or by locally-based charitable organizations. In 1971, and indeed today, all of the basic decisions in these areas are made by senior governments and local authorities have either lost all influence or have been reduced to a purely administrative role. In education, the appearance of local decision-making has been maintained, but its substance has been largely removed by growing provincial intervention.

The Manitoba government, for example, prescribes curricula and textbooks and decides whether and where new schools or school expansions will be permitted. It also allocates a portion of education funding, in the process deciding on the amount to be made available. In at least a couple of cases, school boards, having apparently given up the last pretense of being anything more than administrative agents for the province, have actually called upon the Minister of Education to decide, in cases where enrolment was declining, which schools would be closed.

Even in the area of land use control, which, on paper, remains primarily a local prerogative, senior governments have become increasingly prominent actors whenever important decisions are being made. In Winnipeg, many of the most important initiatives of the past 50 years – the expansion of roads in the 1950s, the Core Area Initiative (Clatworthy and Associates, 1990; Dector & Kowall, 1990), the convention center, the Winnipeg Development Agreement of the late 1990s and the decision in 2003 to tear down the landmark Eaton building and replace it with an arena, to name only a few examples – have been subject to substantial senior government intervention.

A less conspicuous, but even more significant way in which local governments are deprived of power is through the legalistic rigidity of provincial enabling legislation. Thus, such ordinary, every-day activities of government as passing regulations, requiring licences and taking enforcement action typically cannot be undertaken without the permission of the provincial government unless they are specifically authorized in provincial legislation – legislation that, typically, also specifies the precise circumstances under which they can be undertaken.

The practical effect of such a welter of detail is often that, on those rare occasions when municipal councillors work up the courage to propose an imaginative solution to a local problem, it is as likely as not that the municipal solicitor will tell them that the authority for their proposed action does not exist in the legislation, in short that they cannot do it. This can have the effect not only of blocking needed action, but, more damagingly, of discouraging initiative and blocking thought and imagination. The apparent assumption is that, although provincial governments can trust municipal politicians to manage city governments, they cannot be trusted to figure out how best to do it.

Much of the political weakness of local government, therefore, stems, not from the way it is organized, but from its lack of authority. Given that reality, the idea of trying to restore local governments' political strength through the establishment of parliamentary-style institutions, without giving local authorities more decisions to make, is clearly over-optimistic. This is a serious oversight, and is a major contributor to the unrealistic expectations raised by the Unicity reform, as well as to the ensuing disappointment.

Unification and participation
Still, the institutional reforms were carried through, boldly and with finesse, and those that have survived the storms of the 1980s and 1990s are worthwhile achievements. The Unicity legislation unified Winnipeg's urban area under a single political authority, a rarity in North America, and a feature that undoubtedly strengthens the hand of municipal government.

For example, a local leader interviewed in 1985 – a prominent conservative and a good friend of the development community – argued that the existence of unified government had done much to strengthen the municipal government's hand in its dealings with developers, both by making better planning expertise available to it and by depriving developers of their ability to play municipalities off against each other – an ability that has been restored by urban growth in recent years.

The legislation also established a council of 50 members, each representing a ward with a population of about 10,000. The wards were grouped into areas of the city, called communities, and a variety of local matters were brought in the first instance before a so-called community committee, a subcommittee of council that held public meetings regularly in neighborhood offices (Hefferon, 1972; Manitoba, Urban Affairs, 1976). *[handwritten margin note: structure]*

Community committees, as well as the relatively large council, were intended to ensure that the unification of the metropolitan area under a single government did not produce an over-centralized government. Another provision intended to promote grassroots participation was Resident Advisory Groups, which soon became known as RAGs, each chosen at an annual community conference to advise its community committee on issues arising within the community. Since these bodies were intended to reflect the community voice in a very direct way, each community was empowered to determine the manner of election and the size of its RAG, as well as the length of members' terms.

The establishment in the Unicity legislation of a relatively large council based on wards was an initiative that remains defensible today. And the idea of combining this city-wide representative system with community committees, which help maintain neighborhood identity without political fragmentation, is an ingenious feature that has proven its utility for both citizens and leaders. Numerous disputes between neighborhoods and the central municipal government – over expressways, library branches, swimming pools, halfway houses and video arcades, to name just a few – testify to the fact that citizens made use of the representation Unicity affords them, and would presumably regard themselves as worse off without it. Even when the number of wards was subsequently reduced, this local representation remained important (Figure 1).

The RAGs were a different matter. From the beginning, they were perceived by some city councillors as a training ground for future electoral competition, and given an unfriendly reception when they made representations at community committees. Their attempts to marshall the case for their concerns also ran up against a deeply-rooted habit of secrecy in Winnipeg's municipal government, and they were blocked, sometimes by outright refusals to make information available and sometimes by such devices as being allowed access to documents, but only through photocopying at exorbitant rates.

Nor were they provided with funding to allow them to secure necessary secretarial or research assistance, or assistance in maintaining communication with their constituents and placing their positions before the public (Brownstone & Plunkett, 1983; Wichern, 1984).

In addition, as the Taraska Commission observed in 1976 (Manitoba, Urban Affairs, 1976; Wichern, 1984), the Unicity legislation failed to define a concrete role for RAGs. The Taraska Report recommended that the provincial government try to revive them by giving them a role in the city planning process, but the provincial government chose to pursue a policy of benign neglect. RAGs continue to exist where community members opt to organize them, but they have not been a significant factor in city politics.

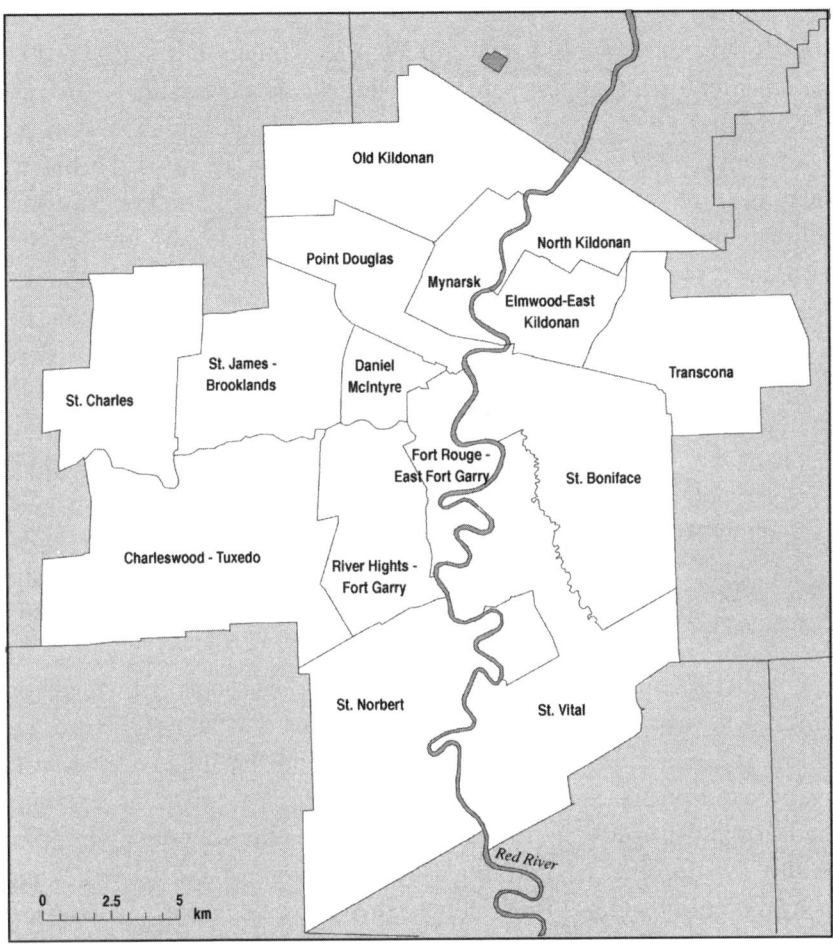

Figure 1: City of Winnipeg Ward boundaries

At various times, RAGs in some communities have been able to maintain good working relations with their community committees, and were seen by some councillors as a constructive feature of city government. Thus, though they obviously failed, in part because of design flaws in the original Unicity legislation, they were never really given a serious chance to succeed. In short, although Unicity's provisions for metropolitan unification and its structures of representation and participation have fallen short of the extravagant expectations of their creators, they measure up reasonably well when judged by more realistic standards.

Equalization

Some of the excessively harsh criticism that Unicity has suffered was the creators' own fault, brought on by unrealistic expectations – driven by sweeping change – that structural reforms would open up new vistas of effective, responsive government. However, a share of the blame must also be borne by the critics, whose ill-will and/or partisan political motivations have led them to focus a great deal of attention on those aspects of Unicity most vulnerable to criticism – notably the ill-fated resident advisory groups – while taking for granted its achievements (Axworthy, 1980).

This seems especially true of one of the most obvious and notable achievements: the equalization of general municipal revenues, as a result of the creation of a single municipality unifying what was then an entire metropolitan area, which eliminated the unseemly spectacle of impoverished and wealthy municipalities existing side by side. Equalization was and is a major political accomplishment, as important as it is rare and difficult. It deserves at least to be recognized for what it is.

In practical terms, equalization has been instrumental in a major shift in development policy, from a focus on suburban arenas, swimming pools, roads and other facilities on the urban fringe to a renewed emphasis upon preservation and improvement of existing facilities in the heart of Winnipeg. Major upgrading of public facilities in the low-income neighborhoods of Brooklands and North Point Douglas during the 1970s are part of this trend, as was the Core Area Initiative of the 1980s, the Winnipeg Development Agreement of the 1990s and current programs for the renewal of downtown residential neighborhoods and then revival of the commercial core. To be sure, many factors besides equalization share credit for these changes, but it seems likely that equalization is among them. If, in another generation, history records that Winnipeg managed to avoid the kind of downtown deterioration so lamentably familiar in many other cities, equalization may be given part of the credit.

"Repatriation" of special-purpose bodies.

Another major political achievement of Unicity's creators – one which has gone virtually unnoticed – was their success in enhancing the control of council over a variety of municipal functions without unleashing the political storm which might well have been expected had the coup been carried off less skilfully (Leo, 1987). During the urban reform movement at about the turn of the last century, such bodies were created in great numbers, partly in order to achieve more effective administration, but also as part of a calculated effort to undermine municipal politicians who were seen in business circles as being dangerously representative of the interests of immigrants, petty traders and working people (Anderson, 1979; Weaver, 1977).

Although the specific ideological impulses of the turn-of-the-century reform movement have been diluted somewhat, the idea that it is desirable to keep municipal politicians weak is still very much a part of the municipal conventional wisdom, and special-purpose bodies are still helping to deprive municipal politicians of their effectiveness and prestige by removing large slices of municipal authority from them.

Any attempts to reverse this state of affairs are seriously hampered, both by the conventional wisdom that sees municipal activities as being somehow sanitized when they are "removed from politics," and by pressures from specific groups (educators, librarians, lawyers and so forth) whose interests are served by the fact that the activities most important to them (schools, libraries and police forces, for example) are insulated from the public scrutiny focusing upon and emanating from city hall.

The authors of the 1970 white paper and the Unicity legislation – Meyer Brownstone and a Toronto lawyer named Dennis Hefferon in particular (Hefferon, 1972; Leo, 1987; Manitoba, Urban Affairs, 1971) – decided to restore the powers municipal politicians had lost to the authorities and had the political shrewdness to find a way of doing it without directly confronting either the interest groups or the conventional wisdom.

The Brownstone-Hefferon strategy for overcoming these obstacles was to retain the appearance of the bodies' independence while deftly removing its substance, simply by providing that the majority of board members be members of city council. The strategem worked. Although initially there were sporadic complaints from interest groups that their favorite boards had lost their independence, the fact that the boards were still manifestly in existence made it difficult to mount a concerted attack on the new order of things. In the meantime, the new order has become the status quo, and the complaints have died out.

This little bit of shrewd manipulation is a genuine tour de force, and with luck a permanent achievement. The virtual elimination of special-purpose bodies from Winnipeg's municipal scene has removed what has long been regarded as a major source of fragmentation and blurred accountability.

R.I.P. Unicity

Nevertheless, Unicity was not the breakthrough its creators clearly hoped it would be. Meyer Brownstone's original concept had called for full parliamentary government, with election of the mayor by the council, instead of the public at large, mimicking the responsibility of the prime minister to parliament. This proposal failed even before the Unicity legislation was passed, for a couple of reasons.

One was that a mayor elected by the council was suspect in the eyes of a public and a leadership accustomed to city government modelled on presidential rather than parliamentary traditions. Possibly an even more important factor was the provincial government's anxiety to secure the support of then-mayor Steven Juba, who had ambitions to become Unicity's first mayor and who was more noted for his skill as a cultivator of voter support than as a leader of political colleagues (Brownstone & Plunkett, 1983: 97–100)

Successive revisions of the Unicity legislation reduced the size of the council, first to 29 in 1977 and then to 15 in 1992, and the citizens of Winnipeg now have twice as many representatives in the provincial legislature as they have in city hall. The accompanying increase in the costs of running for the council, as well as in the budgets of individual councillors, has seriously reinforced the staying power of incumbents, and in the 2002 election the only two councilors replaced were ones who had retired. The next civic election is in 2006.

As we saw, resident advisory groups have not lived up to the hopes of the creators of unicity and of many citizens who, at the founding of Unicity, hoped for a new era of greater citizen participation and government responsiveness. As we will see, a recent revision of the legislation has given the council the power to abolish community committees if it chooses. The term "Unicity" itself has fallen into disuse. Twenty-first Century Winnipeg Unicity is, quite simply, Winnipeg.

However, if Unicity was less than a success, it was not as much of a failure as its detractors made it out to be. Three achievements stand out.

- First, the equalization of general tax revenues, though it is now being eroded by a fresh round of exurban growth, remains in place for more than 600,000 citizens of a Census Metropolitan Area with a population of a little less than 700,000 (StatsCan, "Community profiles," 2001 Census).
- A second lasting achievement is the subjection of special-purpose bodies to council control.

Both of these features are no longer subject to direct political challenge. But the exurban population, which is exempt from Winnipeg taxes – though only 12 per cent of the CMA population so far – grew more than six per cent between 1996 and 2001, 38 times as fast as the population of the city, which grew a mere 2/10 of one per cent in five years. If those growth rates continue, it will not be long before a significant proportion of the metropolitan population is once again slipping free of tax equalization (authors' calculation from ibid.).

As for the special-purpose bodies, there are periodic calls for their re-establishment, on the basis of the time-honored assumption that one function or another will be better performed if it is freed of "political interference," which is otherwise known as democratic governance. Thus gradual re-establishment of special-purpose bodies remains a possibility.

- Finally, there are the community committees, which remain a lively forum for political debate whenever a controversial matter comes before them, one of the few elements of Winnipeg government that are genuinely open to voter participation.

The Counter-Revolution

Thus ended the revolution. The counter-revolution began in 1997, with the publication of Reshaping our Civic Government, adopted by the City Council in March 1997, in response to a report of George B. Cuff

Associates, an Edmonton consulting firm (City of Winnipeg, 1997; Cuff and Associates, Ltd., 1997: 9). The document represents the belated empowerment of Mayor Susan Thompson, who had been swept into office in 1992 on the one-word slogan "Change," promising a hard-nosed, cost-cutting, businesslike approach to government, had been repeatedly thwarted in her attempts to carry out her planned reforms, but was nevertheless re-elected in 1995.

After her second election she gave up her long-cherished notion that a businesslike mayor should abstain from politics, developed an effective, if dictatorial and widely resented, leadership style and began to get her way. In retrospect, Reshaping our Civic Government, a commitment to "affordable government," marks the turning point.

In addition to a variety of contracting-out initiatives already underway – such as park mowing, transit for disabled people and refuse collection – the document committed the city to a list of further initiatives designed to bring about a drastic reduction in the size of the public service establishment through privatization and alternative forms of service delivery. It is this set of initiatives that is at the heart of the "Cuff" round of reforms.

With the help of the so-called Cuff Report, which spelled out the political and administrative implications of the new policies (ibid.), Mayor Thompson and her newly compliant council set about the task of eliminating obstacles to the desired changes, beginning with golden handshakes for the existing administrative leadership, a four-member board of commissioners, and its replacement by a single chief administrative officer. These changes were followed by a thoroughgoing shake-up in the ranks of the public service, together with corresponding changes in the council committee system.

Under the new system, the mayor became arguably the most powerful municipal executive in Canada. She chaired the executive policy committee (EPC), the equivalent of a cabinet, and appointed its members, four of whom she simultaneously appointed as chairs of the standing committees. She also has the power to suspend the chief administrative officer (CAO) for up to three days, by which time the EPC must either extend the suspension for 30 days, reinstate the CAO or recommend dismissal to council (City of Winnipeg Charter Act, 2002, Sections 57–59, 98).

The council continued to have 15 members, elected by wards, and the term of the council and the mayor was extended from three to four years. The council has the power to appoint members of standing committees, not including the chairs. It decides how many members the EPC will have, up to a maximum of 7 (ibid., Sec.63).

All of these changes help to ensure the accountability of the administration to the council, and especially to the mayor and the EPC. However, as has been the case ever since the first flush of enthusiasm over Unicity died, this enthusiasm for political control and administrative potency is not matched by a similarly strong commitment to effective representation of the public in political decision-making.

Capping a succession of reductions in the size of the council – each of which necessarily increased the cost of campaigns and reduced the intensity of representation[1] – the latest legislation gives the council the power to abolish community committees. These committees of the council, which, as we have seen, were one of the more successful parts of the Unicity concept, comprise, respectively, the councillors from each of Winnipeg's five communities and become the first political forum for deliberation of such local issues as subdivision and demolition approvals, rezoning, snow removal issues, parking issues, construction and maintenance of recreation facilities, and so forth.

These committees have been lively forums for debate, in noisy meetings that sometimes extend far into the night. It is their duty to produce recommendations to the council, and the recommendations have been influential. The council has generally been reluctant to overturn a community committee recommendation, unless it was felt that pressing city-wide concerns justified overriding the local community's expressed will.

In the original Unicity legislation, there were 13 community committees. As the size of the council dwindled, the community committees likewise dwindled to five, and now they could disappear. The replacement in 1998 of the conservative Susan Thompson by Glen Murray, formerly a left-wing councillor, and North America's first openly gay big city mayor, made their abolition appear less likely, but

---

1   The compensation for reduced intensity of representation is that councillors receive a pay increase and their positions are designated as full time. Whether they are spending their extra time staying in touch with and responding to constituents remains open to debate.

the legislative provision remains on the books. Murray announced his resignation as mayor in May 2004 – the first city mayor to quit mid term – to run for the Liberals in the June 28, 2004, federal election. He was defeated. Under his successor, Sam Katz, the city's first Jewish mayor, the continued existence of the community committees is currently under review by the Winnipeg council (www.winnipeg.ca, accessed March 1, 2005). However, in the meantime, the community committees continue to operate in their present form and have the same powers and duties as they did under the City of Winnipeg Act before it was amended in October, 1998 (www.winnipeg.ca, accessed March 3, 2005).

The Charter Act

The 1998 revisions of the City of Winnipeg Act were legislated in the twilight of Progressive-Conservative government in Manitoba. In 2002, the provincial New Democrats, who had won power in 1999, introduced legislation to provide the city of Winnipeg with a new charter in January 2003. While the city has had its own charter since 1972, the latest effort by the provincial government sought to modernize many aspects of the old Unicity Act.

Murray, then mayor of one of Canada's self-designated five "hub cities,"[2] was a vocal advocate for substantial increases in the power and independence of the governments of major cities. Murray, who, unlike Susan Thompson, was able to cultivate good relations with the provincial government, called the new city charter an acknowledgement on the part of the province of the responsibility and accountability of Winnipeg's local government (Province of Manitoba, *News Release*, 2002).

Following are some of the act's key features:

---

2   The C5 was originally conceived by renowned urbanist and economist Jane Jacobs and Toronto-based businessman and philanthropist Alan Broadbent. It first met in Winnipeg in May, 2001, with Murray acting as host, in order to develop a strategy for Canada's economic hub cities. The mandate of the C5 is to push for a legislative reform agenda and renegotiate a new relationship for municipalities with senior levels of government. See Christopher Leo, "Rethinking Urban Governance in the 21st Century," Halifax, Canadian Political Science Association paper, 2003, pp 1-2.

- A significant expansion of the city's powers to act independently of provincial control.
- Provisions to increase the city's ability to buy and sell goods and services in innovative ways.
- Authorization to undertake tax increment financing.
- A miscellany of measures billed as mandating an increase in the city government's accountability to the public.

Regional governance

The Unicity reforms of 1972 were revolutionary by Canadian municipal standards, but they were Manitoba's last revolutionary venture. Despite revisions of the City of Winnipeg Act in 1977, 1992 and 1997, there had, until 2003, been no far-reaching reform of the powers delegated to the city, nor a shift in municipal boundaries. Unlike Ontario's recent efforts to "disentangle" provincial and municipal functions in the 1990s,[3] no similar attempt were made to do so in Manitoba. Considering the contrast between the prudence and "wait and see" attitude of the Manitoba Progressive Conservatives and the ideologically motivated neighboring Ontario Conservative government then led by Mike Harris (Premier, 1995–2002) , this is hardly surprising (Piel & Leo, 2005).

The province's reluctance, since 1972, to wade into very deep political waters is also evident in the contrast between a number of major municipal amalgamations across the country on one hand and the Manitoba government's unwillingness on the other to undertake any serious initiatives in the governance of the Winnipeg region. The provincial government's efforts at regional governance have eschewed substance in favor of appearances. The province established a Capital Region Committee in 1989 to address regional issues affecting

---

3   On this, see, for example, Province of Ontario, Report of the Advisory Committee to the Minister of Municipal Affairs on the provincial-Municipal Relationship (Toronto: Government of Ontario, January, 1991; something wrong with these paretheses David Siegel, "Disentangling Provincial-Municipal Relations in Ontario," Management (Toronto: IPAC, Fall, 1992); Canadian Urban Institute, Disentangling Local Government Responsibilities – International Comparisons (Toronto: January, 1993); and the former Toronto Mayor/MP chaired David Crombie Who Does What Panel – appointed by Ontario Premier Mike Harris in 1996. Its final report was in December, 1996.

Winnipeg and 15 surrounding municipal jurisdictions. Each municipality is allowed one member on the committee.[4]

Thus, one person represents more than 600,000 citizens and the other 15 represent an average of about 5,000 each. Most of the 15 fringe municipalities have an incentive to build their own tax revenues through low-density urban development with minimal service levels, resulting in a very competitive tax rate. Under those circumstances, it is clear that the committee of 16 will not meaningfully control exurban growth. The committee's real role has been limited to minor housekeeping matters.

The do-nothing status of the committee has been enough of an embarrassment to motivate both the previous and the current provincial government to commission investigations into the state of regional governance.[5] So far, however, neither the committees nor the successive governments themselves have proved willing to take regional governance beyond hollow exhortations to the 16 municipalities to cooperate.

Legalistic rigidity and natural person powers
In looking at Unicity, we made the point that the 1972 reforms concentrated on structures of government and overlooked functions, with the result that Winnipeg's government, like other municipal governments, continued to be shackled by the legalistic rigidity of provincial legislation.

In the 1990s, the Government of Alberta caused a buzz in municipal circles by granting "natural person powers" to its municipalities, allegedly addressing the problem of legalistic rigidity (Government of Alberta, 2005). British Columbia added a similar provision in its Community Charter, passed in May, 2003 and in effect since January 1, 2004; according to the BC Ministry responsible, the new Charter would "replace a provincial tradition of rigid rules and paternalism with flexibility and co-operation, ... will encourage municipalities to be

---

4   See also, Golden and Slack, this volume, on the GTA for a comparison.
5   For recent reports regarding the Capital Region Committee, see The Province of Manitoba, Department of Intergovernmental Affairs, Strengthening Manitoba's Capital Region (2002), The Province of Manitoba, Department of Intergovernmental Affairs, Planning Manitoba's Capital Region: Next Steps (2001) and The Province of Manitoba, Department of Intergovernmental Affairs, Final Report of the Capital Region Review Panel (1999).

more self-reliant ... [and] presents simple, concise legislation that balances broad municipal abilities with public accountability and protection of province-wide interests in key areas like the economy, environment and public health (BC Ministry of Community, Aboriginal and Women's Services, 2002: 3). What difference the BC changes have meant remains less certain.

The previous Manitoba government, in revising legislation covering municipalities other than Winnipeg, opted instead to grant corporate powers to its municipalities (Manitoba, *Municipal Act*, 1996), which sounds a great deal like the power municipalities have always had. Does that mean, as has been suggested, that Alberta, in a bold stroke, expanded the autonomy of local government, while Manitoba, in the 1990s, proceeded more cautiously?

It is our argument that in this, as in so many other things, both the devil and the angels are in the detail, and that the labels "natural person powers" and "corporate powers" tell us very little about what is actually going on. For what it is worth, the previous Manitoba government argued that they considered Alberta's approach and rejected it after concluding that, far from being too radical, it was quite simply inappropriate (Nesbitt, 1999) A number of considerations speak for their argument.

In the first place, since municipalities more nearly resemble corporations than individuals, corporate powers can be seen as providing a more straightforward path than "person powers" toward the objective of expanded powers. Secondly, natural person powers are expressed primarily through the language of rights, powers and privileges, with little mention of limitations, obligations and duties.

Some of the broad categories that could be described as natural person powers include: (1) contractual powers; (2) commercial powers; (3) instruments of commerce; (4) rights of expression and philanthropy, such as selling services, goods or land below market value; (5) general powers such as the right to sue or be sued including the ability to sue and be sued for more "personal torts" like defamation of character and the like.

Council by-laws, meanwhile, are necessarily limited to municipal purposes, whereas natural person powers are in no way subject to such limitations. Finally, individuals do not have the ability to pass legislation or collect taxes, things which are of obvious importance for municipal jurisdictions.

In short, once natural person powers have been granted, a great deal of further legislation is needed to clarify what that means for municipalities, and it is this clarifying legislation, together with court decisions, which determines what the original grant of power actually means. The previous Manitoba government apparently concluded that the Alberta approach was as likely in practice to fatten the bank accounts of lawyers as it was to enhance the powers of municipalities.

Undoubtedly Alberta authorities could respond to this argument by pointing out that municipalities, in reality, are neither persons nor corporations, and that Manitoba too has had to specify in legislation what the expanded powers actually consist of. In fact, the argument will not be settled by reference to the general strengths and weaknesses of competing legal concepts.

The current Manitoba government has undertaken an apparent reversal of the previous government's stance on the question of natural person powers vs. corporate powers, but a closer examination suggests that it is in fact corporate powers that are being granted (City of Winnipeg Charter Act). As we have argued, the test of what either theory implies for the actual powers municipal government is able to wield can be found, not in the broad theory chosen, but in the detail, to which we now turn.

In the City of Winnipeg Charter Act, the powers of municipal government, instead of being set out in a wide array of detailed grants of very specific powers, are consolidated into 14 broad categories of powers (City of Winnipeg Charter Act, 2002, Sections 128–223). The 14 are: public convenience, health, safety and well-being, activities in public places, streets, activities of businesses, buildings, equipment and materials, floodway and floodway fringe areas, waterways, water, waste, public transportation, ambulance services, fire protection and police.

So far, so good, and there is more. In the earlier act, the city only had powers explicitly granted. And they were so scattered throughout the act that only a lawyer could venture a meaningful interpretation. In addition to the many detailed grants of power, there were process clauses that specified exactly how these powers might be wielded.

In the new Charter Act, which took effect at the beginning of 2003, everyday government actions – such as joining an organization of municipalities, passing regulations, requiring licences and taking enforcement action – are permitted, provided they are taken in pursuit of the specified powers. For a city council accustomed to deferring routinely to the solicitor, and going frequently and on bended knee to the provincial government with pleas for specific powers, it is a potentially dizzying grant of power, but whether it consists of natural person powers is another question.

A section entitled "Natural Person Powers," located at the beginning of the act, states: "The city has the capacity, rights, powers and privileges of a natural person for the purpose of exercising its authority under this or any other Act" (ibid., Part I, 7[1]). But that is the only mention of natural person powers in the act, while 22 sections (202–23) are devoted to corporate powers. In any event, it is clear on the face of it that such matters as licensing and enforcement are corporate powers, not those wielded by a person.

It seems likely, therefore, that when the dust raised by the current round of grants of natural person powers to Canadian municipalities has settled, we will conclude that the term contains more politics and public relations than legal substance. Despite fine words, the City of Winnipeg remains subject to a heavy provincial hand. The excision of 275 pages of restrictions in the City of Winnipeg Act still leaves the Charter Act with a weighty 328 pages. Moreover, Part 5, which is devoted to powers, contains many sections setting out qualifications on the powers granted.

Nevertheless, early indications are that the City of Winnipeg will enjoy a great deal more authority than it has in the past and, even if there are no layoffs in the solicitor's department, perhaps the solicitors will be able to say Yes more often than they have in the past. More to the point, council may be in a position to respond more meaningfully to its constituents and to the city's needs.

Procurement and provision of goods and services
As we enter the third millenium, the term "innovative solutions" is often synonymous with public-private partnerships, not least in municipal government. Municipalities routinely discontinue offering services in favor of contracting these services out to private enterprises,

and expanded municipal powers will provide new opportunities for such activity in Winnipeg.

Alternatively, two or more municipalities can jointly establish an arms-length special purpose body to administer the service for the combined geographical area. There are numerous reasons for this: (1) in many cases a municipality does not have the bureaucratic expertise in administering and delivering a given service in the most efficient and effective manner; (2) if a municipality does have that expertise, it is often thought to be more cost-effective to contract out to companies that are subject to market discipline, in hopes that this will drive down costs; and (3) if a municipality is an efficient and cost-effective provider of a service, it may benefit by offering that service on contract to other municipalities.

All of these possibilities are opened up in Sections 214–16 of the City of Winnipeg Charter Act, in which broad powers are granted to the city to procure goods and services and to create special service units that can supply goods and services both within and outside the city.

Tax increment financing
The Charter Act contains provisions that, it is claimed, would make Winnipeg the first city in Canada authorized to adopt tax increment financing (TIF), a financial tool that has been in use in a number of American cities for some time. It has generated some debate in the U.S. on its usefulness as a municipal development financing technique (Johnson & Man, 2001). What follows is a short description of TIF: the Charter permits the use of TIF to raise funds for urban development or infrastructure projects (City of Winnipeg Charter Act, Section 222). TIF is designed to ensure that the benefits of new development accrue to the area in which the development took place.

TIF, in effect, creates a revenue shelter for a geographical area within a city. Property values are first assessed in the designated area, and then those values are frozen. Increases in tax revenue due to investment and development in the area are channeled into a reserve fund to pay for future infrastructure projects or development subsidies in that district. Johnson and Man (2001) write: "The creation of a TIF district assures private investors that their property taxes are used to pay for infrastructure needs and development expenditures in the district which directly benefit their businesses, rather than to pay for the general cost of local government services. In the absence of TIF, these costs would be borne by those investors."

(handwritten margin note: TIF essentially saves investors)

There are draw-backs to such a program of development financing. Should the tax revenue from development projects fall short of initial estimates, the city will have to finance the project from general tax funds, creating a heads-I-win-tails-you-lose situation in which the beneficiaries of the development program get help from the rest of the city in dealing with costs, but do not have to share benefits. TIF can be used to finance infrastructure, but insofar as the benefits accrue to private investors, it may actually be little more than another subsidy shell game.

More positively, and at its best, TIF can serve as a viable way of financing projects in inner-city redevelopment, urban revitalization, affordable housing, or other worthy projects the funding of which might otherwise prove difficult or impossible. Portland, Oregon, for example, used it for downtown housing before TIF's were subsequently abolished there.

(handwritten margin note: TIF ex)

Increased accountability?
In the original version of Unicity, the large council – 50 ward-based councillors – was part of the plan for achieving a more democratic, responsive and accountable municipal government. What some called a bloated representative system was designed to ensure that wards were small enough to keep public office within the financial reach of ordinary citizens, and that each councillor knew her or his ward well enough to provide effective representation.

The Charter Act empowers city council to increase the number of wards by by-law. In theory, therefore, the act permits restoration of increased accountability via more intensive representation (City of Winnipeg Charter Act, Section 17[1]), but a significant change along these lines is unlikely. There is little appetite in Winnipeg for a return to a council comparable in size to the original Unicity council, and even much more modest increases are not high on the political agenda, especially since any boundary change is likely to jeopardize incumbent political bases.

In any event, many in Winnipeg would disagree with the suggestion that a larger council represents greater accountability. More readily saleable is the suggestion that greater direct citizen involvement in decision-making is tantamount to greater accountability. Part of the claim that the Charter Act increases accountability, therefore, rests on a provision that allows council to appoint citizens to appeal bodies empowered to adjudicate such questions as taxes and land use planning decisions (ibid., Sec.83), theoretically making council more responsive to civil society.

The practice may prove very different. Considering how cozy council and the business community are, it would hardly be the workings of a paranoid mind to assume committees may become excessively representative of the business leader. In reality, this so-called accountability measure could prove to be the thin edge of the wedge for a reversal of Unicity's "repatriation" of special-purpose bodies, discussed earlier in this article.

While the idea of appointing citizens to council committees sounds good, there is no protection against membership on such committees becoming exclusive. In the worst case scenario, Winnipeg might find itself once again suffering the fragmentation of powers that the Unicity legislation greatly reduced by bringing special-purpose bodies under council control. The Charter Act, therefore, could initiate the erosion of one of the few enduring legacies of Unicity.

Also billed as an accountability measure is a provision allowing the council, in the words of a government press release, "to identify those matters it thinks are of such importance that more than the normal 50% majority vote of Council is required." If the entrenchment of questions beyond the reach of majority rule is an accountability measure, it is certainly some variety of accountability other than democratic accountability. Aside from Manitoba New Democrats thinking, this idea of "super majorities" is reflected in the May 17, 2005 referendum on electoral reform in neighboring British Columbia. Here, reform required the support of 60% of the May, 2005 BC General Election total vote, plus a 50%+1majority in 60% of the province's constituencies, or 48 of the 79 BC ridings (www.gov.bc.ca/referendum_info, accessed February 28, 2005).

Two other measures, somewhat more likely to have a positive impact in the promotion of democratic governance are a provision requiring the council to adopt a code of conduct for employees (ibid.,

Sec. 89 [1]) and one extending the jurisdiction of the provincial ombudsman to municipal government (ibid., Secs 462–463).

New Revolution, or Counter-Revolution Continued?

The reforms of 1972 tried to build a serious concern with democracy into municipal institutions that have a long tradition of sacrificing democratic accountability to administrative strength. Much of what was attempted in 1972 failed, though, as we saw, a couple of those innovations have endured to the present.

The 1998 reforms constituted a fully-fledged return to the pre-1972 traditions. While the reforms may have achieved greater administrative effectiveness and efficiency they did nothing to support, let alone expand, democratic accountability, indeed they undermined it further by raising the possibility of a future abolition of community committees. The Charter Act reinforces the 1998 drive to greater efficiency and effectiveness by widening municipal powers in the area of procurement and provision of goods and services and authorizing the city to undertake tax increment financing.

At the same time, it perpetuates the 1998 approach to democratic accountability through reforms that, while they are labelled accountability provisions, in fact look more likely to undermine genuine democratic accountability than to support it. In this respect, Winnipeg's situation is similar to that of BC municipalities under its 2004 Communiuty Charter (Smith & Stewart, 2005b; Smith and Oberlander, this volume).

However, the elimination of a great deal of detail from the provincial legislation governing the City of Winnipeg – in other words the attempt to free the council from the shackles of legalistic rigidity – is a different matter. It is too early to tell whether the Charter Act has actually succeeded in granting wider powers to the council. We will have to await the results of practical experience in the operation of the city government under the new act, as well as court rulings to test the interpretation of the wording in the act, before we know whether the council is indeed significantly freer to act than it was before. Early 21st century results suggest no dramatic shifts.

These reservations are important ones. It is a lamentable fact of political life that our representatives would sometimes rather refrain from exercising power than take action on our behalf and risk being held responsible for it. Likewise, anyone who has a motive for limiting the power of the city council can bring the matter before a court system deeply habituated to very strict interpretations of municipal acts. Here judicial rulings, such as on Ontario's Megacity Toronto amalgamation challenges, continue to underscore the significance of the province in such matters (Golden and Slack, this volume).

But if experience proves that the redefinition of powers in the Charter Act really does leave municipal government freer to set priorities and pursue them, then the Manitoba government will deserve credit for at last having addressed the problem the designers of Unicity overlooked: the expansion of the functions of municipal government in such a way as to enable it, more meaningfully than in the past, to serve as an effective government, able to be genuinely accountable to its constituents.

References

Anderson, J. D. (1979). The municipal reform movement in Western Canada. In: A.F.J. Artibise & G.A. Stelter (eds.), *The Usable Urban Past: Planning and Politics in the Modern Canadian City.* Toronto: Macmillan, pp. 73–111.

Axworthy, L. (1980). The best laid plans often go astray: the case of Winnipeg. In: M.O. Dickerson, S. Drabek & J.T. Woods (eds.), *Problems of Change in Urban Government.* Waterloo: Wilfred Laurier Press.

Brownstone, M., & Plunkett, T.J. (1983). *Metropolitan Winnipeg: Politics and Reform of Local Government.* Berkeley: Institute of Governmental Studies, University of California.

Canadian Urban Institute (1993). *Disentangling Local Government Responsibilities – International Comparisons.* Toronto: CUI.

City of Winnipeg (1997). *Reshaping our Civic Government: Executive Policy Committee's Strategic Direction for City Government,* Winnipeg.

Clatworthy, S. and Associates (1990). *An Evaluation of the Winnipeg Core Area Agreement Tripartite Model*. Winnipeg.

Crombie, D. (1996). *Who Does What Panel* – Final Report, December.

Cuff, G.B. and Associates Ltd. (1997). *Organizational Review and Performance Assessment Report*. City of Winnipeg.

Decter, M.B., & Kowall, J.A. (1990). *The Winnipeg Core Area Initiative: A Case Study*. Ottawa: Economic Council of Canada.

Government of Alberta, (2005) *Municipal Government Act*, Section 6.

Government of Manitoba (1996). *Municipal Act.*

Gutkin, H. with M. Gutkin (1987). Meyer Brownstone, grassroots activist. In: H. Gutkin with M. Gutkin, *The Worst of Times, the Best of Times: Growing up in Winnipeg's North End*. Markham, ON:: Fitzhenry and Whiteside, pp. 145–157.

Hefferon, D.C. (1972). Notes on Bill 36, the City of Winnipeg Act. In: L.D. Feldman & M.D. Goldrick, *Politics and Government of Urban Canada: Selected Readings* (Second Edition). Toronto: Methuen.

Johnson, C.L., & Man, J.Y. (eds.) (2001). *Tax Increment Financing and Economic Development. Uses, Structures, and Impacts*. Albany: State University of New York Press.

Leo, C. (1986), *Strong Government, Weak Government: Classifying Municipal Structural Change*. Research and Working Paper #23: Winnipeg: Institute of Urban Studies.

Leo, C. (1987). *Revising the City of Winnipeg Act: A Discussion Paper*. Winnipeg: Institute of Urban Studies, University of Winnipeg.

Leo, C. (2003). Rethinking urban governance in the 21st Century. Halifax, Canadian Political Science Association.

Lipset, S.M. (1950). *Agrarian Socialism*. Berkeley: University of California Press.

Manitoba, Department of Urban Affairs (1971). *Proposals for Urban Reorganization in the Greater Winnipeg* Area. Winnipeg.

Manitoba, Department of Urban Affairs (1976). Committee of Review, City of Winnipeg Act (Taraska Commission), *Report and Recommendations.*

Manitoba, Department of Intergovernmental Affairs (1999). *Final Report of the Capital Region Review Panel.*

Manitoba, Department of Intergovernmental Affairs (2001). *Planning Manitoba's Capital Region: Next Steps.*

Manitoba, Department of Intergovernmental Affairs (2002). *Strengthening Manitoba's Capital Region.*

Manitoba, Government News Release, June 20, 2002: http://www.gov.mb.ca/chc/press/top/2002/06/2002-06-20-07.html

Manitoba, *City of Winnipeg Charter Act*, Bill 39, (2002).

Nesbitt, L, (1999). Research Co-ordinator for the Review Panel, Policy and Special Projects Unit, Manitoba Rural Development, Personal communication with authors, May 17.

Piel, M., & Leo, C. (2005). Governing Manitoba's communities: legislative reform in the 1990s and beyond. In: J. Garcea & E. LeSage Jr. (eds.), *Municipal Reforms in Canada: Dimensions, Dynamics, Determinants.* Toronto: Oxford University Press.

Province of Ontario (1991). *Report of the Advisory Committee to the Minister of Municipal Affairs on the Provincial-Municipal Relationship.* Toronto: Government of Ontario.

Siegel, D. (1992). Disentangling provincial-municipal relations in Ontario. *Management*, Toronto: IPAC, Fall.

Smith, P., & Stewart, K. (2005a). Policy analysis for whom? Institutional inadequacy and the potential for democratic policy-making deviation in eight Canadian cities. In: L. Dobuzinskis, M. Howlett & D. Laycock (eds.), *Policy Analysis in Canada: The State of the Art.* Toronto: University of Toronto Press.

Smith, P., & Stewart, K. (2005b). Local government reform in British Columbia – 1991–2005: one oar in the water. In: J. Garcea & E. LeSage Jr. (eds.), *Municipal Reforms in Canada: Dimensions, Dynamics, Determinants.* Toronto: Oxford University Press.

Statistics Canada (2001). *Community Profiles,* http://www12.statcan.ca/english/profil01/PlaceSearchForm1.cfm

Weaver, J.C. (1977). *Shaping the Canadian City: Essays on Urban Politics and Policy, 1890–1920.* Toronto: Institute of Public Administration of Canada.

Wichern, P.H. (1984). *Evaluating Winnipeg's Unicity: Citizen Participation and Resident Advisory Groups, 1971–1984.* Winnipeg: Institute of Urban Studies, University of Winnipeg, 11–16.

PATRICK J. SMITH AND H. PETER OBERLANDER

Greater Vancouver: *l'exception canadienne métropolitaine*

The first thing to say about Vancouver in terms of the theme of metropolitan governing is that British Columbia's major metropolitan region is unlike the other city regions of Canada. Despite being Canada's third largest city region, Greater Vancouver is the essential "odd-one-out" in the Canadian re-metropolitanization trend line of bigger is better. Whether in Halifax, Ottawa, Toronto, Hamilton, Winnipeg, Calgary or Edmonton, and – perhaps – even Montreal, the Canadian experience is toward a more amalgamated, megacity model. In Greater Vancouver, this Canadian trend has yet to take hold; indeed it is being resisted. Metropolitan Vancouver is a federated system with all its weaknesses and difficulties versus a centrally-imposed amalgamation. Greater Vancouver, thus, remains "l'exception canadienne metropolitaine."

One of the other things to add about metropolitan governance is that the constitutional order Canadians work under is a product of the 1860s – when three-quarters of Canadians lived in rural/agricultural settings and "local" really **was** local – whether in building schools or maintaining public roads (with the exception of "the King's highways"). Today, as noted in our most recent 2001 decennial census, 80% of Canadians live in urban centers of 10,000 people or more, and rural population has continued to decline. More importantly, by 2001, almost two-thirds (over 64%) of Canada's population, or about 19,500,000 people, lived in 30 census metropolitan areas (CMAs) (see Appendix 1). Yet the constitutional order of the 1860s remains.

Finally, by the last 2001 decennial census, 51% of Canada's population concentrated further in just four broad metropolitan regions (Figure 1) – up from 49% in 1996:

- the extended/Toronto-centered Greater Golden Horseshoe in southern Ontario;
- Montréal and environs;
- the Calgary-Edmonton corridor. and
- Vancouver/BC's Lower Mainland & southern Vancouver Island (Statistics Canada, 2001)

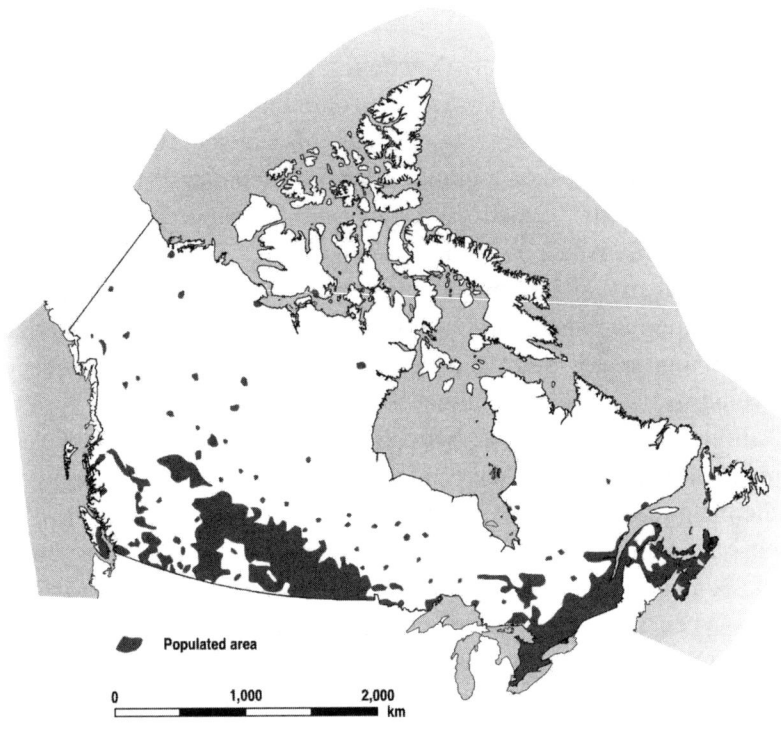

Figure 1: Where Canadians live
Source: http://www.canadainfolink.ca/canadian cities.htm

The Setting: British Columbia and the Vancouver Metropolitan Region

British Columbia is Canada's third most populous province – 4,196,383 citizens (July 1, 2004) (BC Stats, Ministry of Finance, 2005) – representing just over 13% (13.032%) of the total Canadian (31,825,400) population (ibid.). Despite being Canada's third largest province (948,600 square kms.), 85% (about 3.548 million) of the provincial population resides in 156 incorporated municipalities encompassing just one percent of BC provincial territory. Over half of the citizens of the province (2.393 million people – 57.5% – BC` Stats, 2005) reside in the "Lower Mainland" – comprised of two regional districts along the Fraser River Valley adjacent to Vancouver. This "Lower Mainland" [bounded on the south by the United States border, on the north by mountains which extend virtually without interruption to Alaska, and on the east – at Hope, approximately 160 kms. away – by similar mountain ranges, with its western extremity, including the City of Vancouver, the gulf waters of the Pacific Ocean] represents the economic center of the province (Bond 1996; Smith, et al., 1996; Hutton 1997). Politically, the region elects just over half (50.7%) of the members of the legislative assembly of the province. In Jacobs' terms, this Vancouver-centered "Lower Mainland" forms one coherent "city region. (Jacobs, 1984; Oberlander & Smith 1993).

Greater Vancouver is Canada's third largest metropolis. It is one of the four fastest growing urban areas in North America, Canada's fastest. The Greater Vancouver region has grown to over 2 million (2.133 million as of 2004 – BC Stats, 2005). It is the core of British Columbia's "Lower Mainland." The Vancouver census metropolitan area now essentially corresponds with the redefined Greater Vancouver Regional District (Figure 2). Established in 1967, the GVRD is a federation of 21 municipalities and one unincorporated electoral area, covering 3,250 sq. kms. The Greater Vancouver Region contains a little over half (51.3% – 2.133 million people) of the provincial population and a majority (6 of 9) of the largest (over 100,000 population) and 11 of 19 (over 50,000 population) local authorities in the province (BC Stats, 2005). For the May, 2005 BC general election, this "Lower Mainland" has 47 legislative seats (59.5%) and the Vancouver metropolitan region has 39 of the 79 legislative seats, 49.4% of the provincial total.

Whatever its substantial growth potential, the fastest growing areas in the Vancouver metropolis are in the Fraser Valley suburbs within and beyond the eastern boundaries of the GVRD. By 2025, for example, GVRD projections have the Greater Vancouver suburb of Surrey surpassing the central city Vancouver in population. (The City of Vancouver's population is currently 583,296, close to neighboring

Seattle's 580,800, BC Stats, 2005). Adjacent non-GVRD metropolitan/ outer suburbs, such as Mission, Abbotsford and Chilliwack are the fastest growing areas in the province; and "next door" municipality Abbotsford (126,634 population, BC Stats, 2005) is "in" the GVRD for its parks functions.

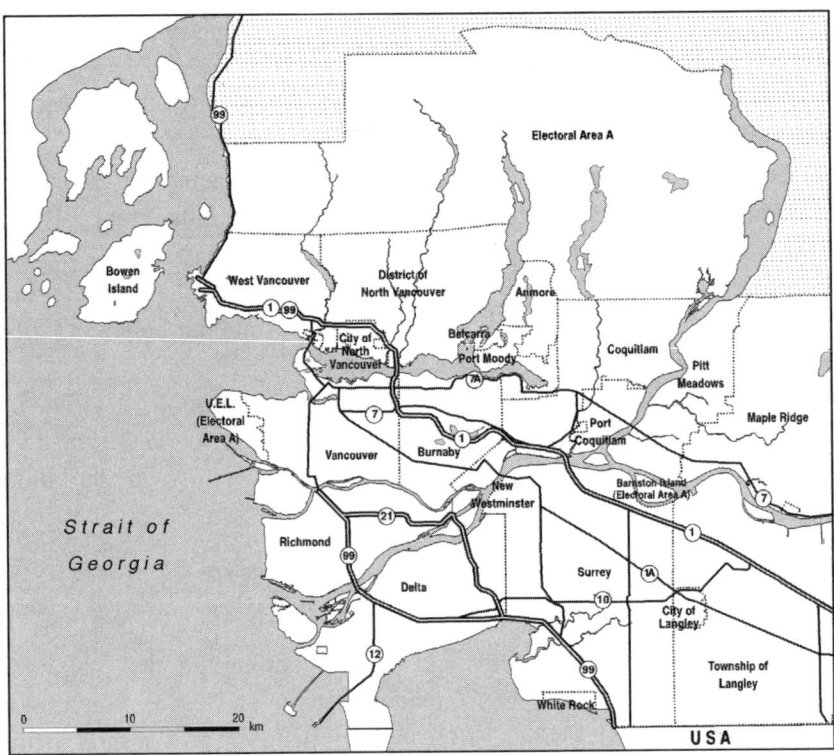

Figure 2: Greater Vancouver Regional District
Source:GVRD

One byproduct of the rapid growth of the Vancouver metropolitan area is that the ethnic makeup of the region's population has become increasingly multicultural; more than half of the public school population of Vancouver has English as a second language, for example; other municipalities are not far behind. This translates, increasingly, into politics around who will represent these communities. In metropolitan Vancouver, that has produced new representatives for the Indo-Canadian communities, and the first provincial representatives from the Chinese community (in the May

1996 and 2001 BC general elections). The June 2004 Canadian general election also included an increased number of ethnic/visible minority community candidates; this trend continued in the May 17, 2005 BC General Election.

In terms of the development of metropolitan Vancouver's economy, there has also been a growing dichotomy between the "Lower Mainland"/Southwestern BC and the rest of the province: much of the BC economy has been resource extractive, with heavy reliance on logging, mining and fishing, and a limited manufacturing component. The economic base of the "Lower Mainland," on the other hand, is increasingly service-oriented, with a strong reliance on personal and corporate services, including sectors such as tourism and the film industry, and province-wide distribution of goods and services (Howlett & Brownsey, 1992; Smith, 1994; BC Stats, 2005). Combined with its significant internationalist population, a more interdependent – and internationally oriented – regional economy, and its Pacific port location [the Port of Vancouver is the second busiest in North America, and the busiest on the west coast of the Americas] (Smith, 1992; Bond, 1996; Port of Vancouver, 2005), metropolitan Vancouver has become an "international city" (Smith & Cohn, 1994, Smith, 2002); and the provincial economy has become even more internationalist (Cohn, Merrifield & Smith, 1989; Cohn & Smith, 1996; Smith, 2004; BC Stats, 2005).

One additional factor that impacts on economic development decision making and intergovernmental relations in the Vancouver-centered region is the fact that most of the best arable land in British Columbia is found in the "Lower Mainland." Only one-quarter of the land in the province is suitable for any form of farming – and most of the prime agricultural land is in the Vancouver-centered region. Thus, the potential for policy conflicts and the necessity of devising regional solutions – including on cross border issues like air quality – to resolve urban development problems as part of any economic development strategy – domestic or international – become immediately apparent (Smith,1996; Smith & Oberlander, 1998). Cross-boundary disputes such as the one created by plans for a Sumas II electrical generator in Washington State, approved after several rounds of hearings in Washington in 2002/4, but not in Canada, suggest regional Cascadia-based activity can be an irritant as well as cooperative (Smith, 2004).

The increasing nature of such intra- and trans-regional activity also demonstrates the need to look beyond existing territorial boundaries for "metropolitan Vancouver" solutions: the Cascadia option – variously defined – has provided a new territorial – and institutional – dimension for problem solving on a range of economic, social and environmental issues. Examples such as the Cascadia Mayors' Council, which meets on issues of regional concern, from the regional environment to crime, and meetings of the three regional/metropolitan authorities for Vancouver, Seattle and Portland to develop metropolitan policy learning capacities attest to the growing interest in Cascadia-based solutions to regional policy dilemmas. As such, these also represent an inclination to develop capacity outside of more traditional local-senior governmental settings.

collaboration

Themes

Four themes stand out in examining metropolitan governing in Greater Vancouver:

- In terms of brief comments on the notion of *Levels of Management in Metropolitan Vancouver*, the regional district model, in place since the mid-1960s, has offered a fairly flexible and efficient form of management for the Greater Vancouver region. The combination of limited *mandated* functions and a long list of *voluntary* functions has left much to be decided locally/regionally; this approach to governance has, until recently at least, worked fairly well for "Vancouver."
- On the theme of *Developing and Implementing Metropolitan Reforms*, two factors stand out in metropolitan Vancouver: first, historically, the development of regional institutions was locally-inspired – and solutions were the result of local negotiations at the regional level; second, the senior (provincial) governmental approach largely has been what two commentators have described as "gentle imposition" (Tennant & Zirnhelt, 1973).
- On the idea of *Coordinating Actors at the Metropolitan Level*, what has been a generally successful model of consensus decision-making, through the regional district's two-tiered indirect election

form, has begun to show signs of reaching the limits of its "best-before date." Tensions within, and critiques from outside the GVRD suggest increasing need to rethink the current form of coordination and governance for metropolitan Vancouver.

• Finally, on the theme of *Linking Central/Senior Government Policies and Metropolitan Initiatives*, an ability to adjust metropolitan boundaries to generally reflect population/growth patterns on the ground has helped in metropolitan Vancouver and reflected senior/provincial governmental support for regional capacity. As noted below, there has been a range of shifts in the Vancouver region's ability to act independently: sometimes these have reflected an increase in metropolitan competence; in other, more recent, instances, it has been reflected in a re-assertion of senior (often provincial) ascendancy. Here the Richmond-Airport-Vancouver rapid transit (RAV) line decision, discussed below, or the provincial-West Vancouver dispute over Sea-to-Sky 2010 Olympic highway rebuilding, are good exemplars.

There have been innumerable social and economic prognostications about challenges for the 21st century, but few on governance or global metropolitanization. Yet solutions to the problems of a now highly urbanized world will not occur without a reconceptualization of the future network of metropolises based on an assessment of some of the governance forms which have worked, those which have failed and those which need to be tried. Can metropolitanization based on a dynamic governance process contribute to national well-being and to global sustainability, as Savitch and Vogel (1996) have concluded in their assessment of an emerging "post-city age"? (see also Savitch and Vogel, this volume). Sancton and Rothblatt (1998) think so: in their Revisit of Metropolitan Governance, they came to the conclusion that regional/ metropolitan governing forms – and attendant intergovernmental reforms – may provide the most helpful answers to the challenges of governance for the new millennium.

This suggests a series of related questions – both for Greater Vancouver and beyond:

▪ What are the comparative governance lessons for the 21st century across metropolitan city regional settings?

- What comparative lessons can be learned from *changes* in metropolitan government and governance over the past six postwar decades of the 20th/21st centuries?
- How have these changes occurred?
- What forms and outcomes have resulted?
- What have we learned about attendant local/regional – senior/central intergovernmental relations?
- Where are our "best metropolitan practices"?
- Are there identifiable city-regional experiences and global threads on which to base a new metropolitan – and urban intergovernmental – reconceptualization for the 21st century?
- What has the metropolitan Vancouver experience contributed to this debate?

As noted in the introduction to this volume, the notion of "one size does not fit all" increasingly has become part of the discourse on metropolitan reform. Comparative studies of the metropolitan experiences over the last half of the 20th century and the beginning decade of the 21st offer the best possibility of identifying needed governance options for this still new century. Only then might there be real urban solutions to global problems.

This article, on "Greater Vancouver Experiences," poses the above questions for the metropolitan Vancouver region. Here, one conclusion is that despite a history of some considerable success – and indeed a perception that to date this has offered one best practice model – there are limits to the regional district system found in British Columbia; metropolitan Vancouver appears increasingly past that limit.

As researchers who have argued for much of the last quarter century that regional districts and regional planning in British Columbia represents one of the most successful policy initiatives and governance forms, this conclusion may seem somewhat heretical. And the critique of Greater Vancouver's current governance model does not extend to all the other 27 regional districts in the province; it is largely Vancouver-specific.

The intention here is to make four simple points:

- Governance matters – and its adaptability in the Vancouver city-region has been one of its strengths;

- Regional districts in British Columbia – and earlier regional organizational forms – have worked well over the past 40 plus years; and in all but the largest metropolitan region, Vancouver, regional districts continue to provide an efficient, flexible and effective form of regional governance;
- In British Columbia's largest – Vancouver – metropolitan region, an accountability crunch has come to challenge regional district efficiency arguments and claims. This might result in the conclusion that for metropolitan versus regional governance in British Columbia, indeed "one size does not fit all";
- "What next, in metropolitan Vancouver?" at least, would appear to require legislative reform toward a new, more politically accountable Greater Vancouver Authority (GVA). That has implications for how senior governments and metropolitan initiatives might be linked – and how Greater Vancouver is governed.

Retrospective

The history of regional planning in metropolitan Vancouver is both long and short with a variety of regional authorities created, dating from near the beginning of the 20th century. Initially, these represented "ad hoc" (and often single purpose) responses to a number of local/regional service dilemmas. Almost without exception, the early regionalization experiences were premised on locally-perceived necessity. Actual "regional" beginnings date from 1911, just 25 years after Vancouver's founding, when the City of Vancouver with its Point Grey, South Vancouver and Burnaby municipal neighbors formed the Burrard Peninsula Joint Sewerage Committee. The Committee funded a study which recommended "an ongoing co-operative response," and by 1914 had convinced the provincial government to pass legislation to create a Joint Sewerage and Drainage Board. Subsequent local action resulted in a regional Water District being created in 1926; this was followed by the establishment of four area health/hospital boards between 1936 and 1948 (Oberlander & Smith, 1993).

Modern regional structures best date after the Second World War: in 1948 – a year of significant flooding in the Vancouver-centered Lower

Mainland/Fraser River Valley, amendments to the Municipal Act were passed, allowing contiguous local authorities in a metropolitan region to develop a joint planning capacity. As a result, the Lower Mainland Regional Planning Board (LMRPB) was formed. It covered the whole physical region – from Vancouver, up the Fraser Valley to the mountains and Hope. In some ways this was a recognition – and extension – of a voluntary planning association (of Vancouver, Burnaby, Port Moody, Coquitlam, North and West Vancouver) created in 1937 (North & Hardwick, 1992; Oberlander & Smith, 1993: Case Three, 356–366).

Despite these various local initiatives, provincial action on regional government was slow. Tennant and Zirnhelt (1973) have persuasively argued that the proliferation and success of these early joint boards and authorities did lead the way to provincial consideration of more broadly-based regional solutions to urban development problems, particularly with regard to their application in metropolitan Vancouver. The process of reform, they called "gentle imposition" by the province.

The thinking of W.A.C. Bennett's Social Credit provincial Government (first elected in 1952) was obviously affected by the early experience – and publicity – of metropolitan government reform in Toronto in 1954. As a result, community and regional planning provisions were added to the Municipal Act in 1957, empowering the Minister to direct adjacent municipalities in "Metropolitan Areas" to establish a joint committee "to study and report on such matters of an inter-municipal nature as shall be set out by the Minister..." The already established LMRPB was able to undertake such a process, leading to an official regional plan for the whole of British Columbia's "Lower Mainland" by the mid 1960s. *Chance and Challenge*, the "official regional plan," was approved in August 1966; but as the LMRPB was moving toward this success, the provincial government, perhaps feeling threatened by a jurisdiction representing half the province's population, and reflecting on some intra-regional tensions, determined that administrative and political diffusion was a more appropriate response.

Accordingly, a regional district system for the entire province was created between 1965 and 1967. As stated by then Municipal Affairs Minister Dan Campbell, the British Columbia government's intention was clear: "regional districts are not conceived of as a fourth level of government, but as a functional rather than a political amalgamation" (Campbell, 1976).

As a result, the "Lower Mainland"/LMRPB was divided into four separate regions. Within the Greater Vancouver Regional District (GVRD – originally incorporated as the Regional District of Fraser Burrard on June 29, 1967), as elsewhere in the new provincial system, functions given to the regional districts were of two types:

(i) To carry out **mandated functions** from the province to the new regional districts. These mandated functions included general planning for the region as well as responsibility for governing of the hospital district. In Greater Vancouver, mandated functions also included Water Board and Sewage and Drainage District responsibilities.

(ii) **Voluntary functions** were the second category of responsibilities for the new districts. These voluntary functions were established by Letters Patent. They included 78 functions from A to W (ambulance and animal control to unsightly premises and weed control), and each district could choose the function it was to perform (Statistics, 1989: 3).

In the 1970s, the new Greater Vancouver Regional District successfully completed a Livable Region Plan (LRP). It set out growth planning ideas such as regional town centers and preservation of agricultural and green space which guided regional development into the 1980s (Oberlander & Smith, 1993). This capacity to plan regionally continued despite the loss of formal planning authority in 1983 – through a direct provincial legislative intervention removing the regional planning authority from regional districts due to a land-use dispute between the GVRD and the Province (Magnusson, Carroll, Doyle, Langer & Walker, 1984) – but by the 1990s, significant growth pressures confronted the region.

In metropolitan Vancouver and British Columbia, the response to regional growth management problems and issues of metropolitan democracy were to seek to build on the successes of prior regional agreements. In 1995, under a leftist/NDP administration, new provincial planning legislation – a Growth Strategies Act – was passed for British Columbia. This legislation required municipalities to plan regionally (Smith & Oberlander, 1998) and allowed the province to establish mediative forms when local-regional agreement was not forthcoming. This new provincial legislation was the result of an extensive provincial-municipal consultative process which included consideration of other planning and governance models comparatively.

In 1995, the Greater Vancouver Regional District (with recently enlarged boundaries generally equivalent to the Vancouver Census Metropolitan Area) arrived at the end point of a five year long local-regional process of consultation and discussion to establish a new Livable Region Plan. This "Creating Our Future" process produced broad agreement, one initial major suburban dissent – Richmond – and the possibility of the first use of the province's "mediation to closure" procedures under the Growth Strategies Act. In early 1996, local-regional resolution of this dissent – and minor ones with Surrey and Langley Township – was arrived at without such provincial mediation. Greater Vancouver's "Livable Region Strategic Plan" (LRSP) was approved by the provincial government in Spring, 1996 (Smith & Oberlander, 1998). Translating that "on the ground" – with "context statements" by the region's 21 municipal units was the next task. That was followed by a review of the regional plan and subsequent adjustments. In 2005, the GVRD has been involved in a full review of the LRSP (www.gvrd.bc.ca/growth/lrsp).

The Region had already undertaken a "Cities Plus" (for "Cities Planning for Long-term Urban Sustainability") initiative along with 30 other Canadian cities. In June 2003, Greater Vancouver's was named the Grand Prix winner at the International Sustainable Systems Design competition in Tokyo for its 100-year plan for the region (Cities Plus, 2005). This initiative has led to a range of ongoing initiatives focusing on sustainability in the region: including awards from the International Gas Union on energy sustainability, work for Vancouver's hosting of the World Urban Forum in 2006, a Green guide for the region, and work on risk management (see Sheltair, 2005 www.sheltair.com) and the Sustainable Region Initiative (SRI).

——— Vancouver's Sustainable Region Initiative is a partnership of the GVRD, GVTA (Greater Vancouver Transportation Authority), the Fraser Basin Council, and NGOs – the Business Council of BC, the United Way of the Lower Mainland and Smart Growth BC – focusing on three aspects of sustainability: economic, social and environmental. This "three-legged stool" involves short, intermediate and long-range plans/strategies. It does not include the increasingly prevalent notion that "governance" is a fourth, and necessary leg in sustainability (www.sustainability.ca; www.gvrd.bc.ca/sustainability).

Both the mid-1990's British Columbia provincial planning legislation and the GVRD's planning process/resolution spoke directly to arguments about metropolitan governance, local/regional-provincial intergovernmental relations and growth management reform. It also spoke about the extent of "senior governmental interest or capacity" to address major urban issues (Frisken, 1994), and proposed suggestions that a "consensual model," as exemplified by Greater Vancouver, suffered from a "lack of mandate," lack of representation and "an inability to achieve consensus on matters of specific policy." While Golden and her GTA Commissioners concluded that "differences in regional political culture helped explain the relative success of "consensual decision-making" in the Greater Vancouver case, such an approach in other settings was "inherently weak" (Golden, 1996). Subsequent to the GTA Task Force Report, Tindal and Tindal (2004) reminded students of local governing of the continued benefits of this flexibility, while also noting that accountability concerns had increased in prominence:

> The regional districts have proven to be a flexible structure for dealing with a variety of considerations. They have assumed direct responsibilities for...municipal services...in unorganized areas. They have also acted as the administrative agency for certain functions or projects which some of their member municipalities wished to pursue jointly. In addition, they have assumed responsibility for various functions delegated to them by their constituent municipalities.... (But while) the flexible structure of the regional districts allows diversity and preserves a sense of community, ... accessibility concerns exist.

The Greater Vancouver and British Columbia experience of the 1990s suggested an alternative to metropolitan restructuring being pursued in other jurisdictions like Ontario – with Metropolitan Toronto Megacity, and the Greater Toronto Area, in Ottawa-Carleton, in Nova Scotia, with a new metropolitan Halifax, and elsewhere. The British Columbia experience also supported a notion of metropolitan governance as a clear alternative to metropolitan government, and to ideas such as "bigger is better."

That was then, and this is now: this article explores some of the more recent experience of British Columbia and metropolitan Vancouver and comments on the relationship between turn of century restructuring forms such as the creation of a new Greater Vancouver Transportation Authority (popularly known as TransLink), the creation of new provincial legislation – the Community Charter – and arguments put forward in rethinking metropolitan government and governance for Greater Vancouver in the early 21st century. (www.thinkcity.ca).

Contemporary Greater Vancouver: challenges not yet met

(I) Simply put, the first contention here is that much of the success of regional planning in British Columbia has been tied to reform of local governing structures: whether locally inspired before World War I and II, in the 1940s with the provision that adjacent municipalities might begin to plan together to establish regional planning, through the legislation of a first Municipal Act – and provisions for official regional plans in the 1950s or the creation of regional districts themselves in the 1960s, the first three decades of regional planning in British Columbia were closely tied to structural – governance – reforms.

(II) And it worked! It worked so well that regional planning did either commence or continue in the 1960s and 1970s, and perhaps more importantly, often continued (certainly in Greater Vancouver), albeit under a different guise, even when legally abolished in a provincial pique in the 1980s (Oberlander & Smith, 1993; Magnusson et al., 1984). It did so largely because of a number of governance factors: as Richard and Susan Tindal (1995) have noted, "municipal government reform in British Columbia ... resulted in one of the most imaginative and flexible governing arrangements found anywhere in Canada. The regional structure allow(ed) existing municipalities to continue, with whatever communities of interest they represent(ed), provide(d) for the delivery of a variety of services by the regional authority, and avoid(ed) the bureaucratic build-up and duplication often associated with full-blown two-tier regional governments."

Former British Columbia Municipal Affairs Minister Dan Campbell, provincial spokesperson on regional districts in the 1960s, 1970s and 1980s, argued consistently that regional districts were **not** regional governments, preferring a regional service delivery definition. Not all agreed: Donald Higgins (1977, 1986), following the "if it waddles and quacks like a duck test," concluded that regional districts had indeed become regional governments. Bob Bish (2000) came to the same conclusion more recently, but noted that the regional system in British Columbia has allowed "the division of responsibility – ...'who does what'... – between municipalities and the regional government (to be) made by the municipalities themselves."

That aspect – both local recognition of the value of, and often local initiation of particular regional solutions and resultant local buy-in – produced a positive regional experience of success, often following success. It is a view largely shared by Andrew Sancton (1995), even in the context of major urban-regions:

> Can a large city-region contain a number of municipalities, establish a regional-local government institution and avoid the pitfalls of two-tier municipal government? This is the biggest structural question facing urban government today..... All... Canadian city-regions require an institution similar to the GVRD (Greater Vancouver Regional District): one that is comprehensive in territory and flexible in function. Such institutions do not require large bureaucracies. In fact, they will probably work best if they have no operational responsibilities at all. Their aim should be to provide a forum where regional issues can be discussed, to act as a catalyst for the creation of inter-municipal agreements and special purpose bodies and to enact planning documents with sufficient legal status to coerce municipalities into adhering to broad strategic objectives for the use of land.

(III) The questioning here is not of where metropolitan Vancouver has been, however, but where Greater Vancouver is going. The much less certain future of British Columbia's largest regional structures, as they take on more and more responsibilities, lies on bedrock of what has been largely a positive, locally-inspired, policy, governance and intergovernmental experience. While not a rejection of the success represented by the past 50+ years of regional planning and governance in British Columbia, it is time to raise serious questions about whether that achievement of the last half century can endure long into the 21st century.

Current assessment is that increasingly citizens in British Columbia's largest city-region, Greater Vancouver, (2,132,824 population, 2004) have come to resemble Butch Cassidy and the Sundance Kid looking back at their pursuers and asking "who are those guys?" Citizens in the GVRD increasingly are wondering who is responsible for making more important and more expensive decisions – on transportation, infrastructure, maybe policing and beyond, and on new forms of taxation – and have begun to ask the same question as Butch and Sundance.

Perhaps this is illustrated nowhere more obviously than in the recent experience of Greater Vancouver's Transportation Authority – TransLink. In June 1998, the second NDP/Clark Government, under Minister of Finance/Deputy Premier Joy McPhail, initiated the Greater Vancouver Transportation Authority (Ginnell & Smith, 2001; Smith & Stewart, 2005). Under this act, responsibility for transportation and related services in metropolitan Vancouver was passed from the provincially-appointed British Columbia Transit to the Greater Vancouver Transportation Authority (popularly known as TransLink). The Act mandated that TransLink and the GVRD "work together to establish a mutually agreeable strategic transportation plan and growth management strategy." But while the provincial act legally established TransLink as a separate entity from the GVRD, the two organizations were joined in many formal and, most importantly, informal ways. For example, members of the indirectly elected GVRD hold 12 of the 15 TransLink board positions and the other three – Provincial appointments – have remained unfilled.

The functional mandate of TransLink has been to "plan and finance a regional transportation system that moves people and goods efficiently and supports the regional growth strategy, air quality objectives and economic development of the Greater Vancouver Regional District." Total funding for TransLink's operations in 2004-5 was approximately $680 million dollars. The province "contributed" 37.5% of that from the provincial motor fuel tax from the region, 2.5% from a provincial-regional levy on electricity accounts and 2% from the provincial sales tax on off-street paid parking (TranksLink @ www.translink.bc.ca/About_TransLink/Financing_Annual_Report 2001); this was to increase to over $1billion by 2009. TransLink was also given the ability to increase revenues through several other "taxation" instruments – though in many instances, such as a vehicle levy, it needed provincial assistance to collect this revenue. The TransLink board's institutional image is one of an almost at-arms-length provider of management for the several subsidiary companies and programs it established under its jurisdiction. It has described its role or management style as "steering not rowing" (Rock, 2001).

In creating GVTA/TransLink, the province recognized that the needs of the Vancouver region were different from those of other regions in the province. That was a small step forward. BC Transit is a purely provincial entity under the supervision of the appropriate minister, TransLink can be said to be a new addition to the family of regional governing bodies in metropolitan Vancouver because its board, while a separate entity, is controlled by indirectly elected GVRD members. With that change in structure came a corresponding change in function – in that the Greater Vancouver Transportation Authority Act moved responsibility for the Vancouver area's transportation into the hands of locally elected officials. Financially, the capacity to toll and tax – even if still needing provincial assistance on its collection in many instances – marked a change in the de facto financial power of those holding seats on the GVRD/GVTA as well.

In terms of efficiency and accountability, moving control over transit to a regional body continued the trend of decentralization begun in British Columbia in 1997 that an optimist might describe as an attempt to unleash the innovational power of local officials and make transit more efficient. However, in terms of accountability, TransLink has created a new problem: it has more fully empowered indirectly elected officials who are now two steps removed from their constituents. While the GVRD has been primarily a forum where locally elected mayors and councillors could discuss, negotiate and make voluntary agreements on issues such as regional growth, there was little need for them to be directly elected. But now that these same officials are vested with the power to make decisions over service provision and taxation with little provincial supervision, a stronger argument can be made for more accountability such as through democratic reforms like direct elections.

This was demonstrated late in 2000 when TransLink attempted to use one of its new revenue generating instruments to levy a vehicle tax directly. The proposed levy generated widespread public opposition from many different sectors and was ultimately abandoned when the Province of British Columbia refused to collect the new tax. This underscored the fact that while GVRD/TransLink now has the jurisdictional capacity to impose such charges, they often lack the administrative capacity to collect such taxes. More importantly, the public outcry against the vehicle levy highlighted the ongoing regional accountability gap. This accountability gap became a ravine during the summer 2002 Vancouver bus strike; lasting over several hot summer months, no one could find any accountable politician at TransLink, which had turned management of its buses over to a subsidiary, Coast Mountain Bus Company Ltd. (Fershau, 2003). The lack of an accountability oar to match the one intended for efficiency was clearly apparent.

This Vancouver metropolitan governance dilemma has had several impacts on linking senior governmental policies and metropolitan initiatives. Perhaps two recent examples illustrate this best: (1) the senior governmental pressure to ensure regional building of a rapid transit airport-to-downtown Vancouver link – the Richmond-Airport-Vancouver (RAV) line, as part of senior (Federal and Provincial) efforts for the 2010 Winter Olympics in Vancouver; and (2) the clash between the values of local initiatives/home rule included in the new British Columbia Community Charter Act and subsequent provincial legislation, re-asserting its jurisdictional ascendancy with the Significant Projects Streamlining Act (Bill 75, the Significant Projects Streamlining Act was introduced November 3, 2003) (www.gov.bc.ca and www.dogwoodinitiative.org/SignificantProjects StreamliningAct.htm). The Act was given Royal Assent Dec. 2, 2003 (www.civicnet.bc.ca).

On the RAV line decision-making, after considerable local lobbying to get transportation planning authority from the province, the GVRD finally achieved this goal in mid-1998. Coupled with earlier efforts, such as the Long-Range Transportation Plan for Greater Vancouver (Transport 2021 [1993] – a joint GVRD/BC project) which reported in

September 1993, and the development of the land-use based LRSP in 1996, the intention was that metropolitan Vancouver would be able to plan for both metropolitan land-use and transportation aspects as the region saw fit.

The regional plan (the LRSP) was clearly set out – for both land use and transportation. It did not include a RAV link in the early stages – certainly not before one additional cross-regional link – and a subsequent spur to the Northeast was completed. Then came the decision – promoted particularly by the provincial and federal governments – to award Vancouver the 2010 Winter Olympics. Both senior governments came offering additional funds for the RAV-line, with provincial support tied to a P-3 (Public-Private Partnership) option, unlike the two prior lines' public enterprise aspect. The dollars offered by the senior governments were substantial – $300 million from the province, $450 million from the federal government, combined with $300 million each from Vancouver's airport authority and $300 from TransLink itself. These monies were tied to the RAV project going ahead of other already established regionally-defined rapid transit needs.

As a case study in linking senior and metropolitan initiatives, RAV tells much about the relative lack of change in British Columbia. The new rapid transit "skytrain" RAV-line addition is costed at $1.5 – $1.7billion. The federal government provides $450 million, the province now $370 million, an anticipated private builder/operator and the region and airport authority picking up the rest. In spite of the clear desire of both levels of senior jurisdiction to have the RAV line built in time for the 2010 Winter Olympics in Vancouver, the regional authorities (GVRD and TransLink) had serious reservations about the proposal. Their concerns were threefold:

- the P-3 requirement imposed by the provincial government;
- the question of anticipated cost-overruns – particularly for a then anticipated tunneled section in the City of Vancouver – and the fact that these would have to be covered by metropolitan taxpayers;
- the fact that the RAV-line itself was not the top transit priority as identified by more than a decade of discussion within the Greater Vancouver region.

That combination of local/regional concerns led to a TransLink decision (7–5) on May 7, 2004, "not to precede work on the RAV line due to projected cost overruns." Provincial disappointment in the metropolitan authority's decision led the Premier to announce on June 15, 2004, that British Columbians collectively would cover any cost overruns as well as contribute $170 million to the RAV-delayed Northeast Skytrain connector. On June 18, 2004, TransLink again defeated the RAV proposal with a 6–6 vote.

The province's Transportation Minister, Kevin Falcon, MLA for Surrey (Greater Vancouver's "second city," south of the Fraser River, and an area subject to considerable commuting stress) announced that the provincial dollars were lost for RAV/TransLink and would instead be used for a provincial "Gateway Project" – including the twinning of suburban portions of the Trans Canada Highway and twin the Port Mann Bridge crossing the Fraser River into the older inner suburbs and the City of Vancouver – an area of considerable private auto congestion for his constituents and those in government-friendly ex-urban municipalities beyond. Such a proposal ran completely counter to more than a decade of land-use and transportation planning by the region (Steffenhagen, 2004).

The combination of senior governmental dollars and overt political pressure resulted in an unprecedented third vote on the same issue. The result was that the senior governmental priorities overruled regional policy decisions – with a vote of 8–4. RAV is being built; regional priorities were altered.

On the clash between the new Community Charter legislation and the Significant Projects Streamlining Act, the juxtaposition of competing values is just as stark: the Community Charter Act (Bill 14), "commenced" January 1, 2004; it set out its purpose in language recognizable to advocates of modest home rule; for Canadian urbanists, British Columbia's Community Charter legislation also includes language which students of Section 92–8 recognize as maintaining provincial jurisdictional oversight potential; American local governance observers might simply recognize this as Dillon's Rule Lite – or "Home Rule Extra Lite."

This is clearest in the purposes of the new Community Charter:

Purposes of the Act

3. The purposes of this Act are to provide municipalities and their councils with

    (a) a legal framework for the powers, duties and functions that are necessary to fulfill their purposes,

    (b) the authority and discretion to address existing and future community needs, and

    (c) the flexibility to determine the public interest of their communities and to respond to the different needs and changing circumstances of their communities. (Community Charter Act, proclaimed May 29, 2003)

The principles of the Act sound closer to the views of local autonomy/home rule advocates. They reflect a stated desire to clarify both the municipal and the provincial components of the provincial-municipal relationship in British Columbia, and, potentially, to add to local autonomy:

Bill 14 – May 2003

COMMUNITY CHARTER

HER MAJESTY, by and with the advice and consent of the Legislative Assembly of the Province of British Columbia, enacts as follows:

Part 1 – Principles, Purposes and Interpretation

Principles of municipal governance

1 (1) Municipalities and their councils are recognized as an order of government within their jurisdiction that

    (a) is democratically elected, autonomous, responsible and accountable,

    (b) is established and continued by the will of the residents of their communities, and

    (c) provides for the municipal purposes of their communities.

    (2) In relation to subsection (1), the Provincial government recognizes that municipalities require

    (a) adequate powers and discretion to address existing and future community needs,

    (b) authority to determine the public interest of their communities, within a legislative framework that supports balance and certainty in relation to the differing interests of their communities,

    (c) the ability to draw on financial and other resources that are adequate to support community needs,

    (d) authority to determine the levels of municipal expenditures and taxation that are appropriate for their purposes, and

    (e) authority to provide effective management and delivery of services in a manner that is responsive to community needs.

Principles of municipal-provincial relations

2 (1) The citizens of British Columbia are best served when, in their relationship, municipalities and the Provincial government

    (a) acknowledge and respect the jurisdiction of each,

    (b) work towards harmonization of Provincial and municipal enactments, policies and programs, and

    (c) foster cooperative approaches to matters of mutual interest.

  (2) The relationship between municipalities and the Provincial government is based on the following principles:

    (a) the Provincial government respects municipal authority and municipalities respect Provincial authority;

    (b) the Provincial government must not assign responsibilities to municipalities unless there is provision for resources required to fulfill the responsibilities;

    (c) consultation is needed on matters of mutual interest, including consultation by the Provincial government on

    (i) proposed changes to local government legislation,

    (ii) proposed changes to revenue transfers to municipalities, and

    (iii) proposed changes to Provincial programs that will have a significant impact in relation to matters that are within municipal authority;

(d) the Provincial government respects the varying needs and conditions of different municipalities in different areas of British Columbia;

(e) consideration of municipal interests is needed when the Provincial government participates in interprovincial, national or international discussions on matters that affect municipalities;

(f) the authority of municipalities is balanced by the responsibility of the Provincial government to consider the interests of the citizens of British Columbia generally;

(g) the Provincial government and municipalities should attempt to resolve conflicts between them by consultation, negotiation, facilitation and other forms of dispute resolution.

The language hides as much as it illuminates, however: for example, despite talk of limiting interference by the senior provincial authority, should local governments under British Columbia's Community Charter decide to raise local taxes – such as on businesses – rather than opt for the province preferred user-fees and the like, the province reserves the right to impose limits on property tax rates – in direct contradiction of the Community Charter's "empowering local autonomy" intent. And under a re-defined provincial-municipal relationship, the Community Charter reminds local governments that apart from acknowledging and respecting each other's jurisdiction, the legislative intent is to "work towards harmonization of provincial and municipal enactments, policies and programs." This may work in many instances, but not where a local government wishes to take a rather divergent policy tack. Here, the intergovernmental game becomes more perilous for local authorities (Smith & Stewart, 2005).

The past dismissal of some school boards in British Columbia and the "over a weekend" order-in-council elimination of the GVRD's authority over the region's watershed when it tried to block provincial implementation of a natural gas pipeline through that watershed to Vancouver Island, serve as historical reminders of senior provincial powers (Smith & Oberlander, 1998). The more recent provincial overturning of a local governmental (Delta) bylaw to limit negative air quality impacts of large greenhouses by requiring them to utilize natural gas or propane vs. wood waste (Penner 2003) is a good case in point: in this case, the Municipality of Delta had passed a bylaw to provide some local controls of large (e.g., in this case 18 acres) greenhouse operations, in particular their use of less-clean fuel sources for heating. The British Columbia Government intervened when a grower challenged the bylaw, citing provincial Right to Farm legislation over the right of a municipality to legislate on local businesses. The province also argued that the local bylaw contradicted the provincial Waste Management Act that exempts agricultural operations. Urban-Rural issues of this sort are not new to Delta, a Vancouver suburb. In the late 1980s and 1990s, Delta held the longest land use dispute hearing in Canadian history over efforts by developers to build on farmland for urban use. The debates over the so-called Spetifore lands near the Tsawwassen ferry terminal to Vancouver Island initially led to the Bill Bennett Social Credit government abolishing regional planning in 1983 when the GVRD initially prevented development plans by a Delta Social Credit supporter (Magnusson et al., 1984, on this latter issue).

The BC Minister of Agriculture/Fisheries has since precluded use of local bylaws to prevent/regulate coastal fish farms in British Columbia as well, to prevent local coastal municipalities from using their bylaw powers to limit possible negative environmental impacts from fish farms; the provincial "return" of fines to fish-farm operators continue to serve as current reminders that constitutional authority does matter when significant policy differences arise between local and provincial players (Anderson, 2004).

Perhaps most stunningly, in the era of a new Community Charter is British Columbia's Bill 75, the Significant Projects Streamlining Act, introduced and passed in just three weeks in November 2003; it allows the provincial government to override any local governmental opposition on any project deemed of significant provincial interest. Over half of the Union of BC Municipalities' (UBCM) member municipalities passed motions condemning Bill 75. Then-Minister of State for Deregulation, Kevin Falcon, noted that the Act was to "cut red tape," "remove unnecessary and costly delays" and "create new economic activities." Run out of the Premier's Office, the Significant Projects initiative produced an official, highly critical UBCM response:

> The UBCM Executive is shocked by the degree of intrusion of this legislation into local affairs. It allows <u>any</u> Minister … to replace <u>any</u> local government bylaw, plan, regulation, policy, etc. to facilitate the approval or development of a "provincially significant project." Cabinet can make that determination without <u>any prior</u> notice to the local government or the community. The Community Charter… promised us recognition as an independent, accountable and responsible order of government…. The Community Charter touted public accountability and openness but Bill 75 replaces local, publicly developed plans (including those developed through public hearing processes) with fiats from the provincial Minister.
> We recognize there is a need to balance local and provincial interests…. This is just not the way to achieve it. The Executive is calling on the provincial government to remove local government from Bill 75 (UBCM, 2003).

Similar school board experience in several of Ontario's largest cities in the latter period of Harris/Eaves Tory rule in the late 1990s/early 2000s mirror these lessons. If the test is in puddings, it would appear necessary to go back to basic recipe ingredients on local empowerment and accountability and start again in British Columbia.

Other recent reminders include the year 2004 also starting with the province again showing a disregard for local decision-making: in another example of provincial interference in local affairs, local police forces found out on December 30, 2003 that all bars and restaurants in British Columbia would be allowed to stay open until 4 a.m. on

December 31, 2003 – January 1, 2004 and thereafter. The provincial Liquor Control and Licensing Act was amended in late 2002 allowing for this change, but it was not implemented. Local police forces first learned of it less than 48 hours before its impact, resulting in expensive overtime/shift changes – all costs borne by the municipalities. The provincial legislation over-rode municipal by-laws and even when the changed hours were decided by the provincial agency, no one informed municipal/policing officials until they found out the day before; the reason given by the province for this oversight: the legislation "did not require" notification to local governments (CKNW News, December, 2003).

In 2004–2006, one other dispute has highlighted the assertion of provincial powers over locally defined preferences in Greater Vancouver: as part of its Olympic bid, the province committed to "fixing" the "Sea to Sky" highway linking Vancouver and Whistler; it also committed to a "sustainable Olympics" (www.eagleridgebluffs.ca). Within Greater Vancouver's portion of the highway, the District of West Vancouver has objected to the form of routing, requesting a tunnel vs. an overland route through the ecologically sensitive undeveloped Eagle Ridge Bluffs, Larson Creek Wetlands and part of the North Shore Baden Powell Trail. BC's Minister of Transportation, citing costs announced the 2.4 km. overland route vs. the 1.4 km. tunnel strongly preferred by the municipality. The municipality undertook court action vs. the federal government's environmental assessment approval of the province's plan. That case was heard in February 2005 (www.westvancouver.ca). In May 2005, Canada's Federal Court ruled in favor of the province and the federal government, rejecting West Vancouver's claim. It did require the federal environmental assessors to ensure that provincial promises to mitigate impact were fulfilled when that phase of the highway is built over the next three years (Federal Court of Canada, 2005).

Meanwhile, as part of the political skirmishing, the District of West Vancouver has insisted that all work on the Sea to Sky highway within the municipality be subject to municipal bylaw controls (e.g., over blasting, noise control, etc.). The BC Transportation Minister says "municipal regulations do not apply to the province." In that, he is correct; however, their own Design Build Agreement compels all contractors to comply with all laws *and bylaws* (www.westvancouver.ca/article?a=3864c=677).

With the provincial general election on May 17, 2005 and BC municipal elections in November, 2005, the political debate over the attempts of the province to override municipal interests continued to pit Community Charter commitments vs. Significant Projects Streamlining powers well into 2006–2010.

Conclusions

The Regional District system that has worked admirably for the last almost 40 years may well continue to provide a highly successful, negotiated and flexible model of decision-making for another half century in most regional districts in British Columbia. Even in the Capital Region/Victoria – if Bish is correct – this may remain true, though the Province of Nova Scotia thought not for the Halifax region, a metropolitan region equivalent in size to Victoria's capital region (Sancton, 1996, 2000; Meech & Vodicka, 1997; Poel, 1999; Evans, 2001). And Mike Harris's Ontario – in Toronto, Ottawa Carleton, Hamilton Wentworth, Sudbury, Kingston and beyond – came to the same conclusion (Golden & Slack and Andrew, this volume).

In metropolitan Vancouver, the crunch has come. The GVRD and related regional authorities such as TransLink increasingly lack the mandate to take regional decisions without an appropriate political accountability base. For 26, and probably 27, of British Columbia's regional districts, as William Shakespeare noted, "past is prologue" (Shakespeare, *The Tempest*, Act 2, Scene 1, line 261). For Greater Vancouver, it is probably simply past. While not all agree (Cameron, 2005), that leaves the question, "what next?" If not now, then very shortly, the Province of British Columbia and the GVRD/GVTA will be forced to recognize that accountability concerns may overwhelm the considerable regional successes of the past century in British Columbia's largest metropolitan district. It will be public reactions to new regional charges/taxes for regional services that will be the tipping point. That may come with GVTA/TransLink improvements such as RAV. Already RAVCO, the line developer has moved from high cost tunneling to a cut and cover construction prompting local area businesses to state that they were lied to and to try – unsuccessfully – for a judicial injunction. It may also result from higher charges for the more traditional range of services such as water or parks; or it might be precipitated by financial pressures toward regional policing (and other public safety) services. With a continued right-wing provincial government/agenda following the May 17, 2005 BC General Election, it could also be pushed by a substantial downloading of social service or other responsibilities as occurred in Mike Harris' Ontario. Whatever the back-breaking straw, the regional camel in metropolitan Vancouver will increasingly be under structural pressure and citizen scrutiny over its governance.

That should not seem surprising. A central debate is taking place about accountability in public governance. On the one side, the argument is made that accountability is one half of an equation – the other side being efficiency. Governance theorists such as Peter Self (1977) have contended that the relationship between accountability and efficiency is zero-sum: as you add to one, you subtract equally from the other. Self further asserted that the relationship between accountability and efficiency is the central dilemma in public administration; it is also a dilemma which has grown considerably more complex with time. Certainly, all governments in the late 1990s and now the 2000s are under increased pressure on the efficiency side. For the regional district in the largest urban setting in British Columbia – Greater Vancouver – however, there is now need for more accountability.

The most obvious "what next" in terms of improving accountability for Greater Vancouver – the only regional district over 400,000 in population in BC and the only region with multiple municipal units over 100,000 – is democratic electoral reform. That might imply a shift to a megacity or to some new/other form of directly elected Greater Vancouver Authority. This has already been suggested (Smith & Stewart, 1998: 47–49). In spring 1998, a Report for the Ministry of Municipal Affairs on Making Local Accountability Work in British Columbia recommended "the creation of a Greater Vancouver Authority, with a directly elected Greater Vancouver Assembly and a Regional Mayor elected across the whole region." The Report noted that "with ... eleven municipal units of 50,000 and more than half of these at or over 100,000 population size, a shift to direct elections would appreciably enhance local-regional accountability" (Smith & Stewart, 2000b). Greater London, after Margaret Thatcher's *Streamlining the Cities* annihilation of the GLC and six other Metropolitan County Councils (MCCs), had a regional authority re-established – with the GLA; part of the rationale of the Blair government was to provide a broader regional structure to compete more effectively internationally ("Who Represents 'London'?" vs. "Who Does What?"). For Greater Vancouver, the international dimensions of regional governance reform would be a significant collateral benefit (Smith, 1992; Andrew & Smith, 1999; Smith, 2002; Smith, 2004; Smith & Stewart, 2005). Britain's New Labour reforms creating a Greater London Authority suggest both regional **and** international benefits (Dunleavy & Margetts, 1998).

Democratic reforms to Greater Vancouver could include other electoral notions as well: if direct elections were introduced, these might include broader electoral system changes including some form of proportional representation; it could include electoral expense/spending limit reforms (Smith & Stewart, 2000a); and it could involve a clearer disentangling of who does what. Bill 31, the Local Government Statutes Amendment Act (1998) recognized local government as an independent, responsible and accountable order of government. Subsequent unilateral action by the province on cuts to municipal grants generally, on required skytrain technology and its Sea to Sky Highway in Greater Vancouver, rather suggested a continued senior governmental paternalism versus legislative efforts to make local governments both more independent **and** accountable in British Columbia. The policy failures of past NDP Municipal Affairs Ministers Jenny Kwan, Jim Doyle and Cathy McGregor suggested more pessimism than optimism on the reform front at the turn of the century. As (then) Deputy Premier Joy MacPhail said – to the agreement of NDP leadership colleagues in 2001 – on municipal accountability reform "we chickened out" (Smith & Stewart, 2000b). The Liberal administration, first elected in 2001, has done no better. On October 2, 2004, TransLink Directors criticized the "province's unilateral approach to regional transportation planning." Their concerns reflected the stance of Transportation Minister Kevin Falcon "to consult (the region) but... then push ahead with the Gateway (highway/bridge twinning) project" (Boei, 2004). In late January, 2006, provincial Transportation Highways Minister Kevin Falcon, formally announced his Gateway project

Certainly, equally important to international benefits of regional governance reform, would be the accountability benefits of renewed Greater Vancouver governance. TransLink and GVRD directors face an uncertain future in ignoring the increasingly obvious public accountability concerns. (Smith & Stewart, 2005) Little short of democratic reform will be required of TransLink and other regional authorities in Greater Vancouver. It is a view increasingly understood within the GVRD as well. Some senior staff have concluded the following:

- there is no entity capable of governing in the interests of the entire metropolitan area;
- people assume the GVRD handles all metro issues, but it does not and is often uncomfortable with the suggestion that it should do more;
- parochial interests outweigh areas where cooperation would be obvious (e.g., regional policing, regional economic planning, regional land use planning);
- financial circumstances vary among local governments;
- GVTA has been a source of public controversy and has exposed an urban-suburban divide on some issues. (GVRD, March, 2005)

Finally, it is arguable that with a clearer link to its regional citizenry, metropolitan Vancouver might be better able to resist senior governmental pressures and blandishments – at least where these threats and inducements ran counter to policies determined by, and for, the region itself (Smith and Stewart, 2004) In its past, one of the great successes of local-regional interests and institutions in the Lower Mainland was the ability to anticipate and recognize the need for change; failure to do so now – or in its short-to-intermediate-term future – may threaten the longer-term prospects for another 50 years of regional planning and governance success in Greater Vancouver. Ironically, this challenge comes just as the British Columbia Regional District model is being held up as a "best case" in governance over government for metropolitan regions elsewhere.

References

Anderson, C. (2004). Auditor-General to look into return of (fish-)farm fines after a complaint by the Sierra Legal Defense Fund; The Province, February 15, p. A6.

Andrew, C., & Smith, P.J. (1999). World class cities; can – or should – Canada play? In: C. Andrew, P. Armstrong & A. Lapierre, eds, World Class Cities: Can Canada Play? (pp. 5–25). Ottawa: University of Ottawa Press.

BC Stats (2005). www.bcstats.gov.bc.ca/data/pop.pop.htm; accessed March 5.

Bish, R. (2000). Evolutionary alternatives for metropolitan areas: The capital region of British Columbia. Canadian Journal of Regional Science 23, 1, 73–88.

Bish, R. (2001). Local government amalgamations: discredited Nineteenth-Century ideals alive in the Twenty-First. Commentary, Toronto: C.D. Howe Institute, no. 150, March.

Boei, W. (2004). Victoria's traffic plans upsets some mayors. *Vancouver Sun*, 2 Oct. 2, p. B9.

Bond, D. (1996). Maintaining the metropolitan economy. In: P. Smith,H.P. Oberlander & T. Hutton, editors, Urban Solutions to Global Problems: Vancouver-Canada-Habitat II, Vancouver: UBC/CHS & SGU/IGS, 68–71.

Cameron, K. (2005). Vancouver: United Nations – World Urban Forum.

Campbell. Hon. Dan, (1976). Former Minister of Municipal Affairs, BC, personal interview with author, (Smith), March.

Cities Plus (2005). @ www.citiesplus.ca (accessed March 11, 2005).

CKNW News (2003). (BC Radio 980), December 30, 2003.

Cohn, T., Merrifield, D., & Smith P. (1989). North American cities in an interdependent world: Vancouver and Seattle as international cities , In: E. Fry, L. Radebaugh & P. Soldatos, editors, The New International Cities Era: The Global Activities of North American Municipal Governments, Provo, Utah: Brigham Young University.

Cohn, T., & Smith P., (1996). Constituent Diplomacy Policy Determinants In: British Columbia: Developing A Global Region In The Pacific Northwest. *BC Studies*.110, Winter, 25–59.

Dunleavy, P., & Margetts, H. (1998). Report to the Government Office for London: Electing the London Mayor and the London Assembly. London: LSE Public Policy Group, June.

Evans, T. (2001). Amalgamating Halifax, MA Thesis, Political Science, Simon Fraser University.

Federal Court of Canada (2005). Corporation of the District of West Vancouver vs. the Queen (BC Ministry of Transportation and Attorney General of Canada) Docket T–1310–04; Citation FC593, May 4, Justice Francois Lemieux.

Fershau, J. (2003). Translink Governance, MA Thesis, Political Science, Simon Fraser University.

Frisken, F. (1994). Metropolitan change and the challenge to public policy. Introduction in F. Frisken, ed., The Changing Canadian Metropolis (pp 1–35). Berkeley, Cal..: Institute of Governmental Studies, University of California Press.

Ginnell, K., & Smith, P. J. (2001). Habitat @ 25: Lessons (still) From Vancouver. Paper for the United Nations General Assembly Special Session for the Overall Review and Appraisal of the Implementation of the Habitat Agenda. New York, June, 32 pp.

Golden, A., (1996). Greater Toronto: Report of the GTA Task Force, Toronto: Queen's Printer.

Higgins, D. (1986). Local and Urban Politics in Canada. Toronto: Gage.

Higgins, D. (1977). Urban Canada: Its Government and Politics. Toronto: Macmillan.

Howlett, M. & Brownsey, K. (1992). British Columbia: Public sector politics in a Rentier resource economy. In K. Brownsey & M. Howlett, eds., The Provincial State: Politics in Canada's Provinces and Territories (pp. 265–295). Toronto: Copp Clark Pitman.

Hutton, T. (1997). The Innisian core-periphery revisited: Vancouver's changing relationships with BC's staple economy. BCStudies1, 13, Spring, 69–100.

Jacobs, J. (1984). Cities and the wealth of nations: Principles of economic life, New York: Random House.

Magnusson, W. , Carroll, W.K., Doyle, C., Langer, M., & Walker, R.B.J., editors (1984). The New Reality: The Politics of Restraint in British Columbia. Vancouver: New Star.

Meech, K., & Vodicka, R. (1997). Hindsight is 20/20: Planning for amalgamation in the Halifax regional municipality. Cordillera Institute Journal 1, 1.

North, R., & Hardwick, W. (1992). Vancouver since the Second World War: An economic geography. In: G. Wynn & T. Oke, eds. Vancouver and its Region (pp. 200–233).Vancouver: UBC Press.

Oberlander, H. P., & Smith, P. J. (1993). Governing metropolitan Vancouver: Regional intergovernmental relations in British Columbia (pp. 329–373). In: D. Rothblatt & A. Sancton, editors. Metropolitan Governance: American/Canadian Intergovernmental Perspectives. Berkeley, Cal.: Institute of Governmental Studies Press, University of California.

Penner, D. (2003). Tomato King cheers right to burn wood: Court overturns bylaw that restricted growers fuel – Delta bylaw 'set undue restrictions'. Vancouver Sun, April 19, C1–2.

Poel, D. (1999). (Not) thinking regionally: Citizen responses to municipal consolidation, Canadian Regional Science Association paper, Montreal, November.

Port of Vancouver, (2005). Annual Report, Vancouver: Port of Vancouver.

Rock, C. (2001). Senior Planner, Translink. Class Presentation to Simon Fraser University Political Science class, February.

Sancton, A. (1995). Governing Canada's City-Regions: Adapting Form to Function (pp. 98, 100). Montreal: IRPP.

Sancton, A. (1996). Reducing costs by consolidating municipalities: New Brunswick, Nova Scotia and Ontario. Canadian Public Administration 3, 3, 267–289.

Sancton, A. (2000). Merger Mania: The Assault on Local Government (pp. 89–101). Westmount, Que.: Price-Patterson – since re-published – same title (2000), by Montreal: McGill-Queen's University Press.

Sancton, A., & Rothblatt, D., (1998) eds., Metropolitan Governance Revisited: American/Canadian Intergovernmental Perspectives. Berkeley, Cal.: IGS Press, University of California.

Savitch, H. V., & Vogel, R. K. (1996) eds., Regional Politics: America in a Post City Age. Thousand Oaks, Cal.: Sage/Urban Affairs Annual Reviews, 45.

Self, P. (1977). Administrative Theories and Politics. Boston: Allyn & Unwin, Chap. 8.

Sheltair, (2005). @ www. Sheltair.ca (accessed March 10, 2005).

Smith, P. J. (1992). The making of a global city: Fifty years of constituent diplomacy. The case of Vancouver, Canadian Journal of Urban Research 1, 1, 90–112.

Smith, P. J. (1994). British Columbia: Public policy and perceptions of governance. In J. Bickerton & A.-G. Gagnon, eds. Canadian Politics (pp. 506–526). Peterborough: Broadview.

Smith, P. J., Oberlander, H.P. & Hutton, T. eds. (pp. 156–168). Urban Solutions to Global Problems: Vancouver, Canada. Habitat ii. Vancouver: University of British Columbia, Center for Human Settlements.

Smith, P.J. (2002). Cascading Concepts of Cascadia: A Territory or a Notion? In International Journal of Canadian Studies, vol.25, Spring, 113–148.

Smith, P.J. (2004).Transborder Cascadia: Which Borders Matter? Journal of Border Studies, 19,1, 99–121.

Smith, P. J., & Cohn, T. H. (1994). International cities and municipal paradiplomacy: A typology for assessing the changing Vancouver metropolis. In: F. Frisken, ed. The Changing Canadian Metropolis, Berkeley, Cal.: Institute of Governmental Studies, University of California Press, pp. 725–750.

Smith, P. J., & Oberlander, H. P. (1998). Restructuring metropolitan governance: Greater Vancouver – British Columbia reforms. In: A. Sancton & D. Rothblatt, eds.Metropolitan Governance Revisited: American/Canadian Intergovernmental Perspectives. Berkeley, Cal.: IGS Press, University of California, pp. 371–406.

Smith, P. J., & Stewart, K. (1998). Making Local Accountability Work in British Columbia, Report 2: Reforming Municipal Electoral Accountability, for the Ministry of Municipal Affairs and Housing, British Columbia, June, pp. 41–42.

Smith, P. J., & Stewart, K. (2000a). Local democracy and local government: Policy impediments and legislative reform proposals – British Columbia cases, British lessons. Making Votes Count, conference paper, Vancouver, May.

Smith, P. J., & Stewart, K. (2000b). Up the policy stream without a champion? Local democratic legislative reform in British Columbia: 1991–1996 and 1996–2001. British Columbia Political Studies Association paper, Victoria, May.

Smith, P.J., & Stewart K. (2004) Beavers and cats revisited: Has the

Local-Intergovernmental Game Shifted to the Mushy Middle? Canadian-American Comparisons, Korean Local Government Review, .6,1: 123–156.

Smith, P. J., & Stewart, K., (2005) Local Government legislative reform in British Columbia: 1991–2005: One Oar in the Water, In: J. Garcea & E. Lesage Jr. (eds.). Municipal Reforms in Canada: Dimensions, Dynamics, Determinants (pp. 25–56). Toronto: Oxford University Press.

Smith, P. J., Oberlander H. P., & Hutton. T. (1996). Urban Solutions to Global Problems: Vancouver – Canada. Habitat II. Vancouver: University of British Columbia, Center for Human Settlements.

Statistics (1989) relating to regional and municipal governments in British Columbia. Victoria: Province of British Columbia, June, p.3.

Statistics Canada (2002), 2001 Canadian Census, Ottawa; "About Vancouver" at www.city.vancouver.bc.ca and Seattle, Datasheet, (City of Seattle, 2002) at www.ci.seattle.wa.us. (both accessed 11 Sept.).

Steffenhagen, J. (2004). RAV foes promote light rail line. *Vancouver Sun*, 21 June.

Tennant, P., & Zirnhelt, D. (1973). Metropolitan government in Vancouver: The politics of "Gentle Imposition." Canadian Public Administration 16, Spring, pp. 124–138.

Tindal, R., & Tindal, S. (1995). Local Government in Canada. 4th edition (pp. 123–124). Toronto: McGraw-Hill Ryerson.

Tindal, R., & Tindal, S. (2004). Local Government in Canada. 6th edition. Toronto: Nelson.

TransLink, (2001), About Us, http://www.translink.bc.ca/aboutus/gvrd.htm. (accessed May, 2003).

Transport 2021 (1993): A Long-range Transportation Plan for Greater Vancouver. Burnaby: GVRD, September, 86 pp.

Union of BC Municipalities, Press Release, Frank Leonard, President, 7 Nov. 2003. Accessed 14 Feb. 2004.

www. sustainability.ca (accessed March 2, 2005)

www.thinkcity.bc.ca. (accessed February 28, 2005)

www.eaglebluffs.ca (accessed March 17, 2005)

www.westvancouver.bc.ca (accessed March 12, 2005)

Appendix 1

30 Major metropolitan/urban centers in Canada

	2001	Rank 2001	Rank 1996	Area[1]	Density[2]
Toronto** (Ontario)	4,682,897	1	1	5,902.74	793.3
Montreal (Quebec)	3,426,350	2	2	4,047.35	846.6
Vancouver (British Columbia)	1,986,965	3	3	2,878.52	690.3
Ottawa–Hull (Ontario–Quebec)	1,063,664	4	4	5,318.36	200.0
Calgary (Alberta)	951,395	5	6	5,083.00	187.2
Edmonton (Alberta)	937,845	6	5	9,418.62	99.6
Quebec (Quebec)	682,757	7	7	3,154.35	216.4
Winnipeg (Manitoba)	671,274	8	8	4,151.48	161.7
Hamilton (Ontario)	662,401	9	9	1,371.76	482.9
London (Ontario)	432,451	10	10	2,333.37	185.3
Kitchener (Ontario)	414,284	11	11	826.98	501.0
St. Catharines–Niagara (Ontario)	377,009	12	12	1,406.2	268.1
Halifax (Nova Scotia)	359,183	13	13	5,495.54	65.4
Victoria (B.C.)	311,902	14	14	695.34	448.6
Windsor (Ontario)	307,877	15	15	1,022.53	301.1
Oshawa (Ontario)	296,298	16	16	903.23	328.0
Saskatoon (Saskatchewan)	225,927	17	17	5,192.22	43.5
Regina (Saskatchewan)	192,800	18	18	3,407.84	56.6
St. John's (Newfoundland Lab.)	172,918	19	19	804.63	214.9
Greater Sudbury (Ontario)	155,601	20	20	3,536.10	44.0
Chicoutimi–Jonquière (Quebec)	154,938	21	21	1,753.67	88.4
Sherbrooke (Quebec)	153,811	22	22	1,108.16	138.8
Barrie (Ontario)	148,480	23	29	897.46	165.4
Kelowna (British Columbia)	147,739	24	25	2,904.00	50.9

	2001	Rank 2001	Rank 1996	Area[1]	Density[2]
Abbotsford (British Columbia)	147,370	25	26	625.94	235.4
Kingson (Ontario)	146,838	26	23	1,906.82	77.0
Trois-Rivières (Quebec)	135,507	27	24	880.47	156.2
Saint John (New Brunswick)	122,678	28	28	3,359.61	36.5
Thunder Bay (Ontario)	121,986	29	27	2,548.16	47.9
Moncton (New Brunswick)	117,727	30	31	2,177.23	54.1
Source: Statistics Canadaq				[1] in km^2	[2] per km^2

http://www.canadainfolink.ca/canadian cities.htm

Part III
Comparative Lessons

KENNEDY STEWART

Why Insulate New Institutions?
Evaluating Pre- and Post- Change Support for Metropolitan Reform in General London and Totonto

Recognizing that policy outcomes are affected by the rules and procedures by which they are generated, governments alter institutions in ways that support their preferred policies both during and beyond their mandates. To insulate new institutions against future tampering these same governments often make significant efforts to build elite and grassroots support prior to initiating reforms. Recent regional government reform processes in London and Toronto provide an opportunity to test the value of this insulation strategy. Where British Prime Minister Tony Blair used a "Big Tent" approach to build widespread pre-change support for the Greater London Authority (GLA), Ontario Premier Mike Harris's use of a "Big Stick" to create Megacity Toronto spawned strong opposition. Despite radically different reform processes, elite support is now high for both new legislative bodies. More surprisingly, post-change opinion poll evidence shows that public support for the once hated Megacity is higher than for the GLA. These results appear to undermine the insulation strategy and suggest that local elite will reverse strongly held beliefs to take full advantage of new environments. They also suggest that consultation is unnecessary as long as the public believe progress is being made on an issue of concern. But where local leaders may always sell-out to stay in power, those who believe in the value of public participation should not despair. Additional evidence demonstrates that the public does not reward upper-tier governments that make empty promises or rely on bully tactics.

Governing Greater London

To cope with the 18th-century population explosion during which Greater London's population grew from one million in 1801 to nearly six million in 1891, the Conservative Government in Whitehall created the London County Council (LCC) in 1888 to coordinate and deliver services for Londoners. Elected LCC councillors and aldermen were responsible for the management, planning and coordination of transportation and sewage. Recognizing that urban areas require micro and macro attention, 28 metropolitan boroughs were created in 1899.

By the early 1950s the capital's population had outgrown the LCC's capacity to provide urban solutions to regional problems as only 3.35 million of the region's 8.35 million inhabitants lived within the LCC's jurisdiction. Established to address the LCC's lack of effectiveness, the Royal (Herbert) Commission recommended that a new and larger regional body be created. Introduced in the *London Government Act 1963*, the boundaries of Greater London were widened to contain parts of Essex, Kent, Surrey, Hertfordshire, Croydon, East Ham and West Ham, the number of metropolitan boroughs increased to 32, and an elected, upper-tier metropolitan authority with broad planning powers called the Greater London Council (GLC) was brought in to replace the LCC (Byrne, 1990; Chandler, 1991; Foley, 1972; Rogers & Fisher, 1992; Thornley, 1992).

Unlike the Labour dominated LCC, power on the GLC swung back and forth between Labour and Conservative majorities. Labour won the first election in 1964, the Conservatives the next two in 1967 and 1970. Labour regained control in 1973, but then again lost to the Conservatives in 1977. Concerned that past Labour GLC governments had frequently overstepped their mandates, the 1977 Conservative GLC administration commissioned a report into the scope and jurisdiction of the regional body. The resulting Faulk Report recommended that the GLC's strategic role be enhanced but direct service delivery powers be reduced. However, no immediate action was taken.

After gaining control of the GLC in 1981, the radical left Labour leader Ken Livingstone came into constant conflict with Conservative Prime Minister Margaret Thatcher – elected to national office in 1979. Partly in reaction to Livingstone's constant taunts and defiance,

Figure 1: The Boroughs of Greater London (1964-Present)

1. City of London	12. Brent	23. Bexley
2. Westminster	13. Ealing	24. Havering
3. Kensington and Chelsea	14. Hounslow	25. Barking &
4. Hammersmith & Fulham	15. Richmond	Dagenham
5. Wandsworth	16. Kingston	26. Redbridge
6. Lambeth	17. Merton	27. Newham
7. Southwark	18. Sutton	28. Waltham
8. Tower Hamlets	19. Croydon	Forest
9. Hackney	20. Bromley	29. Haringey
10. Islington	21. Lewisham	30. Enfield
11. Camden	22. Greenwich	31. Barnet
		32. Harrow
		33. Hillingdon

Source: UK Department for Transport, Local Government and the
Regions

Thatcher's cabinet tabled *Streamlining the Cities* – a 1984 White paper proposing the abolition of the GLC (and the other six British metropolitan county councils). A year later, the GLC was disbanded with most its powers and responsibilities transferred back to central government, appointed boards or local borough councils. While the Thatcher reforms were justified in the name of efficiency, Ian Loverland (1999: 91) states, "one need not be unduly cynical to conclude that their primary purpose was to remove a potentially significant source of opposition to central government."

Calls for a new regional governance body practically began the day the GLC was abolished, but detailed proposals took some time to develop. In preparing their 1992 election Manifesto, Tony Blair's New Labour began a consultation process by launching a discussion paper entitled *London: A World Class Capital* (Labour Party, 1992). Responses were collected and announced in *An Elected Voice for London* (Labour Party, 1996), in which Labour endorsed an elected, London-wide strategic authority. Failing to win in 1992, New Labour used a similar strategy to develop their 1997 election manifesto. In 1996 a public discussion paper entitled *A Voice for London* (Association, 1996) was launched in which the party reiterated its commitment to a London-wide strategic authority that would speak up for London within Britain, Europe and globally – a pledge that broadly corresponded with the wishes of the public. The proposal was sketchy and issues such as boundaries, structure and electoral system were left open for debate (Labour Party, 1996). In their 1997 Manifesto New Labour took their commitment one step further, promising a referendum on this issue.

Two months after winning the May, 1997 General Election, Tony Blair issued the *New Leadership for London* Green Paper (Great Britain, 1997) that proposed a new London Authority with a directly elected, executive mayor and scrutinizing assembly. Over 1,200 individuals and organizations responded to the proposal. On March 28, 1998, a White Paper, entitled *A Mayor and Assembly for London* (Great Britain, 1998a), was released in which the mayor and assembly's power were detailed. In the foreword, John Prescott – Deputy Prime Minister and Secretary of State for the Department of Environment, Transport and Regions – stated that London needed a new regional government to "...fill the democratic deficit created by the abolition of the GLC in 1986, to provide strong strategic leadership and restore accountability...," and to find solutions to "...many pressing issues – congestion and pollution poverty and social exclusion – all of which reduce the quality of life for Londoners and visitors and threaten to undermine London's international competitiveness" (Great Britain, 1998a). The proposal was advertised widely on billboards, radio and newspapers and a summary of the White Paper posted to every London household.

After passing a city-wide referendum, New Labour introduced the *Greater London Authority Act* (Great Britain, 1998b) that received Royal Assent on November 11. The Greater London Authority has the general power to enact policies that further any one or more of its principal purposes: (1) promoting economic development and wealth creation; (2) promoting social development; and, (3) promoting the improvement of the environment. In addition to pursuing these goals, the GLA must take into consideration how their policies will affect health and sustainable development. The key player in the GLA is the mayor who sets the budget and develops the overall strategies for transport, planning and the environment and approves strategies for economic and cultural development. The mayor also appoints many committee heads and members of four new pan-London bodies: Transport for London, London Development Agency, Metropolitan Police Authority and the London Fire and Emergency Planning Authority. Much like New York City Council, the Greater London Assembly scrutinizes the actions and non-actions of the executive mayor. The Greater London Assembly's main power is the ability to overrule all or part of the mayors' budget with a two-third majority.

On May 4, 2000, former GLC leader Ken Livingstone took up where he left off when three quarters of a million voters elected him to office. Following a bitter dispute and split with New Labour, Livingstone was elected mayor as an independent. Twenty-five Assembly members were elected using a "mixed" style Additional Member System (AMS) in which 14 are elected from single-member constituencies and 11 top-up members on a London-wide basis through proportional representation. No party was elected with a majority – with the Conservatives holding nine, New Labour holding nine, Liberal Democrats four and Green Party three of the 25 available Assembly seats. Livingstone controls an approximately £32 million operating budget as well as directs £3.3 billion previously spent by central and borough governments on police, fire, transport and economic development, with which he directs the actions of 55,000 employees.

Ken Livingstone was readmitted to the Labour Party following his

2000 electoral victory. He was then re-elected mayor in 2004 with a sizeable majority. In the June 10, 2004 Greater London Assembly elections, the Conservatives elected nine members – maintaining their numbers from 2000, Labour seven – a drop of two, Liberal Democrats five, and the Green and UK Independence Parties two members each (www.londonelects.org). The next Greater London elections are in 2008 (www.electoralcommission.org.uk/elections/gla.cfm).

Assessing pre- and post-change institutional support in Greater London

The above section provides the basic structural form and developmental progress of the GLA. This section begins to assess the value of building pre-change elite and public support for new institutions. Support in the pre-change period is measured by assessing elite and public opinion prior to Livingstone and the Assembly members taking office. Post-change support is assessed by gauging later attitudes and behavior. These data are later compared to similar information from Greater Toronto.

Pre-change support for the GLA: Blair's "Big Tent"
Prior to and after their 1997 General Election victory New Labour used a "Big Tent" strategy to build support for changing London's governance structure which included anticipating and accommodating demands of opponents and conducting widespread public consultation before implementing change.[1] These tactics were seen as necessary as New Labour knew it would face opposition and demands from other national parties. According to Bob Neill, leader of the GLA Conservative group, New Labour's fears of Conservative Party opposition were well founded:

> We'd always been opposed to a London-wide Authority as a party and that was the manifesto from which we fought the election. We'd accepted it largely as a voice for London, but not the proposed structure and not necessarily a directly elected

---

1   The term "Big Tent" was first brought to my attention during an interview with Bob Chilton – former Chief Executive Officer of the GLA.

mayor. It may have been an early acceptance, there might be an argument on that one, but it was inherited and we stuck with it.[2]

Less hostile than the Conservatives, but still demanding, one of the longest held Liberal Democrat policies has been electoral reform as under the single member plurality system they suffer more than any other major party in the United Kingdom.[3] By highlighting the need for more sustainable environments, the blossoming Green Party also captured Labour's attention – especially since the Greens planned to field a strong slate of candidates in the first GLA elections. While detrimental to their own immediate election fortunes, New Labour attempted to gain support from the Liberal Democrats by incorporating a more proportional electoral system into the *Greater London Authority Act* (Dunleavy & Margetts, 1988: 2). To accommodate the Green challenge New Labour required that every piece of legislation passed by the GLA be assessed for potential impact on sustainability. As Blair began to build consensus support for the GLA among traditional rivals even the Conservatives changed their strategy – eventually running a full slate of candidates. According to Bob Neill:

> Should we continue with absolute opposition or should we change? The evidence seemed to suggest that on balance it (the current process) would lead to some kind of London-wide structure. So the first thing to do was to turn round the party's attitude to that…. A consensus emerged pretty quickly: *it wouldn't do our electoral prospects…any good to be seen to be rigidly opposed to the idea of a Mayor.* Then there was a poll on the same day. So that's why the Tory Party started shifting.[4]

To support their attempts to build elite consensus through concession, New Labour also made great efforts to win public favor on this issue. Part of this effort included providing the public with ample information on the proposed arrangements and time to contribute to the GLA

2   Interview, Bob Neill, Leader of Greater London Authority Conservative Group, August, 2000.

3   For an explanation of the effects of Britain's single-member plurality system, see Dunleavy, et al., 1998.

4   Interview, Bob Neill, Leader of Greater London Authority Conservative Group, August, 2000.

debate. In addition to the previously described pre-election consultation documents and government papers, the issue generated a huge amount of media coverage with the London-focussed *Evening Standard* and *Guardian* each running almost 1,000 articles on the Greater London Authority between New Labour's election in May1997 and when the GLA took power in July 2000.[5] Perhaps most importantly, New Labour twice gave the public the final say on the GLA by campaigning on the idea during the 1997 General Election and holding a London-wide referendum in which 72 % of those who voted supported the new institutions (Table 1).

New Labour continued to consult even after the Act had received royal ascent. For example, the *Shape of Things to Come*, a consultation paper setting out the proposals for the initial organization of the GLA, garnered 44 detailed responses from London boroughs, organizations later absorbed into the GLA, organizations later transformed into functional bodies, academics, professional groups, trade unions, and non-governmental organizations (Government Office for London, 1999). Far from an empty consultation, the follow up report entitled *Shaping Up for the Mayor and Assembly* shows that some of the recommendations were used to change how transition would take place and how some specific organizational arrangements would be handled (Greater London Authority, 1999).

Post-Change Support for the GLA
Like the pre-change period, post-change support for the GLA can be garnered from elite and public points of view. On the first, there are two key relationships within the GLA – among the members of the assembly and between the assembly and the mayor. Assembly voting patterns show a high level of consensus within the new chamber. Of the 161 motions raised in the Assembly during 2001, 142 (88 %) were passed. This high percentage shows that despite the presence of four strong minority groups – one of which was hostile to the very idea of a new government for London – only 12% of the tabled motions were voted down. At the very least, this high level of agreement indicates that no party was working to systematically undermine the Assembly.

---

5   Based on a FT Profile count of articles in these papers including the words "London Mayor," "Mayor for London," "Greater London Authority" or "GLA."

Table 1: 1999 GLA Referendum Results by Borough (%)

Borough	Yes	Turnout	Borough (cont'd)	Yes	Turnout
Barking &Dagenham	74	25	Houslow	75	32
Barnet	70	36	Islington	82	35
Bexley	63	35	Kensington &Chelsea	70	28
Brent	78	37	Kingston upon Thames	69	41
Bromley	57	40	Lambeth	82	32
Camden	81	33	Lewisham	78	30
City of London	63	31	Merton	72	38
Croydon	65	38	Newham	81	29
Ealing	77	33	Redbridge	70	36
Enfield	67	33	Richmond upon Thames	71	45
Greenwich	75	33	Southwark	81	33
Hackney	82	35	Sutton	65	35
Hammersmith & Fulham	78	34	Tower Hamlets	78	36
Haringey	84	30	Waltham Forest	73	34
Havering	61	34	Westminster	72	32
Hillingdon	63	35	Total	72	34

Question: Are you in favor of the government's proposals for a Greater London Authority, made up of an elected Mayor and a separately elected Assembly?

However, the early relationship between the mayor and the Assembly has not been as congenial. The Assembly used its major scrutiny power to reject the Mayor's initial budget proposal in 2001. According to Pimlott and Rao (2001: 167), "…members of all parties…rejected the budget by 24 votes to one, eliminating all but the provision for additional police officers and reducing the precept increase to about one third of that originally proposed." The following year Labour and Liberal Democrat Party members cooperated to force the mayor to cut his budget by £85 million to £2.5 billion.[6] These stands by the Assembly show that some tension exists within London's

6   GLA Press Release, London Assembly agrees to Mayor's "sensible compromise" on budget 13-2-2002.

newest city hall, but to claim that this dissention indicates widespread dissatisfaction with the institutions would be a stretch. In sum, while the Assembly has made the mayor's life difficult at times, all parties seem to have adapted to and embraced the new institutions.

Public support for the GLA can be measured through public votes and opinion surveys. Starting with 1999 referendum, while 72% voted "yes" to the Greater London Authority, only 34% of registered voters cast a ballot. This result indicates that the institution was popular with those who voted, but the low levels of turnout do not indicate that the GLA captured the imagination of the local populace. The same holds for the 2000 GLA elections where only 35% of Londoners chose to vote in a widely publicized and dramatic race that saw Livingstone split with New Labour and Steve Norris replace a disgraced best-selling author Jeffery Archer as the Conservative mayoralty candidate.

Table 2: Satisfaction with London Mayor

Question: Are you satisfied or dissatisfied with the way Ken Livingstone is doing his job as Mayor of London?				
Response	**2000 (%)**	**2001 (%)**	**2002 (%)**	**2002–2000**
Very satisfied	5	6	4	-1
Fairly satisfied	25	29	23	-2
Neither atisfied nor dissatisfied	40	31	29	-11
Fairly dissatisfied	5	9	14	+9
Very dissatisfied	3	5	13	+10
Don't know	23	19	17	-6
Satisfied (very + fairly satisfied)	30	35	27	-3
Dissatisfied (fairly + very dissatisfied)	8	14	27	+19
Unsure (neither + don't know)	63	50	46	-17
Source: MORI The London Survey 2002. Results are based on 1452 face-to-face interviews conducted in the Greater London area between October 18 and December 10, 2002. Data are weighted by gender, age, work status and ethnicity.				

Opinion polls reinforce the idea that despite New Labour's efforts, Londoners have little connection to the GLA. Table 2 shows results from MORI *London Survey* polls conducted in 2000, 2001, 2002. When aggregated into "Satisfied," "Dissatisfied" and "Unsure" categories, the poll shows that 27% of those surveyed were satisfied and 27% dissatisfied with the performance of the mayor in 2002. Overall the poll suggests that Londoners are growing more familiar with the mayoral position moving from 63% or 46% being "neither satisfied or dissatisfied" or "unsure" between 2000 and 2002. This swing indicates that people are becoming more aware and opinionated about the office of mayor, but from an institutional perspective the position of mayor seems only relevant to a bare majority of Londoners.

Table 3: Satisfaction with Greater London Assembly

Question: Are you satisfied or dissatisfied with the way the London Assembly is doing its job?				
Response	2000 (%)	2001 (%)	2002 (%)	2002– 2000
Very satisfied	2	2	1	-1
Fairly satisfied	17	15	8	-9
Neither satisfied nor dissatisfied	39	35	31	-8
Fairly dissatisfied	4	7	6	+2
Very dissatisfied	3	5	4	+1
Don't know	36	37	50	+14
Satisfied (very + fairly satisfied)	19	17	9	-10
Dissatisfied (fairly + very dissatisfied)	7	12	10	+3
Unsure (neither + don't know)	75	72	81	+6
Source: MORI The London Survey 2001. Results are based on 1,458 face-to-face interviews conducted in the Greater London area between October 31 and December 14, 2001. Data are weighted by gender, age, work status and ethnicity.				

The results from Table 3 should be even more worrying for those who thought a "Big Tent" strategy would cause citizens to embrace the GLA. When asked about how satisfied they were with the new London Assembly in 2002, 9% responded positively and 10% negatively. That 81% were unsure about the mayor's legislative counterpart indicates a very low level of attachment to the Assembly. More seriously, this

category of respondents is 6% higher than when first asked in 2000 –
signifying a lessening of support and or knowledge of the new
institution. In another question from the same 2002 MORI survey a
staggering 86% answered that they knew "Not very much," "Nothing
at all" or "Don't know" when asked "How much, if anything would
you say you know about what the London Assembly is doing for
London?"

Table 4: Public Scepticism about GLA Devolution

Q1: Do you think that London's new Mayor SHOULD or SHOULD NOT have power to… Q2: Do you think that London's new Mayor WILL or Will NOT in actual fact have the power to …		
Topic	Q	Yes %
…run London's schools?	1	42
	2	24
	1-2	-24
…run London's Hospitals?	1	48
	2	25
	1-2	-23
…decide whether fares on London's tubes or and buses should go up or not?	1	74
	2	62
	1-2	-12
…decide whether motorists should pay to drive in the city center?	1	64
	2	59
	1-2	-10
…raise or lower significantly the amount of council tax that Londoners pay?	1	53
	2	41
	1-2	-12
Source: ICM/Evening Standard Mayor Poll, March 2000. Telephone sample of 1,005 London adults.		

An ICM/Evening Standard pre-election poll helps explain the origins
of this public disaffection. Over 1,000 Londoners were asked questions
pertaining to what powers they thought the mayor *should* be endowed
and what powers they thought he *would* be endowed. Although a
majority of those polled thought that the mayor should control transit
fares, congestion charges and tax rates, fewer people believed that
central government would actually devolve these powers. As shown in
Table 4, this skepticism about decentralizing control prevails in all

categories, suggesting that the reason Londoners may be less than fully embracing the new institutions is because they do not feel that the central government will give the GLA the power it needs to do its job.

The recent tussle over how to finance improvements to London underground demonstrates that Londoners were perhaps correct to be skeptical of Blair's commitment to decentralization. Although management of the London underground was transferred to Livingstone and his Transport for London Commissioner Bob Kiley on July 15, 2003, the New Labour central government delayed the handover in order to sign a number of long-term private-public partnerships. Livingstone had fought a long legal battle against the partial privatization, claiming that splintering the management of London's underground services was unsafe and would not provide the public value for money. But Blair went ahead and new contracts with Metronet and Tubelines that will see £16 billion in new investment in the underground over the next 15 years. Despite his vehement opposition to the scheme, Livingston is now forced to honor these agreements. So although Livingstone now has complete managerial control over London's transportation network, it is under conditions he opposes yet cannot alter.

In sum, that the Greater London Assembly passes 88% of its motions demonstrate that local parties and officials have bought into the GLA experiment. Blair's "Big Tent" approach of accommodating the demands of various factions and incorporating them into the new institution deserves at least some credit for building this cohesion. While evident, budget-day derision between the mayor and the Assembly should not be seen as this revolt against the new institutions but rather as the Assembly exercising its only significant power. However, from the public perspective Blair's "Big Tent" approach failed to win the average Londoner's heart and mind. The vast majority of local residents did not participate in the local referendum or the first GLA elections and have no knowledge about the workings of the Greater London Assembly. And only a bare majority has an opinion about the workings of the now highly visible mayor's office. Part of this disconnect may be due to the fact that Londoner's do not believe that the GLA will have the power it needs to address their woes. While Blair's "Big Tent" might have been a successful elite brokering exercise, it largely failed at the grassroots because of New Labour's reluctance to release its grip and adequately devolve policy-making power.

Governing Metropolitan Toronto

By the 1950s, Greater Toronto began to exhibit all symptoms usually associated with metropolitanism. To provide regional solutions to health, transport and planning dilemmas for a region of over one million inhabitants, in 1953 the Ontario Provincial Government brought in "Metro" – a new metropolitan level governing body that assumed control over major land-use planning decisions and the main transportation and sewage routes. This indirectly elected upper-tier governmental body was composed of representatives chosen from the councils of the then 13 lower-tier governments of various sizes ranging from the village of Swansea (population 9,628) to the City of Toronto (population 672,407) (Filion, 1999: 428).

Initial response from most municipal units was negative, but Metropolitan Toronto eventually gained wide praise for its contribution to solving regional problems. A subsequent Goldenberg Commission in the 1960s (which reduced the number of municipal units to 6) and a Robarts Commission in the late 1970s (which recommended additional democratic reforms leading to direct election of metropolitan Toronto councillors) completed the governmental restructuring (Ontario, 1965; Ontario, 1977). Between 1961 and 1991 the population of the Greater Toronto Area (GTA) grew to 4.2 million - of which just 54% fell under the jurisdiction of Metro. Reducing the number of lower-tier Metro municipalities from 13 to 6 in 1967 did not aid in managing extra-jurisdictional growth, nor did changing from indirect to direct elections in 1988 (Filion, 1999: 432). In 1995 a provincially appointed "Task Force on the Future of Greater Toronto" was launched under the direction of Dr. Anne Golden to once again tackle what were perceived as regional coordination problems. Completed in 1995, but not publicly released until January 16, 1996, the Golden Report recommended that the five existing regional governments (see map below) be merged into a single, Greater Toronto regional governance body and that the number of local municipalities be reduced for an estimated annual savings of approximately $1 billion (Ontario, 1965; Golden, 1999).

However, a change in provincial governments late in 1996 preempted these recommendations and marked a shift in views as to how regional government in Toronto should be structured.

Defeating an urban-friendly New Democratic Party government on June 8, 1995, Conservative Premier Mike Harris's more suburban and rural electoral focus abruptly altered the flow of the regional governance debate. On May 30, 1996 Harris appointed David Crombie – a former Toronto mayor and federal cabinet minister – to head the "Who Does What" advisory panel. With a mandate to make policy recommendations on property tax assessment, transportation, utilities and municipal administration issues, Crombie's focus fell squarely on municipal government. Working throughout the summer, the panel rapidly delivered a large number of recommendations to the Harris cabinet. Perhaps of most importance, on December 6, 1996, Crombie made three broad recommendations concerning the existing governance structure including:

- replacing the five upper-tier (regional) municipalities with a Greater Toronto Services Board (GTSB);
- consolidating member (lower-tier) municipalities into strong cities;
- consolidating Metro Toronto to create a strong urban core for the GTA (Ontario, 1996a).

is this not the same as the Golden Report recommend's?

Before the Crombie recommendations were even tabled, Harris had set his restructuring plan in motion. On November 25, 1996 – almost two weeks before Crombie tabled his report – Harris paid Klynveld, Peat, Marwick and Goerdeler (KPMG) to estimate what savings would be gained from amalgamating the six lower tier municipalities – East York, Etobicoke, North York, Scarborough, Toronto, and York – as well as Metro regional council into a single region-wide government (Ontario, 1996b). Released on December 10 – a mere ten days after the Crombie report – KPMG announced that a merger would reduce the number of staff required to run municipal services and save taxpayers up to $865 million in the first year and $300 million per year every year thereafter. KPMG argued that many of the potential savings were not at all attributable to the amalgamation, but rather up to two-thirds were to come from "efficiency enhancements," possible even without radical organizational change (Milroy et. al., 1999: 163). When later

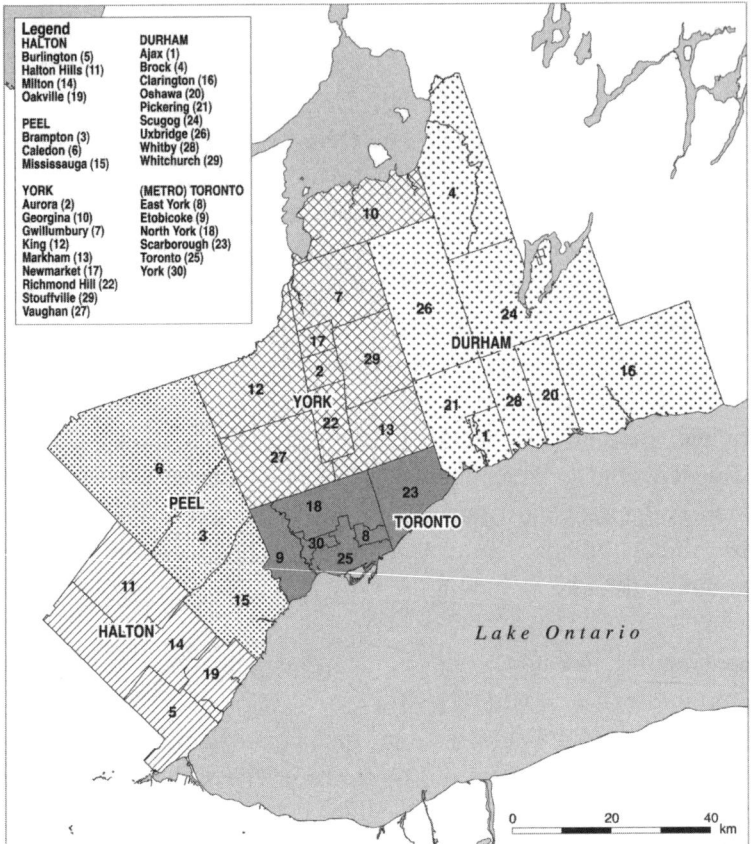

Legend

HALTON	DURHAM
Burlington (5)	Ajax (1)
Halton Hills (11)	Brock (4)
Milton (14)	Clarington (16)
Oakville (19)	Oshawa (20)
	Pickering (21)
	Scugog (24)
PEEL	Uxbridge (26)
Brampton (3)	Whitby (28)
Caledon (6)	Whitchurch (29)
Mississauga (15)	
YORK	(METRO) TORONTO
Aurora (2)	East York (8)
Georgina (10)	Etobicoke (9)
Gwillumbury (7)	North York (18)
King (12)	Scarborough (23)
Markham (13)	Toronto (25)
Newmarket (17)	York (30)
Richmond Hill (22)	
Stouffville (29)	
Vaughan (27)	

Figure 2: Greater Toronto Area (Pre-1997 Amalgamation)
Source: School of Applied Geography, Ryerson Polytechnic University

pressed the company admitted that "it's possible that the amalgamation could produce significantly lower savings than we have talked about or even a negative result, a net increase in expenditures." However, this additional information did not enter into the debate as the report was issued one day prior to the tabling of Bill 103 (ibid.).

On December 17, days before the legislature was to rise for the winter holidays, Municipal Affairs Minister Al Leach tabled the *City of Toronto Act, 1996*. The Bill proposed replacing the seven existing municipal governments of Metropolitan Toronto with a new single-tier on January 1, 1998. The first city council was to consist of a mayor and one member from 44 wards elected in 1997, but would not take office until early 1998. A board of trustees was to oversee the financial affairs of the seven existing municipal/regional governments while a transition team managed and planned the changeover. In introducing the Bill, Minister of Municipal Affairs and Housing Al Leach stated that the goals of the merger were to "save money, remove barriers to growth and investment and help create jobs." Savings were to come from eliminating duplication of services and were estimated at $208 million annually (Boudreau, 1999: 772; see also Wendell Cox Consultancy, 1997). According to Milroy et al. (1999), the original goals were to: "create a competitive, efficient city government; to keep some services local; and to protect existing neighborhoods." Milroy et al. continue that "the second and third (rationales) were periodically restated, but not developed".

The City of Toronto Act, 1997 passed on April 27, 1997. Immediately following, the provincial government appointed a six-member transition team to carry out certain pre-amalgamation tasks. According to Roda McInnis Contractor – Amalgamation Office Director of the new City of Toronto – the nine months given to ready the city to go "on-line" on January 1, 1998 was inadequate and at least two years were needed to properly address the tasks at hand. While the transition team did not draw up a plan as to how the amalgamation was to take place, they did appoint a number of key senior executives, including a new Chief Administrative Officer, City Clerk, Chief Financial Officer, Head of Human Resources and Fire Chief among others (Contractor, 2000).[7] Elections were also held during the transition period. North York Mayor Mel Lastman – a once vocal opponent of the amalgamation – beat out Toronto Mayor Barbara Hall – another merger opponent – to become Megacity Toronto's first mayor in November 1997.

---

7   In further reflections on the transition process, Contractor goes on to state:

In amalgamating Toronto, the provincial government raised great expectations as to how much money would be saved through consolidation. The new administration found that while a significant amount of money could be saved, including staff reductions, it was unrealistic to expect, in the short-term, the exceptionally high savings predicted by the provincial government. Unfortunately, once the province's numbers were public, they became a political mantra that the new administration had to continuously address...

Assessing pre- and post-change support in Metropolitan Toronto

This section evaluates support for the Toronto metropolitan reform process both before and after changes were effected. In this case pre-change evidence relates to levels of elite and public participation in the change process. Post-change support is measured by assessing legislative cohesion and public opinion. The purpose of this assessment is not only to test for continuity within Metropolitan Toronto but also to generate data to compare with that collected from the Greater London experience.

Pre-change support for Megacity: Harris's "Big Stick"
In contrast to Blair's "Big Tent" approach, Premier Harris and his ministers used a "Big Stick" to drive through their Greater Toronto reforms. The first prong of this strategy was to gain approval for the changes from traditional supporters by developing a clear and coherent message. Harris had relied on a less government, lower taxes, a "Common Sense Revolution" platform to gain office during the 1995 election and continued with this message through the Metropolitan reform period – not only in Toronto, but in other centers like Ottawa. Hamilton, Kingston and Sudbury (Ontario, 1999). Support came from traditional right of center organizations such as the Metropolitan Board of Trade, the Urban Development Institute and the Greater Toronto Homebuilders Association (Boudreau, 1999: 773). Harris was also successful in gaining support from the chair of the soon-to-be abolished Metropolitan Toronto Council and future appointed head of the Greater Toronto Services Board, Alan Tonks.[8] In a pre-appointment period speech to the provincial Standing Committee on Government during the few public hearings on the amalgamation, Tonks stated:

> I support the concept of a united city…. It will be less top-heavy, less bureaucratic and more efficient. Amalgamation doesn't mean bigger government; it means leaner government. Amalgamation won't just make our government more efficient to run; it will make it easier to understand. People will know who

8   Alan Tonks was subsequently elected a Toronto area MP.

to turn to when they need help and they will know who to hold accountable when they are unable to get it.[9]

The second prong of the "Big Stick" was rapidity. The speed with which the reforms were pushed from Bill to Act indicates a deliberate attempt to choke oppositional cries. That Bill 103 was tabled 11 days after the Crombie recommendations and a day after the KMPG report initially limited opposition to legislative opponents. Liberal and New Democratic members of the provincial legislature were firmly against Bill 103 and in tandem the two parties managed to orchestrate a 10-day filibuster during the passing of the legislation (Boudreau, 1999: 775). However, even as the Bill progressed through its brisk readings, grassroots opposition began to form. Lead by former Mayor John Sewell, the Citizens for Local Democracy organized public opposition to the Conservative reforms, as did local mayors – including Barbara Hall from the City of Toronto, and academics – including Andrew Sancton from the University of Western Ontario. Public forums and well-attended demonstrations were held throughout the legislative process until the Bill was passed on April 27, 1997.

Table 5: 1997 Merger Referendum Results

Question: Are you in favor of eliminating [your municipality] and all other existing municipalities in Metropolitan Toronto and amalgamating them into a megacity?			
City	**Yes (%)**	**No (%)**	**Turnout (%)**
Toronto	27	74	36
York	35	65	39
East York	19	82	42
North York	21	79	40
Etobicoke	30	70	19
Scarborough	22	78	18
Total	**24**	**76**	**25**
Source: *Globe and Mail* Tuesday, March 4, 1997, p. A1.			

The most formal evidence of public opposition to Bill 103 can be found from the results of referendums organized by the lower-tier

---

9 Excerpt from presentation to Standing Committee on General Government, 36th Parliament, Session 1, Monday, February 3, 1997, 1:50 am. Hansard Reporting and Interpretation Services, Toronto: Office of the Legislative Assembly of Ontario.

municipalities. Upon the refusal of the provincial government to consult the public on these changes until after Bill 103 had passed, the six lower-tier municipal governments within the Metro area asked citizens the following question: "Are you in favor of eliminating [Area Municipality] and all other existing municipalities in Metropolitan Toronto and amalgamating them into a Megacity?" As shown in Table 5, 76% of the eligible voters casting ballots answered "No" to the question. At first glance the turnout rate of 25% might indicate that citizens did not mobilize in force to stop the merger – especially when compared to the 1997 City of Toronto election turnout rate of 49%. However, it should be noted that the referendum was organized in haste by the lower-tier municipalities, thus it was under-funded and under-organized. Although it is impossible to say with any certainty, as with other public marketing ventures more time and money may have raised participation rates. Beth Moore Milroy captures the spirit of the times with her summary of the hostility toward Bill 103:

> Opposition took many forms: dozens of meetings were held in all six cities (on one hectic Wednesday there were 23 Bill 103-related meetings scheduled in the six cities), six city umbrella organizations coordinated responses to the Bill, letters were sent to the newspapers, experts on the relationship between amalgamation and costs of government were hired, deputations were made to a legislative committee. There were marches, parades, posterings, leafleting, speeches by the politicians in the opposition parties, filibustering in the legislature, threats of legal challenges by all the cities and by citizens, and referendums in each of the six cities. Five of the six mayors were solidly opposed to amalgamation, including the man who would subsequently be elected the first mayor of the megacity. One mayor and the chair of Metro were either equivocal or in favor. John Sewell, a former mayor of Toronto and its most active defender against Bill103, started a network called Citizens for Local Democracy…. It was remarkable for several reasons, one being that its meetings attracted around 1,200 people every Monday night for almost three months and several hundred for most of the rest of 1997. (Milroy, 2002: 161–162).

Post-change support for Metropolitan Toronto

This preceding summary of events shows that the Conservatives planned the amalgamation reforms in secret, built consensus among traditional supporters by claiming the changes would bring massive savings and lower taxes and used blitzkrieg tactics to bypass public input and elite opposition to the changes. Although savvy challengers were able to make uncomfortable the passage of Bill 103, in the end the merger took place on schedule. While successful on paper, Harris's "Big Stick" approach contravened the insulation strategy and created new institutions vulnerable to future attack. As a result, elite challenge and public opposition would be expected to continue in the post-change period. As with Greater London, this section uses legislative voting patterns and election and opinion poll results to test whether post-change Toronto is loathed by its citizens.

Table 6: Legislative cohesion within the City of Toronto (2001)

Date	Total Motions	Motions Passed	%	Votes Recorded	%
12/05/00	101	89	88	31	31
01/30/01	216	199	92	49	23
06/03/01	241	202	84	80	33
04/24/01	459	371	81	209	46
05/30/01	276	256	93	65	24
06/26/01	235	213	91	67	29
07/24/01	347	327	94	85	24
02/10/01	305	279	91	88	29
06/11/01	287	268	93	78	27
04/12/01	322	296	92	70	22
Totals	**2789**	**2500**	**90**	**822**	**29**

Where non-partisan members elected from former lower-tier municipalities might be expected to be disgruntled and non-cooperative after the forced merger, Table 6 demonstrates remarkable cohesion within the Toronto's new city council.[10] Of the motions tabled in the 2001 legislative session, 90% (2,500 of 2,789) were passed by the council. The number of officially recorded votes also provides further evidence of widespread cooperation. The names of those casting yeas and nays are recorded in a very few procedural instances, but mostly upon the request of a councillor. A fractured legislative body would be expected to produce a high percentage of recorded votes, as these records are the only public method by which to identify a member's voting record. However, of the 2,789 motions tabled, only 822 (about one-third) were recorded. This small number of recorded votes indicates a low level of fragmentation and more evidence that the new institutions are widely accepted by local elite.

Table 7: Megacity - Better or Worse Government?

Amalgamation of the six former municipalities of Metro Toronto has provided better government than the previous two-tiered system.			
Response	Total	Metro Area	Rest of GTA
Agree	37	35	41
Disagree	29	28	30
No change/ don't know	34	37	29
Source: Toronto Star/Ekos Poll on the Civic Election 2000. Total results valid within +/- 3.1 percentage points, 19 times out of 20. The margin of error increases when the results are sub-divided: +/-4.0 percentage points for Metro area and +/- 4.9 percentage points for Rest of GTA			

Table 8: Megacity: Right or wrong decision?

Question: Overall, would you say that the amalgamation of the six former municipalities was the right decision or the wrong decision?			
Response	Total	Metro Area	Rest of GTA
Right decision	60	58	64
Wrong decision	27	30	21
Don't know	13	12	15
Source: Toronto Star/Ekos Poll on the Civic Election 2000.			

10   Section 41.2.1 of the Municipal Elections Act, 1996 states that "Only the names of certified candidates shall appear on the ballot." See Ontario, 1996c. For evidence that removing such as clause results in the development of local parties, see Smith and Stewart, 1998.

More surprising than the elite cooperation is the radical shift of public opinion toward the new institutions. As shown in Table 7, according to a November 2000 Toronto Star/Ekos poll a mere 28% of local residents disagreed that the amalgamated city has provided better government than the previous two-tiered system. When asked if the merger was the "right decision," 58% of those living in the merger area responded in the affirmative. When contrasted to the pre-change referendum results in which 76% of those polled where against the merger only three years earlier, it is clear that something had happened to change the minds of local citizens.

Table 9: Satisfaction with Individual Services in Metro (2000)

Question: How would you rate the impact of amalgamation of the six former municipalities of Metropolitan Toronto into the current megacity on the following?					
Topic	Positive	Negative	Difference	No change	Don't know
Response time by fire departments	34	10	24	40	16
Municipal taxes on individuals	24	19	5	43	15
Crime in the streets	24	18	4	51	6
Municipal taxes on business	20	16	4	42	27
Garbage collection	24	21	3	49	6
Availability of Toronto's recreation facilities	27	30	-3	34	9
Public access to City Council Members	19	23	-4	42	16
Source: Toronto Star/Ekos Poll on the Civic Election 2000 (Results from Metro Area only)					

The Toronto Star/Ekos poll also probed citizen satisfaction with post-merger service delivery. Arranged from positive to negative impact in Table 9, citizens reported that the new structure has helped improve fire service and garbage collection, reduce crime, and lower individual and business tax rates. Only questions about accessing local councillors and availability of recreation facilities elicited primarily negative responses. What is also striking is the number of people who state that the amalgamation has had no impact on their lives in relation to these services. One would think that a spiteful citizenry would undoubtedly express their feelings more vehemently.

In sum, where citizens and political elites were strongly opposed to the Conservative's plans for Ontario's largest urban center, voting patterns within the legislature and poll data demonstrate both these groups have reversed the opinion. The public now expresses support for the changes while elected members of Toronto City Council show remarkable cohesion. So despite the top-down, exclusionary method by which the changes were introduced, those elite wishing to survive in the local political scene adapted to the new institutions, where the once angry public was brought onside by what they perceive to be better institutional arrangements.

Conclusions

According to the insulation strategy, post-change support for new institutions grows from attempts to build elite consensus and popular consent before reforms are made. As such, the Greater London Authority should have retained its popularity as it was constructed through elite accommodation and devolved citizen control where Megacity Toronto should remain unpopular because of the dictatorial tactics used to abolish long-standing local institutions. Initial evidence in this chapter suggests that pre-change processes have little effect on later popularity. Even elected officials who vehemently opposed reforms now cooperate within both new institutions – implying that local elites will always reverse evenly strongly-held opinions to survive. In terms of the general public, where heavily courted Londoners now seem indifferent to their new mayor and assembly, once outraged Torontonians appear largely satisfied with Megacity – suggesting pre-change public involvement is unnecessary. However, other evidence demonstrates that Londoners' lack of enthusiasm for the GLA is due to New Labour's failure to devolve necessary powers to the mayor and the Assembly. Thus, it is not the "Big Tent" approach that should be viewed as a failure, but rather Tony Blair's reluctance to back his words with deeds. It would also appear that Mike Harris guessed right when he rammed through his then unpopular legislation, as Torontonians now believe themselves to be better off in a megacity. This victory is something about which the Ontario Conservatives can ponder as they sit on the opposition benches watching a new Liberal Provincial Government put forward its new metropolitan visions.

References

Association of London Governments (1996), *Survey of Londoners*, London: ALG.

Boudreau, J. (1999). Megacity Toronto: Struggles over Differing Aspects of Middle-Class Politics. *International Journal of Urban and Regional Research*, 23:4, 771–780.

Byrne, A. (1990). *Local Government in Britain,* 5th ed.. Harmondsworth: Penguin.

Chandler, J. (1991). *Local Government Today*. Manchester: Manchester University Press.

Contractor, R.M. (2000). The amalgamation of Toronto: Some of the lessons learned. *Municipal World*, May.

Dunleavy, P., & Margetts, H. (1998). *Report to Government Office for London: Electing the London Mayor and the London Assembly*. London: LSE Public Policy Group.

Dunleavy, P., Margetts, H., & Weir. S (1998). *The Politico's Guide to Electoral Reform in Britain*. London: Politicos.

Filion, P. (1999). Rupture or continuity? Modern and postmodern planning in Toronto. *International Journal of Urban and Regional Research*, Sept., 23:3,421–444.

Foley, D. (1972). *Governing the London Region: Reorganization and Planning in the 1960s*. Berkeley: IGS/University of California Press.

Golden, A. (1999). *Remarks at 'Shaping Toronto's Future' Conference*, April 7, 1999. www.city.toronto.on.ca.

Government Office for London (1999). *The Shape of Things to Come*. London: Government Office for London.

Great Britain (1997). Department of Environment, Transport and the Regions. *New Leadership for London: the Government's Proposals for a Greater London Authority*. London: Her Majesty's Stationary Office.

Great Britain (1998a). Department of the Environment, Transport and the Regions. *A Mayor and Assembly for London: the Government's Proposals for Modernising the Governance of London* (Forword). London: Her Majesty's Stationary Office.

Great Britain (1998b). *Greater London Authority Act, 1999, Explanatory Notes*. London: Her Majesty's Stationary Office.

Greater London Authority (1999). Transition Team. *Shaping Up for the Mayor and Assembly*. London: GLA Transition Team.

Greater London Authority (2002). *London Assembly agrees to Mayor's 'sensible compromise' on budget*. Press release, 13 February. http://www.london.gov.uk.

Labour Party (1992). *London: A World Class Capital*. London: Labour Party.

Labour Party (1996). *An Elected Voice for London*. London: Labour Party.

Loverland, I. (1999). The Government of London. *Political Quarterly*, Jan-Mar, 70:1,.91–100.

Milroy, B. M. (2002). Toronto's Legal Challenge to Amalgamation. In: C. Andrew, K. Graham & S. Phillips (eds.) , *Urban Affairs: Back on the Policy Agenda* (pp. 157–178). Montreal: Queen's University Press.

Milroy, B. M., Campsie, P., Whittaker, R., & Girling, Z. (1999). Who Says Toronto Is a "Good" City?. In: C. Andrew, P. Armstrong & A. Lapierre (eds.), *World Class Cities: Can Canada Play* (pp. 159–194).Ottawa: University of Ottawa Press.

Ontario (1965). Royal (Goldenberg) Commission on Metropolitan Toronto. *Report*. Toronto: Queen's Printer.

Ontario (1977). Royal (Robarts) Commission on Metropolitan Toronto. *Report: A Framework for The Future*. Toronto: Government of Ontario.

Ontario (1996a). Crombie, Who Does What Panel. *Recommendations on Local Governance* Toronto: Ontario Ministry of Municipal Affairs and Housing, http://www.mah.gov.on.ca/inthnews/backgrnd/961206ce.asp.

Ontario (1996b). Ministry of Municipal Affairs and Housing. *Fresh Start: An Estimate of Potential Savings and Costs from the Creation of a Single Tier Local Government for Toronto.* Toronto: Klynveld, Peat, Marwick, and Goerdeler (KPMG).

Ontario (1996c). *Municipal Elections Act 1996.* Toronto: Queen's Printer.

Ontario (1999). *Fewer Municipal Politicians Act (Bill 25).* Ontario: Queen's Printer.

Pimlott, B., & Rao, N. (2001). *Governing London.* Oxford: Oxford University Press.

Rogers, R., & Fisher, M. (1992). *A New London.* London: Penguin.

Smith, P., &, Stewart, K. (1998). *Making Local Accountability Work in British Columbia.* Vancouver: Institute of Governance Studies, Simon Fraser University.

Thornley, A. (ed.) (1992). *The Crisis of London.* London: Routledge.

Wendell Cox Consultancy (1997). *Local and Regional Governance in the Greater Toronto Area: A Review of Alternatives. Draft Report prepared for the City of Toronto.* January 10.

(www.londonelects.org), date accessed: January 11, 2005.

(www.electoralcommission.org.uk/elections/gla.cfm), date accessed: March 2, 2005.

H. V. SAVITCH AND RONALD K. VOGEL

Local and Regional Governance: Rescaling the City

Introduction

Urbanists have been rethinking the nature of metropolitan governance over the last decade. In the past, scholars called for metropolitan cities or the establishment of metropolitan *government* as a solution to functional and territorial fragmentation of local government in the metropolis. Metropolitan *government*, which stressed formal, vertical institutions, was viewed as a way to enhance efficiency, effectiveness, accountability and equity. Now scholars talk of metropolitan *governance*, which stresses informal horizontal networks, and they are more concerned with reducing disparities between the central cities and suburbs. Many of these studies are lumped together under the label "new regionalism," reflecting the development of a new paradigm of metropolitan governance.[1]

As Allan Wallis explains, regionalism in the United States has actually gone through successive waves of reform (Wallis 1994a, b, c, d), incorporating varying forms of government and/or governance in

---

1   The classic idea of government entailed formal institutions, elections, established processes of decision-making and administrative structures. Government is an elaborate machine that operates through hierarchical layers of political authority and accountability. Most efforts to introduce metropolitan or regional government meant an addition of brand new layers of authority – staffed by a chief executive, a legislative body and a bureaucracy. Government is a fairly encompassing form of organization – a legitimate monopoly that takes responsibility for both providing and producing public services. By contrast, governance has a different connotation. It conveys the notion that existing institutions can be harnessed in new ways, that cooperation can be carried out on a fluid and voluntary basis among localities, and that people can best regulate themselves in horizontally linked organizations. Governance also recognizes that localities can provide public services without necessarily producing them. That is, localities can provide (arrange for) services by entering into a great variety of contracts and arrangements with other governments, non-profit organizations or private corporations that undertake the production (delivery) of services. On this point see Parks and Oakerson (1989). For this and other discussions of "new regionalism" see Savitch and Vogel (2000a). For a critical perspective on new regionalism, see Frisken and Norris (2001).

different historical periods. We are able to sketch these waves. Associating an innovation with a particular era (what Kuhn called "periodization") deserves some qualifications. As we shall see, ideas about rescaling the metropolis have also been adopted in subsequent eras, despite their earlier origins. In addition, there is some overlap in the themes posited by these waves. Each of them does have its own distinctive characteristics that stress particular problems and offer specific approaches toward their resolution. Table 1 illustrates these characteristics in terms of their essential patterns, problems, solutions, limitations and the like.

First wave of regionalism
In the first wave of *progressive regionalism* in the mid 1800s through the early 1900s, reformers sought to ensure that urban growth on the fringe of the city was brought into the formal city boundaries and under a single municipal jurisdiction (Beard, 1923). Underlying reform was a concern to increase efficiency of public services and provide uniform policies and standards for development. By and large, progressive regionalism responded to what it perceived as a "crazy quilt of fragmented governments." Its advocates came to be known as monocentrists because they assumed that large-scaled, singular institutions could better coordinate and run functions over expanding metropolitan areas. Monocentrists believed they could catch ever-expanding regional economies within a formal governmental structure. They reasoned that the best way to construct public policy was to make the boundaries of a new metropolitan city coterminous with the extent of the regional economy. Older cities in the Northeast and Midwest (New York, Indianapolis) resorted to some kind of consolidation in order to realize this objective. Younger cities in the sunbelt (Houston, Phoenix) were more apt to annex burgeoning suburbs around them.

Table 1: Waves of Regionalism

Waves of Regionalism	Pattern of Urban Development	Problem	Concern	Initiator	Solution	Examples	Limits to Approach
Progressive regionalism (late 1800s-early 1900s to 1960s)	Monocentric	Urban growth on fringe so that city boundary no longer corresponds with urban population	Ensure dominance of central city to promote efficiency	State/central city	Structural reform	Annexation or consolidation (e.g., New York City federated 1899)	No longer politically feasible
Polycentric regionalism (1960s to 1980s)	Declining core and multiple nodes	Uneven development and sprawl, lack of infrastructure and services in unincorporated areas; metropolis crosses county boundaries	Stabilize central cities and establish process to coordinate services and infrastructure in growing suburbs (i.e., coordination)	Federal and state	Procedural or modest structural reform through mandates from above	Comprehensive planning, growth management, metropolitan councils or cogs, special districts, two-tier metropolitan government, urban county, multi-service agencies	Shift in national policy (Reagan 1980; ACIR changes direction), suburbs reject central cities
New Regionalism (1990s-200?)	Continued urban expansion	Economic development (competitiveness of city-region in world economy); regional infrastructure and development policy; growing social and economic disparities between core and periphery	Problem oriented rather than structure	Private, citizen, or government in coalition including state and federal	Governance, (public-private partnerships and negotiated solutions among parties including local government); build civic infrastructure	Strategic planning, MPOs	Selective and weak regionalism; more rhetoric than reality?

Source: Adapted from Wallis (1994 a,b,c,d).

Monocentrists were only partially successful in their efforts. By the 1920s, most states had made annexation more difficult. Consolidation was now subject to referendum rather than imposed by state legislatures (Krane, Rigos & Hill, 2000). These reformers were forced to reduce their aspirations proposing regional planning commissions to engage in comprehensive planning and coordinate city and county development and infrastructure placement. One weak variant of this were Councils of Governments (COGs). A few isolated examples of unification in the form of city-county consolidation or quasi-federated government occurred in this period (Nashville, Indianapolis, Miami-Dade) and in the south and west annexation was still possible even into the 1970s (e.g., Atlanta, Dallas, Phoenix).

Other reform agendas to thwart political machines had led to the development of various kinds of public authorities that were largely independent from government and had come to be known as "functional fiefdoms." Many independent public authorities and boards were created to reduce machine control and to place decisions in the hands of trained professional administrators. An unanticipated consequence was that bureaucrats were insulated from political control reducing accountability to the public and increasing political fragmentation leading to a coordination problem in urban governance (Yates, 1977).

Second wave of regionalism
In the second wave of reform, *polycentric regionalism*, reformers recognized that unification was doubtful. First, the metropolis had become more spread out. Second, new municipalities in the suburbs and the barriers to annexation meant more affluent suburbanites could insulate themselves from central city problems. Thus, comprehensive restructuring such as city-county consolidation or two-tier metropolitan government was unlikely. Moreover, public choice theory highlighted the virtues of fragmentation. As they came to be called, polycentrists placed greater confidence in the ability of localities to act on behalf of their own self-interest and argued that intra local competition actually led to salutary effects. In theory, fragmentation enabled citizens to exit a particular locality and select another that best suited their self-interest. The exit option available to the middle class would ensure city governments were disciplined (Siegel, 1997).

Evidence in the field does support these assertions. Studies have found that a market place of local governments held down taxes, promoted efficient services, and made elites more accountable (ACIR, 1987, 1993). Other research showed that centralized government was not correlated with increased efficiency, economies of scale, or even equity.

More importantly, localities could choose to cooperate with one another by establishing inter-local agreements. So called "crazy quilt fragmentation" was neither crazy nor irrational but in reality a "complex network" of self interested localities that had learned to cooperate in select areas. Logically, governments would cooperate on providing services where they had a common interest through arrangements, like contracting out for services, joint service agreements or creating special purpose districts for problems that overlapped municipal boundaries. Thus, a strategy of cooperation might achieve a modicum of *metropolitan governance* beyond that associated with the formal models of metropolitan government.

Third wave of regionalism

The third and current wave of regionalism, *new regionalism*, is more eclectic, pragmatic and able to adopt techniques from different schools of thought. New regionalists would argue that centralization and decentralization are not at odds with one another and can easily be applied to different scales of the metropolis. New regionalists seek ways in which to gain advantages from centralization as well as decentralization. This reflects a paradigm shift and is evidenced in the new language of *metropolitan governance without metropolitan government*. The major features of new regionalism include a shift from a structural or institutional focus to a problem-oriented approach that addresses urban ills. The policy agenda of new regionalism is concerned with containing sprawl, fostering sustainable growth and development, and addressing the growing disparities between the central city and the suburbs. Thus, new regionalists would rarely advocate city-county consolidation for its own sake and they would place an empirical burden on any new organization to establish its benefits. In effect new regionalists were skeptical about adopting unproven change and they were cautious about the political feasibility of comprehensive reform. They were also optimistic about the capacity of government and governance to resolve larger problems, including government accountability, public transparency and the dilution of minority voting power (Powell, 2000). Finally, new regionalists now question whether consolidation might elevate suburban interests rather than ensure the integrity of the historic core central city and its urban culture (Savitch & Vogel, 2004).

New regionalism is built on adapting and applying lessons of the past. In the early 21st century, city-county consolidation and annexations as solutions to metropolitan fragmentation are no longer practically or politically feasible as city-regions now often extend beyond a single county and even across state or national boundaries.[2] Even existing regional governments with extensive boundaries find they fail to correspond to the real metropolis. In the early and mid-20th century, when county governments generally corresponded to the metropolitan region, city-county consolidation or annexation could reasonably create a metropolitan city under a single jurisdiction. In the latter 20th century and 21st centuries, this no longer seems to be the case.

Rather in this third wave, we are finding common ground among scholars of the traditionally opposed public choice and metropolitan government camps that a new governance approach is needed.[3] The

---

2   As a consequence, there has been a general erosion of the Metro Model which a larger portion of the scholarly community now rejects (see Sharpe, 1995). Empirical studies also challenge the benefits of metropolitan government, there are few examples of real metropolitan government in practice, and it is almost impossible to establish one (see Altshuler et al., 1999).

3   Noted public choice scholar Robert L. Bish argues, "Single governing councils and large organizations are simply incapable of dealing with the diverse range of issues that governments must deal with in urban areas. The diversity of metropolitan areas requires close links to citizens and the ability to handle a wide variety of activities on a small scale. For some activities, on the other hand, the commonality of an entire metropolitan area requires mechanisms capable of integrating local diversity. The current weight of evidence is that no single organization can accomplish these tasks. Furthermore, when there is a multiplicity of small municipalities in metropolitan areas, the costs of governance are lower, not higher, and moreover, the political system is more representative. The issue at hand is how the necessary multiplicity of organizations can be created and how they can relate to one another so that the system as a whole is efficient, responsive to citizens, and adaptable to changing conditions. This organizational challenge also poses an intellectual challenge, but similar intellectual challenges have been encountered before" (Bish, 2001; see also, Parks & Oakerson, 2000). Advocates of metropolitan government have reached similar conclusions (for example, see Downs, 1994).

National Academy of Sciences set up a national commission to review evidence concerning the efficient and effective organization of metropolitan governance in the United States. The committee recognized that the existing fragmented system had been somewhat effective in providing services that crossed local jurisdictional boundaries with respect to system maintenance types of services (e.g., sewers, highways, water systems, air pollution control). This was accomplished through creation of regional authorities and special districts (Downs, 1994:15).

The committee did acknowledge inequalities arising from the present system of financing and urban services. However, the committee departed from traditional reform diagnoses and prescriptions. With regard to efficiency, the committee reported "the preponderance of evidence indicates that small local governments…are more efficient for labor-intensive services, whereas larger units are more efficient for capital-intensive services" (ibid.: 106) The committee found that "consolidation has not reduced costs…[and] it may have even increased local expenditures" (ibid.).

The report moved away from formal metropolitan government as a solution to urban problems and embraced a governance strategy. Regarding the effects of consolidation on reducing disparities between central cities and suburbs, the committee reported "the evidence that does exist…suggests that these efforts have had no significant impact on redistributing income or on addressing the problems of the poor or racial minorities" (ibid.: 106–107). Most telling was the committee's recommendation to improve metropolitan governance.

> [W]hen a supra-local approach is desirable, existing overlaying units of governments can provide services, or special districts can be created to do so. When a regional approach or perspective is more appropriate, creation of such entities as the Portland Metropolitan Service District and the Minneapolis-St. Paul Metropolitan Council is desirable, if locally supported and politically feasible. If such entities are not likely to emerge (i.e., in most metropolitan areas), then we find most appropriate the use and expansion of existing metropolitan forums and agencies, such as councils of governments, metropolitan planning organizations, regional special-purpose authorities, and public-

> private alliances on the metropolitan level. It is possible that, over time, one or more of these will organically emerge into an institution that has the ability to make decisions for the entire region in several functional areas (ibid., 129).

However, the committee does not believe that the existing *nested pattern* of government has "been able to address effectively the life-style and redistributional concerns associated with the problem of severe inequality of opportunity" (ibid., 130). Here the committee recommends reducing barriers to affordable housing in the suburbs and ensuring that the poor and central city residents have access to quality education and jobs often located in the suburbs.

Rescaled city regions

We have now experienced roughly a century of efforts to re-scale local government and variations on these regional themes have taken root across the country. One way to conceptualize these variations is to see them as a series of closed, open or overlapping boxes that range over a continuum of efforts to establish regional cooperation. At one end of the continuum, we have the *progressive regionalist* approach that stresses a single, centralized formal government (consolidation). Moving toward the center of the continuum we find a variation of *progressive regionalism*, which while still holding onto formal government, recognizes the value of grassroots democracy. It does this by retaining smaller local governments, while also coordinating them through a formal umbrella of metropolitan government (tiered government).

Still further along the continuum we have *polycentric regionalism*, which embraces the idea of voluntary, decentralized *governance*. If nurtured this would result in a new form of local interaction based on the self interest of localities, the organic growth of horizontal cooperation and the maturation of a web of inter-local agreements (complex networks). Finally, at the furthest end of the continuum we have *new regionalism*, which incorporates both formal and informal institutions (*government* plus *governance*). Also *new regionalism* attempts to reconcile the centralist impulse of *progressive regionalism* with the decentralizing tendencies of *polycentric regionalism*. We should point out that *new regionalism* is still young and there are no firm examples of its institutional basis in the United States, although Portland and Vancouver in the case of Canada have adopted some of its features. Across the Atlantic, the institutional basis of new regionalism has taken root in France ("urban community" or "community of cities").

Figure 1 displays this continuum of cooperation together with examples from various parts of the United States and France. The figure shows each of these models as either a closed single box (consolidation), a limited number of multiple discreet boxes (tiered government) a multiplicity of open, discreet boxes (complex networks) and a series of overlapping boxes (urban community). These scalar organizations also conform to a particular wave of regionalism.

As mentioned earlier, not all rescaling will neatly fit into a given era. Indeed, it is quite natural for localities to adapt ideas from previous eras, and there is always a lag between the incubation of an idea and its adoption. The saying that national governments often prepare their defenses for the wars of a previous era is no less true of local governments that mistakenly adopt outmoded scalar organizations to meet a new set of challenges. The critical factor for placing a scalar organization within a given period rests on a determination of when the idea first germinated, and Figure 1 reflects that approach.

As we see New York along with Philadelphia and New Orleans turned to consolidation during the latter part of the 19th century. These earlier consolidations were followed by similar efforts more than half a century later. Certainly New York was the largest of these consolidations – a kind of mega consolidation that folded five counties, extending over 200 square miles, into a single city. Other consolidations in New Orleans and more recently in Indianapolis and Louisville were also significant. All of these consolidations make cities coterminous with their central county (or multiple counties in the case of New York City) and all of them represent an effort to capture suburban growth within a single political envelope. Despite these efforts suburbs continue to grow well beyond new municipal boundaries and none of these could successfully contain that growth.

New regionalism

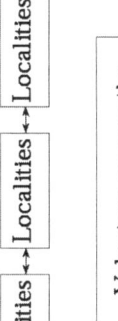

Common Assembly

- Common assembly drawn from existing localities
- Inter local agreements
- Operative concept: "government" plus "governance"

Examples:
Urban communities (Marseille)
Community of cities (Toulouse)

Polycentric regionalism

Complex networks

Localities ↔ Localities ↔ Localities

- Voluntary cooperation
- Horizontal relationship
- Inter local agreements
- Operative concept: "governance"

Examples
Pittsburgh
Los Angeles

Progressive regionalism

Tiered government

Metro council

County (counties)

Localities   Localities

- Separate
- Number of tiers
- Two or more sub tiers
- Operative concept: "government"

Examples
Minneapolis-St Paul (3 tier)
Portland (3 tier)
Miami-Dade (2 tier)

Consolidation

- Single political and legislative bodies.
- May contain service districts, small independent cities, etc
- Operative concept: "government"

Examples
Philadelphia (1854)
San Francisco (1856)
New Orleans (1874)
St. Louis (1876)
New York (1898)
Nashville (1967)
Indianapolis (1970)
Louisville (2000)

Figure 1: Continuum of regional cooperation

Also during the middle of the 20th century more flexible but similar approaches were adopted in Miami-Dade and the Twin Cities of Minneapolis-St. Paul. The idea of multi tiered government is to create mechanisms for larger cooperation, either between a central city(ies) and its county (Miami-Dade) or between an urban core and a larger number of counties (Twin Cities Metro). This tiered system is distinguished by a formal umbrella tier of elected or appointed government, which is responsible for designated functions. While an improvement over consolidation, tiered government has met a number of problems. For one, metro government is often caught between pressures emanating from above in the state houses and pressures welling up from below in the localities. Another problem lies in the existing rigidities of formal government and its inability to absorb new suburbs that lie outside its formal boundaries.

As polycentric regionalism evolved, it also spawned new models of scalar organization. These are represented in Figure 1 by Pittsburgh and Los Angeles. During the 1970s a well known study by the Advisory Commission on Intergovernmental Relations (ACIR) brought the advantages of Pittsburgh's complex networks to light. Other studies showed how localities in and around Los Angeles had begun similar systems of horizontal cooperation (ACIR, 1993; Bish, 1971). This cooperation grew slowly and matured over decades, resulting in regional bodies taking on selective functions for water and waste disposal or environmental regulation. Pittsburgh's regional network has adopted a common tax designed to support investment in culture, science and the arts.

Finally, *new regionalism* has yet to develop definitive institutions in the United States. *New regionalism* is best expressed by the retention of existing local governments, while also using officials from those very same localities to form common structures of local governance. Unlike tiered government, the institutional basis of *new regionalism* combines inter local cooperation with a new incarnation of existing governments, capable of acting in concert. These types of scalar organization also portend new policies for working with private enterprise to leverage local economic and political clout, using marketplace inducements to increase efficiency and respond to citizen demands and adopting new management techniques to ease fiscal strain.

During the 1990s France began to experiment with various forms of inter-local cooperation in designated "urban communities" or "communities of cities." The idea is not to superimpose a brand new umbrella of government upon existing cities, but to take representatives from those localities and recast them into a common assembly. Localities could also form natural webs of cooperation by establishing agreements to trade on each other's strengths. For example, some localities would make cultural facilities available to others in exchange for waste collection or the use of infrastructure. *New regionalism* then combines *government* with *governance*, formal and informal cooperation, centralization and decentralization in altogether new ways. How far this can or will be taken remains to be seen, but the approach is promising.

While the institutional basis of this rescaling is important, we should understand that these are containers for framing problems, adopting policy alternatives and implementing management change. Any discussion of these factors should be preceded by an analysis of the reasons or forces behind territorial rescaling.

Reasons for the rise of regionalism

Underlying the new regionalism agenda is a recognition that the city as a place and a set of institutions fails to comport with the new urban realities. The forces reshaping metropolitan cities today include (1) *metropolitanization*– continued urban expansion, (2) *globalization* – increased economic competition in the world economy, (3) privatization – reduced scale and scope of governmental activity in favor of market-based policies, and (4) *devolution and decentralization* – reorganization of the intergovernmental system to reduce government spending and enhance local autonomy. New regionalism is based on trying to come to terms with increasing metropolitanization. However, the concern with designing a new framework for governing metropolitan cities is also greatly shaped by the other three forces as well. These trends are explored in more detail in this section.

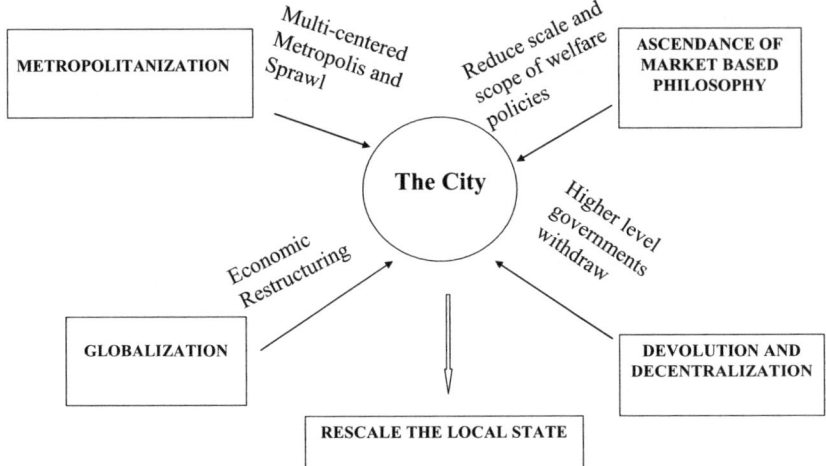

Figure 2: Forces reshaping and redefining cities

Metropolitanization
Growth on the urban edge has outpaced historical boundaries of cities. Looking at the ratio of the city population to the metropolitan or regional population reveals just how dispersed metropolitan areas have become. Table 2 reports the ratios for the 20 largest metropolitan regions in the United States. In 18 of the 20 cases, the central city share of metropolitan population was well below 50%. In 17 of the metropolises, the trend was for slippage in the regional share from 1990 to 2000. Atlanta was at the bottom with only a 10% share of the regional population down from 13% in 1990. The New York metropolitan area had the highest ratio of 87%, up slightly from 1990.

Changes in urban settlement patterns have significant consequences for commuting patterns, urban life, and local and regional governance. The major change in urban form in the United States over the last half century has been the decline of the dominance of the central city in the metropolis. The Federal Highway Administration recently released a study reporting average travel time for commuters in metropolitan areas now is close to 28 minutes. Moreover, greater numbers of workers are living in suburban counties in the metropolitan area and commuting outside their county of residence, but not necessarily to the central city or county. In 2000, 26.6% of workers commuted outside their county of residence for work compared to just 14.5% in 1960

Table 2: City share of metropolitan region, 1990 and 2000

Metropolitan Area	Population of Region, 1990	Population of Central City, 1990	Percentage of Central City to Region, 1990	Population of Region, 2000	Population of Central City, 2000	Percentage of Central City to Region, 2000
Los Angeles-Long Beach, CA PMSA	8,854,200	4,144,698	47%	9,519,338	4,408,869	46%
New York, NY PMSA	8,540,683	7,369,132	86%	9,314,235	8,061,355	87%
Chicago, IL PMSA	7,410,858	3,180,493	43%	8,272,768	3,388,705	41%
Philadelphia, PA-NJ PMSA	4,917,570	1,668,464	34%	5,100,931	1,597,454	31%
Washington, DC-MD-VA-WV PMSA	4,223,404	836,935	20%	4,923,153	833,484	17%
Detroit, MI PMSA	4,266,654	1,222,218	29%	4,441,551	1,147,745	26%
Houston, TX PMSA	3,322,025	1,750,603	53%	4,177,646	2,058,452	49%
Atlanta, GA MSA	2,959,950	394,015	13%	4,112,198	416,629	10%
Dallas, TX PMSA	2,676,248	1,227,340	46%	3,519,176	1,460,393	41%
Boston, MA-NH PMSA	3,226,935	837,924	26%	3,406,835	869,117	26%
Phoenix-Mesa, AZ MSA	2,238,480	1,551,586	69%	3,251,876	2,079,379	64%
Minneapolis-St. Paul, MN-WI MSA	2,538,089	640,615	25%	2,968,806	669,603	23%
San Diego, CA MSA	2,498,016	1,252,183	50%	2,813,833	1,381,095	49%
St. Louis, MO-IL MSA	2,492,525	599,957	24%	2,603,607	543,938	21%
Baltimore, MD PMSA	2,382,177	769,153	32%	2,552,994	686,960	27%
Seattle-Bellevue-Everett, WA PMSA	2,033,156	670,513	33%	2,414,616	763,854	32%
Pittsburgh, PA MSA	2,394,811	369,895	15%	2,358,695	334,563	14%
Miami, FL PMSA	1,937,094	449,326	23%	2,253,362	450,624	20%
Cleveland-Lorain-Elyria, OH PMSA	2,202,069	633,850	29%	2,250,871	602,930	27%
Denver, CO PMSA	1,622,980	467,610	29%	2,109,282	554,636	26%
San Francisco, CA PMSA	1,603,678	723,959	45%	1,731,183	776,733	45%

Source: Data downloaded from Lewis Mumford Center, 2004. The metropolitan region is treated as the Primary Metropolitan Statistical Area in this table.

(McGuckin & Srinivasan, 2003).[4] In larger metropolitan areas, fewer than half and in some cases less than 10% of workers living in suburban counties commute to central counties (ibid.: 6–9).[5]

Decentralizing work patterns contributes to urban decline. Uneven development is also at the heart of concern over inequities associated with existing patterns of metropolitan development and sprawl (Altshuler et al., 1999). These disparities between central cities and their suburbs are the major rationale behind many of the new efforts at city-county consolidation (Rusk, 1995). The Lewis Mumford Center recently released a report comparing cities and suburbs in the largest metropolitan areas on eight variables including median household income, per capita income, poverty, college education, professional/ white collar workforce, unemployment, homeownership and vacant housing. According to the study, "on every indicator, the national average for cities compared to suburbs got worse during the 1990s" (Logan, 2002: 4).[6] In the highest-ranking city Las Vegas, median household income in the city was $1.06 for every dollar earned in the suburbs. And we should point out that Las Vegas is a new boomtown – sprawling through the desert and encompassing the suburbs around it. To this extent, Las Vegas is a statistical artifact that masks the problems of traditional cities. An extreme example of these problems can be seen in the lowest ranking city Newark (50th), where only $.45 was earned in the city for every dollar earned in the suburbs (Table 3).

The dispersed settlement pattern has severe consequences for metropolitan regions and their governance. Historically, reformers called for extending the boundaries of the central city to correspond to the larger city-region. This could be accomplished by annexation or city-county consolidation. In the early 20th century, state legislatures generally toughened annexation laws making it very difficult for central cities to annex with new requirements for a dual majority vote. With mass suburbanization from the 1950s onwards, city-county

---

4   Focusing on the 10 largest metropolitan areas, half had decreases in jobs in the central county between 1990 and 2000 (New York -.01, Los Angeles -6.2, Washington DC -14.3, Philadelphia -11.1, and Boston -1.0). On the other hand, there were large increases in the number of jobs in the central county in other cities (San Francisco 9.5, Dallas 10.1, Houston 11.8). McGuckin & Srinivasan (2003), pp. 2–18.

5   The percentage is as low as 8.4 in San Francisco up to 50.4 in Memphis.

6   http://www.albany.edu/mumford/.

consolidation became rare, especially when coupled with referendum requirements. More affluent suburbanites usually preferred to remain independent of the central cities and their troubles.

Metropolitanization trends have led to a concern for rescaling the city. Often referred to as *reterritorialization*, this rescaling aims to shift the primary unit of analysis and action from the city to the city-region or metropolis. Since most metropolises extend well beyond the core city or even core county, the traditional reform solutions do not apply. Thus, local public and private leaders and citizens focus on existing metropolitan wide institutions that may take on a greater role in shaping and pursuing a metropolitan agenda. The metropolitan planning organizations (MPOs) or council of governments (COGs) are expected to adapt to this new role. Unfortunately, their record in this regard is actually quite mixed. They have been most willing to act in areas of infrastructure planning and development including transportation. They have been least likely to accept the mantle of regional redistributors or to challenge the embedded disparities between the central city residents and the suburbanites arising from the existing pattern of urban development.

hard services are covered
soft services are forgotten
i.e. social services

Table 3: Rank in city-suburb disparity for the 50 largest metro areas

Rank 2000	Rank 1990	Metropolitan Area	2000 City	2000 Suburb	2000 Ratio	1990 City	1990 Suburb	1990 Ratio
1	2	Las Vegas, NV-AZ MSA	$44,069	$41,495	1.06	$40,077	$38,300	1.05
2	3	San Diego, CA MSA	$45,261	$48,389	0.94	$43,883	$46,923	0.94
3	7	Seattle-Bellevue-Everett, WA PMSA	$46,790	$54,911	0.85	$39,968	$50,758	0.79
4	4	Charlotte-Gastonia-Rock Hill, NC-SC MSA	$44,157	$47,164	0.94	$39,741	$40,836	0.97
5	8	Riverside-San Bernardino, CA PMSA	$37,711	$43,284	0.87	$39,273	$44,742	0.88
6	6	Greensboro--Winston-Salem--High Point, NC MSA	$37,867	$41,814	0.91	$35,486	$39,262	0.90
7	1	Phoenix-Mesa, AZ MSA	$42,683	$46,806	0.91	$39,546	$39,040	1.01
8	11	Fort Lauderdale, FL PMSA	$37,887	$41,667	0.91	$35,102	$40,195	0.87
9	9	Tampa-St. Petersburg-Clearwater, FL MSA	$34,950	$37,992	0.92	$30,684	$35,047	0.88
10	5	Raleigh-Durham-Chapel Hill, NC MSA	$43,540	$52,047	0.84	$39,542	$43,581	0.91
11	18	Portland-Vancouver, OR-WA PMSA	$39,799	$51,058	0.78	$34,104	$44,745	0.76
12	15	Orlando, FL MSA	$35,732	$42,141	0.85	$33,761	$39,935	0.85
13	10	Los Angeles-Long Beach, CA PMSA	$37,007	$47,361	0.78	$41,311	$49,146	0.84
14	13	Nashville, TN MSA	$38,519	$50,147	0.77	$35,917	$43,011	0.84
15	17	Norfolk-Virginia Beach-Newport News, VA-NC MSA	$39,493	$50,416	0.78	$38,536	$45,393	0.85
16	16	Fort Worth-Arlington, TX PMSA	$40,450	$51,250	0.79	$38,545	$46,158	0.84
17	32	San Francisco, CA PMSA	$55,221	$70,211	0.79	$43,367	$60,863	0.71
18	14	Austin-San Marcos, TX MSA	$41,510	$56,869	0.73	$33,232	$42,889	0.77
19	26	San Antonio, TX MSA	$36,148	$47,408	0.76	$31,831	$40,881	0.78
20	19	Salt Lake City-Ogden, UT MSA	$36,182	$51,988	0.70	$30,998	$43,367	0.71
21	12	Sacramento, CA PMSA	$37,049	$50,217	0.74	$37,490	$45,773	0.82
22	22	Denver, CO PMSA	$39,500	$54,985	0.72	$32,667	$47,324	0.69
23	24	Oakland, CA PMSA	$42,434	$63,037	0.67	$38,772	$58,447	0.66
24	29	New Orleans, LA MSA	$27,722	$39,556	0.70	$24,775	$36,244	0.68
25	21	Pittsburgh, PA MSA	$28,588	$38,558	0.74	$28,007	$35,969	0.78
26	20	Indianapolis, IN MSA	$38,922	$53,119	0.73	$37,199	$46,114	0.81
27	31	Washington, DC-MD-VA-WV PMSA	$45,498	$64,513	0.71	$44,153	$63,768	0.69
28	28	Kansas City, MO-KS MSA	$38,245	$51,259	0.75	$35,461	$45,695	0.78
29	27	San Jose, CA PMSA	$70,384	$83,314	0.84	$60,160	$69,031	0.87
30	30	Minneapolis-St. Paul, MN-WI MSA	$37,936	$57,661	0.66	$33,512	$52,545	0.64
31	25	Houston, TX PMSA	$36,557	$53,800	0.68	$35,114	$48,327	0.73
32	39	Miami, FL PMSA	$24,495	$39,044	0.63	$21,262	$40,206	0.53
33	33	Columbus, OH MSA	$37,331	$54,093	0.69	$33,868	$47,619	0.71
34	35	Orange County, CA PMSA	$50,252	$60,167	0.84	$52,153	$61,892	0.84
35	23	Dallas, TX PMSA	$38,325	$55,614	0.69	$36,386	$48,954	0.74
36	34	Providence-Fall River-Warwick, RI-MA MSA	$33,232	$49,106	0.68	$34,903	$47,794	0.73
37	36	Cincinnati, OH-KY-IN PMSA	$29,493	$49,027	0.60	$28,169	$43,622	0.65
38	37	Boston, MA-NH PMSA	$40,792	$59,129	0.69	$39,787	$57,149	0.70
39	38	Atlanta, GA MSA	$34,770	$53,268	0.65	$28,846	$48,465	0.60
40	45	Chicago, IL PMSA	$39,568	$58,912	0.67	$35,151	$56,339	0.62
41	40	St. Louis, MO-IL MSA	$29,599	$49,117	0.60	$27,646	$46,223	0.60
42	43	Milwaukee-Waukesha, WI PMSA	$33,738	$55,483	0.61	$32,627	$53,237	0.61
43	46	New York, NY PMSA	$38,069	$64,919	0.59	$38,835	$65,260	0.60
44	42	Buffalo-Niagara Falls, NY MSA	$24,932	$44,740	0.56	$24,666	$43,186	0.57
45	41	Philadelphia, PA-NJ PMSA	$29,947	$55,823	0.54	$31,509	$53,904	0.58
46	44	Baltimore, MD PMSA	$30,268	$56,190	0.54	$31,874	$55,059	0.58
47	48	Cleveland-Lorain-Elyria, OH PMSA	$27,427	$48,366	0.57	$25,332	$45,563	0.56
48	49	Detroit, MI PMSA	$30,397	$54,395	0.56	$26,579	$51,896	0.51
49	47	Hartford, CT MSA	$30,017	$54,884	0.55	$34,344	$57,177	0.60
50	50	Newark, NJ PMSA	$26,913	$60,414	0.45	$30,559	$60,210	0.51

Reproduced from: Logan, 2002, p. 7.

Globalization

Globalization of industry and finance has led to dramatic economic restructuring within cities and city-regions. According to Professor Saskia Sassen (1991), the world economy is now "spatially dispersed, yet globally integrated." That is, there has been a "decentralization of economic activity" around the world. This can be seen in the decentralization of manufacturing operations and office work. At the same time, there is greater concentration of "central control and management" of that world economy in corporate headquarter offices, especially in a few major cities such as New York, London and Tokyo. These global cities were always centers for international trade and banking, but now they have gained new functions as the command points for the new world economy. What distinguishes global cities from other non-global cities is the management and control function that they play in the world economy.

Professor Sassen finds that global cities share certain features. First, the *employment base* of the cities shifted from manufacturing goods to producing services. Global cities produce the "specialized services" such as advertising, accounting, business law, consulting and financial products needed by global corporations. This concentration of command and control functions changed the system of cities or hierarchy of cities within nations. Some cities lost their economic role and declined as a result. For example, Detroit, Liverpool, Manchester, Nagoya, Osaka have been slipping in importance.

Second, these global cities experienced a change in their *spatial organization* with increased business concentration in the central business districts, which crowded out other functions, especially residential. Finally, the *social structure* of the city was altered as jobs and residence radically changed. The middle class rapidly exited the central city, while poor migrants flocked into it. At the same time, large numbers of immigrants from abroad settled in the urban core and found low wage jobs servicing "yuppies" or the new, suburban middle class as restaurant workers, hotel attendants, housekeepers and gardeners.

There has recently been some debate among scholars concerning whether the global cities thesis is overly deterministic and whether all so-called "global cities" are actually experiencing the same phenomenon. For example, manufacturing is still a significant part of the employment base in Tokyo and Beijing. Tokyo has not experienced greater income disparity or immigration like New York and London. The question arises as to whether it is globalization of the economy or distinct local factors, which are shaping spatial organization of so-called global cities (White, 1998).

The focus given to global cities like New York, London and Tokyo may deflect attention from the effects of globalization on all cities, which are linked in some way to the world economy. The shift from manufacturing to services may have been most pronounced and occurred earlier in "global" cities but similar processes occur in most "post-industrial" cities of the advanced developed nations. The important point is to consider how globalization, in particular, economic restructuring, is affecting these cities and not overly focus on the "global" cities. International trade, for example, has become increasingly important for American cities. In 1999, exports from the 253 metropolitan areas in the United States totaled $542 billion and 93 of these metropolises exported more than $1 billion. Overall, exports from American metropolises rose 46% between 1993 and 1999. The top five export metropolitan areas were Seattle ($32 billion), San Jose ($28 billion), Detroit ($28 billion), New York ($25 billion), and Los Angeles ($24 billion).[7]

Globalization has significant implications for municipal and metropolitan governance. Economic and urban development strategy can no longer be focused solely within the municipal boundaries. Labor, airports, industrial locations and the like are located throughout the metropolis. The city needs to access land, labor and capital assets to mount an effective economic development strategy. On the other hand, suburban officials and outlying counties cannot be brought under the city's formal decision-making processes and must be induced to cooperate with the city to maximize the economic health of the region. Suburban reluctance based upon socioeconomic differences must be overcome. The essential task of mayors and other regional actors is to build institutional capacity to develop metropolitan strategies for growth and development (Savitch, 1998). This thickening of institutions links public, private and non-profit actors from the city,

---

7   International Trade Administration, Export Sales of U.S. Metropolitan Areas, 1993-1999, http://www.ita.doc.gov/td/industry/otea/metro/Summary.html 3/22/2004.

neighborhoods, suburbs, outlying counties and state and federal governmental and nongovernmental agencies. Thus, horizontal and vertical integration occurs in a myriad of local and regional forums and associations that overlap and overlay with each other.

Public policy and the new public management

Neil Brenner explains that globalization is leading to reterritorialization meaning "the reconfiguration and re-scaling of forms of territorial organization" (Brenner, 1999: 431). In essence, the historical central city no longer has sufficient space, capital or labor for the new economy. The city and its leaders must find a way for the functional city to act in the world economy and strive to capture economic benefits for its residents and revenues for its operations (Savitch & Vogel, 1996). The city's elite strives to adapt the city to the changes globalization brings (Stone, 1989). This leads to public-private partnerships, strategic planning for economic development, and efforts to redevelop the city. The traditional route to regionalism was for the city to annex more territory or merge with its county, or in a few cases to forge a regional government (one or two-tier) (Savitch & Vogel, 2000a). Elites often continue to advocate this approach (Savitch & Vogel, 2000b). However, in the 21th century, this rescaling of the city and regionalism cannot be accomplished within a single political jurisdiction. Rather, a functional city must be created to provide a strategic planning capacity for the region and to coordinate services.

Ascendance of market-based philosophy and privatization
New regionalism embraced governance, and with that new roles for the private sector and market-based economies. Cities in the United States and the world have seen the emergence of a *new political culture* (NPC) rejecting the role of a strong activist state. A principal trait of the new political culture is a rejection of the strong welfare state whether national or local (Clark & Inglehart, 1998: 11). According to Terry Clark and Ronald Inglehart,

> Some NPC citizens, and leaders, conclude that "governing" in
> the sense of state-central planning is unrealistic for many

services – economic and social. Although not seeking to reduce services, NPCs question the specifics of service delivery and seek to improve efficiency. They are skeptical of large central bureaucracies. They are willing to decentralize administration or contract with other governments or private firms – if these work better. (ibid.: 12)

Peter Self is more critical of the ascendance of market-based philosophies in nations and cities around the world. He argues that the scale and scope of welfare state policies has been dramatically reduced. There is increased cynicism among citizens who no longer hold a positive view of the role of the state – local or national (Self, 1999). Self decries the dominance of market ideology in reducing political choice. According to him,

assumed market "imperatives" now play a dominant role in the politics and policies of almost all countries. The political imperative is to equip the national economy to meet the challenge of global market competition and to maintain or restart the engine of economic growth. Market institutions, methods, and motivations are seen as the essential means to this end – hence the extensive measures of privatization and deregulation, although the latter process may be running out of steam as some counter-measures become inescapable (including not only some degree of social and environmental protection, but the need to keep the market system itself tolerably efficient and workable). Hence too the cutting of government budgets and the sacrifice of collective goods in the assumed interest of freeing resources for the more "efficient" and "productive" market sector. Hence also the reorganization of government itself along market lines and utilizing market motivations. Finally market concepts and motivations are being extended into ever widening aspects of social life, both theoretically and practically. (ibid.: 2)

This ideological shift is apparent in urban management as local governments embrace the *reinventing government* movement or *new public management* (NPM) (Osborne & Gaebler, 1992). NPM focuses on bringing market principles to public management. Thus, public officials are encouraged to give renewed attention to the needs of the customer and adopt *total quality management* processes. Public officials are urged to become more entrepreneurial and to introduce competition into the provision and production of public services. Urban managers are told to monitor and measure performance of local government to ensure services are effective (Morgan & Carnevale, 1997). The city that seems to have most embraced the new public management is Indianapolis under Mayor Steven Goldsmith, who later served as an advisor to President George W. Bush.

The final aspect of the new public management is reliance on public-private partnerships. As cities have faced reductions in federal aid and lost revenue due to the effects of economic restructuring, mayors have increasingly turned to private sector leaders. Indeed, mayors have come to recognize that they share urban governance with private sector leaders (Vogel, 1992). Clarence Stone defines governance as the "informal arrangements by which public bodies and private interests function together in order to be able to make and carry out governing decisions." Governing decisions include "manag[ing] conflict" and making "adaptive responses to social change" (Stone, 1989: 6). Mayors, charged with ensuring that revenues and jobs flow into the city, must work together with private leaders to ensure the city's economic health. Paul Peterson's (1981) city limits thesis focuses on the primacy of development policy on local agendas and stresses the benefits to cities of pursuing development over redistributive policy. A concern for social-centered policies and redistribution is absent from most local agendas in the United States unless framed in the context of welfare reform to encourage individuals to embrace work.

The case for a contraction of the public sphere is probably overstated. A study by the Organization for Economic Cooperation and Development (OECD, 2001: 3) found that:

> [T]he share of public employees of OECD Member countries…decreased during the late 1980s. However, it became stable in some countries or increased in other countries in the early 1990s. In the late 1990s, it has again increased with a few exceptions. This tendency may be attributed to two different reasons: first, many countries still maintain the downsizing policy on public employment; second, due to the economic

booms in recent years, more jobs were created in the private
sector than in the public sector.

However, according to OECD,

> Another interesting finding…is that compared with 1990 data,
> the number of central (or federal) government employees
> decreased while the number of regional (or local) government
> employees increased in some countries such as Canada,
> Germany, and the United States.

This would suggest that local governments are more active even if the
federal government is reducing its responsibilities and even as local
officials delegate or co-produce services with private actors. By some
accounts, cities contract out more than one-fourth of all their services
(Greene, 2002: 375). Nicholas Henry (2002) suggests after reviewing
four books on privatization that "one lesson is that business is not
better than government in delivering public services efficiently and
effectively." However, he does find consensus that competition among
organizations, whether public or private, does increase efficiency and
effectiveness of services (ibid.: 376).

Nicholas Henry (2002) suggests that the emphasis on privatization is
overstated and misleads us as to the true nature of public-private
relations in the United States. Rather, he argues for a new terminology:

> [I]ntersectoral administration which I define as the management
> and coordination of the relations among government agencies
> and organizations in the private and nonprofit sectors for the
> purpose of achieving specific policy goals. To place all this in
> perspective: _governance_ characterizes the current political and
> economic environment of public administration; _intersectoral_
> _administration_ is a method of public policy implementation and
> government service delivery that is unusually compatible with
> that environment; _privatization_ is a subset of intersectoral
> administration that is designed to achieve public goals through
> governments' collaboration with profit-seeking companies (ibid.:
> 377).

Devolution and decentralization

Another force reshaping cities and their governance results from widespread *devolution and decentralization* from higher to lower levels of government. Higher-level governments have transferred programs and responsibilities downwards from central or state to local levels. This has led to fiscal stress. Public sector management has responded to the ascendance of market based philosophies and decentralization by undertaking public-private partnerships, privatizing services, and with strategies such as reinventing and reengineering government. Many efforts at regional cooperation among local governments stem from the need to economize and regionalize services that can no longer be supported by the central city tax base alone.

Movements toward decentralization involve altering the existing pattern by "transfer[ring] of significant powers and functions, along with fiscal responsibility to carry out these powers and functions, from the national to the local level of government" (Stren, 2003: 1). Decentralization trends have to be considered in the light of the situation of local government in the nation's political organization. In a federal system, local government is likely to already have a strong degree of local autonomy. In a unitary system, where the central government is preeminent, there is the possibility of a high degree of local autonomy depending upon the historical experience, political culture, party structure, and system of representation. However, this is an empirical question. It is possible that the central government views local government as a convenient tool to implement the national agenda at the local level to ensure efficient service delivery. In this case, local government is clearly subordinate with little free will.

Gauging the success of decentralization policies requires an operational definition of decentralization. Essential features of local self-governance include (1) sufficient authority for local government to set its own priorities over a broad range of functions; (2) sufficient and stable revenue streams to support basic public services; (3) adequate technical expertise, organizational competence and management skills to efficiently and effectively plan and implement policies and programs and to provide services; (4) democratic legitimacy and accountability to citizens.

If decentralization is intended to substantially bolster local self-government, then it is referred to as *devolution* (Kincaid, 1999).

Central policies aimed at greater administrative discretion being assigned to subnational governments but not significantly altering the intergovernmental relationship would still be viewed as decentralization policies, falling short of devolution. Analysts must be cautious in assessing the degree of decentralization. It is possible that decentralization policies are more rhetoric than reality or that official devolution policies may disguise other policy goals. In addition, national policies often lack coherence. Some national policies promote decentralization while others may lead to greater centralization (Bowman & Krause, 2003). Devolution or decentralization may be a by-product of other higher-level government policies rather than a deliberate effort to realign intergovernmental relations (Kincaid, 1999).

In the United States, cities have substantial local autonomy in spite of limitations imposed by Dillon's rule[8]. This stems from their well-developed revenue sources and professional and bureaucratic capacity. It provides them with a great deal of technical and institutional capacity as they can hire a well-qualified and professional workforce, employ sophisticated management tools to provide services efficiently, and hire expert consultants when confronted with issues beyond their expertise. In addition, the degree of local autonomy found in American local government is bolstered by the high regard for the local in the political culture, and organization of the party and national representation system around local territorial boundaries.

John Kincaid refers to a "de facto devolution" in the United States as the federal government withdraws financial support from cities (ibid.). Here, devolution is not a deliberate policy to bolster local autonomy. Rather, the federal government is moving away from cities and their problems. Peter Eisinger argues that in the "new federal order" city politics in the United States is changing because of this devolution. Cities must be more fiscally and administratively self-reliant (Eisinger, 1998). Thus, local public management takes on increasing importance. This leads urban managers to focus less on issues of social justice and racial equality. Larger cities in the United States operate under the

8   Dillon's rule is a long-standing principle of municipal law in the U.S. which holds that municipal governments can exercise only those powers specifically granted by state legislatures. It states: "Any fair, reasonable, substantial doubt concerning the existence of power is resolved by the courts against the [city government], and the power is denied." (Harrigan and Vogel 2003: 197).

strong mayor model of city government. Thus, mayors in cities like New York, Los Angeles and Chicago embraced the new public management policies and are now hailed for saving the cities (Savitch & Vogel, 2005).

Local governments, including older central cities thrived in the 1990s in the United States as the economy boomed and revenues grew. In this climate, it is easy to see how mayors were successfully managing devolution. Even if mayors were less inclined to pursue redistributive policies, the stronger economy produced jobs and income for all levels of the workforce. However, the recent period of economic recession has changed that. As the National League of Cities reports, "A federal and state fiscal crisis that is the largest the nation has experienced in decades is trickling down to city governments, making it increasingly difficult for city officials to balance their own budgets." The report points out nearly half the states cut revenue for cities in 2003 and 2004 resulting in a 9.2% drop in state aid to cities (Hoene & Pagano, 2003: 1).

Although there has been a de facto devolution in American cities with mixed effects, the national government has continued to play a strong role in domestic policy. The entitlement programs that aid *people* instead of *places* continue to account for a large share of the national budget. This includes programs such as social security and Medicare. The welfare program has been converted from an entitlement program to a block grant to states. Overall, the evidence actually indicates that in spite of the language of devolution and decentralization, the national government has actually centralized policy making even in areas the Constitution traditionally reserves to the states (Bowman & Krause, 2003).

Conclusion

We have focused on metropolitan reform as a product of external stimulus such as higher-level government intervention or the world economy. However, metropolitan reform can also be the result of local initiative independent of these forces. It is important to avoid economic determinism in analyzing cases of metropolitan reform and recognize when institutional change comes from below rather than above. The local impetus for reorganization often stems from selective inducements or benefits (Savitch & Vogel, 2004; Feiock & Carr, 2000a; 2000b).

Together, these forces are leading to a redefinition of the local state in the United States and abroad manifested in the *new regionalism* movement. Local, state and national governments are realigning authority, functions and services among and between themselves and redefining territorial boundaries. This does not take a single form, as leaders have flexibility in how they respond to these challenges. Moreover, these variables are filtered through national and local political cultures and history, which inform and limit the potential alternatives. Rescaling regionalism is an ongoing process rather than a single event.

Studies in regionalism tend to focus on problems associated with metropolitanization of cities and that the fate of the central cities and suburbs are tied together. David Rusk, for example, emphasizes the need for institutional reform (i.e., city-county consolidation) as a solution to disparities between the central city and suburbs (Rusk, 1995).[9] More recently, new regionalists have recognized that metropolitan reform, even if desirable, is unlikely (Altshuler et al., 1999).[10] Moreover, even where institutional reform or boundary expansion occurs, the metropolis still is not contained within a single political jurisdiction.

Since comprehensive government reorganization is unlikely, new regionalists often stress a problem-solving approach.[11] Thus,

---

9   However, Rusk's solutions are now doubtful. Metropolitan government is still the exception in the United States and city-county consolidation is extremely rare. The recent successful referendum to merge Louisville and Jefferson County could lead to another wave of consolidation efforts. However, Savitch and Vogel (2000b) doubt city-county consolidation, at least in Louisville/Jefferson County, will further the new regionalism agenda to redress poverty, reduce sprawl or enhance economic development.

10   Also, not all scholars agree that fragmentation is a problem. For example, see ACIR (1987). And there is doubt that city-county consolidation will reduce disparities between the central city and suburbs. For example, see Savitch and Vogel (2000b).

11   New regionalists may still call for institutional reform if government organization is an impediment to pursuing desired regional policies. New regionalists would tend to avoid comprehensive reorganization of local government in favor of more incremental strategies to better structure the intergovernmental system to achieve new regional goals. To the extent that metropolitan government is part of the new regional strategy, there is a preference for

metropolitan strategies are developed to build more affordable housing in the suburbs (Rusk, 1999), contain sprawl through *smart growth* initiatives (Downs, 1994), adopt tax-sharing policies to ensure adequate revenue flows to the core (Orfield, 1997), and to foster greater regional cooperation on development policies to ensure the economic health of the entire city-region (Barnes & Ledebur, 1998). Regional policy becomes central to ameliorating poverty and inequality in the central city. A strong federal and state role is called for to promote regional cooperation (Altshuler et al., 1999). Some now call for a new politics built upon regional coalitions to bring about a new national agenda for federal renewal of cities (Dreier et al., 2001).

However, voluntary cooperation among local governments in the metropolis does not necessarily occur nor lead to effective metropolitan governance (Frisken & Norris, 2001; Savitch & Vogel, 1996; Vogel & Nezelkewicz, 2002). *Governance* does not imply an absence of government. It is important to recognize that accomplishing regional objectives may require restructuring intergovernmental relations and even institutions in the metropolis (Barlow, 1991). *New regionalism* must be seen in a larger context. Reterritorialization is merely one aspect of the new regionalism. Innovative policies and new management techniques are emerging and could replace over-centralized hierarchies. Cities and city regions are experimenting in how to govern a sprawling metropolitan region and develop collaborative relationships with other governments in the area, state, and nation alongside local and international private and nonprofit organizations. The challenge is to ensure that traditional concerns about efficiency, effectiveness, equity,, and democracy are not lost in building the new regionalism.

"two tier" systems as opposed to unified government. On these points, see Barlow, 1991, and Altshuler et al., 1999.

References

ACIR (1987) (Advisory Commission on Intergovernmental Relations). *The Organization of Local Public Economies*. Washington, DC: author.

ACIR (1993). *Metropolitan Organization: Comparison of the Allegheny and St. Louis Case Studies*. Washington, DC: author.

Altshuler, A., Morrill, W., Wolman, H., & Mitchell, F. (eds.) (1999). *Governance and Opportunity in Metropolitan America*. Washington, DC: National Academy Press·

Barlow, I.M. (1991). Metropolitan Government. London: Routledge.

Barnes, W.R., & L.C. Ledebur (1998). *The New Regional Economies*. Thousand Oaks, Cal.: Sage.

Beard, C. (1923). *The Administration and Politics of Tokyo*. New York: Macmillan.

Bish, R.L. (1971). *The Public Economy of Metropolitan Areas*. Chicago: Markham Publishers.

Bish, R.L. (2001). Local government amalgamations: Discredited nineteenth-century deals alive in the twenty-first. *C.D. Howe Institute Commentary*, 150 (pp. 1–2).Toronto, ON: C.D. Howe Institute, March. http://www.cdhowe.org/.

Bowman, A. O'M., & Krause G.A. (2003). Power shift: Measuring policy centralization in US intergovernmental relations, 1947–1998. *American Politics Research* 31, 301–326.

Brenner, N. (1999). Globalisation as reterritorialisation: The re-scaling of urban governance in the European Union. *Urban Studies* 36, 431–451.

Clark, T.N., & Inglehart, R. (1998). The new political culture: Changing dynamics of support for the welfare state and other policies in postindustrial societies. In: T. N. Clark & V. Hoffmann-Martinot (eds.), *The New Political Culture*. Boulder, Col.: Westview Press.

Downs, A. (1994). *New Visions for Metropolitan America*. Washington, DC: The Brookings Institution.

Dreier, P., Mollenkopf, J., & Swanstrom, T. (2001). *Place Matters: Metropolitics for the Twenty-First Century*. Lawrence, Kansas: University Press of Kansas.

Eisinger, P. (1998). City politics in an era of federal devolution. *Urban Affairs Review* 33, 308–326.

Feiock, R., & Carr, J. (2000a). Private incentives and academic entrepreneurship: The promotion of city-county consolidation. *Public Administration Quarterly* 24, 223–245.

Feiock, R., & Carr, J. (2000b). Incentives, entrepreneurs, and boundary change: A collective action framework. *Urban Affairs Review* 36, 382–405.

Frisken, F., & Norris, D.F. (2001). Regionalism Reconsidered. *Journal of Urban* Affairs 23, 467–478.

Greene, J.D. (2002). Cities and Privatization cited in Nicholas Henry, "Is privatization passé? The case for competition and the emergence of intersectoral administration. *Public Administration Review* 62, May/June, 375.

Harrigan, J.J. & Vogel, R.K. (2003). *Political Change in the Metropolis*. New York: Longman.

Henry, N. (2002). Is privatization passé? the case for competition and the emergence of intersectoral administration. *Public Administration Review* 62: 374-378.

Hoene, C., & Pagano, M.A. (2003). *Fiscal Crisis Trickles Down as States Cut Aid to Cities.* Washington, DC: National League of Cities.

Kincaid, J. (1999). De facto devolution and urban defunding: The priority of persons over places. *Journal of Urban Affairs* 21, 135–168.

Krane, D., Rigos, P.N., & Hill, M.B. (2000), *Home Rule in America: A Fifty-State Handbook*. Washington, DC: Congressional Quarterly Press.

Logan, J.R. (2002). *The Suburban Advantage: New Census Data Show Unyielding City-Suburb Economic Gap, and Surprising Shifts in Some Places*, July 24. Albany, NY: Lewis Mumford Center for Comparative Urban and Regional Research.

McGuckin, N.A., & Srinivasan, N. (2003). *Journey to Work Trends in the United States and Its Major Metropolitan Areas 1960–2000* (pp. 2–12). Washington, DC: US Department of Transportation, Federal Highway Administration [FHWA-EP-03-058].

Morgan, D.R., & Carnevale, D.G. (1997). Urban management. In R.K. Vogel (ed.), *Handbook of Research on Urban Politics and Policy in the United States*. Westport, Conn.: Greenwood Press, pp. 210-221.

Orfield, M. (1997). *Metro Politics: A Regional Agenda for Community and Stability.* Washington, DC: The Brookings Institution.

Organization for Economic Co-operation and Development. (2001). Highlights of Public Sector Pay and Employment Trends. Paper for HRM Working Party Meeting, June 25-26, Paris.

Osborne, D., & Gaebler, T. (1992). *Reinventing Government.* Reading, Mass.: Addison Wesley.

Parks, R.B., & Oakerson, R.J. (1989). Metropolitan organization and governance: A local public economy approach. *Urban Affairs Review* 25, 18–29.

Parks, R.B., & Oakerson, R.J. (2000). Regionalism, localism, and metropolitan governance: Suggestions from the research program on local public economies. *State and Local Government Review* 32: 169–179.

Peterson, P. (1981). *City Limits.* Chicago: University of Chicago Press.

Powell, J. A. (2000). Addressing Regional Agendas for Minority Communities. In: B. Katz (ed.), *Reflections on Regionalism.* Washington, DC: The Brookings Institution Press, pp. 218-246.

Rusk, D. (1995). *Cities Without Suburbs.* Washington, DC: Woodrow Wilson Center Press.

Rusk, D. (1999). *Inside Game/Outside Game: Winning Strategies for Saving Urban America.* Washington, DC: The Brookings Institution.

Sassen, S. (1991). *The Global City: New York, London, and Tokyo* (pp. 3–4), Princeton, NJ: Princeton University Press.

Savitch, H.V. (1998). Global challenge and institutional capacity: or, how we can refit local administration for the next century. *Administration and Society* 30, July, 248–273.

Savitch, H.V., & Vogel, R.K. (eds.) (1996). *Regional Politics: America in a Post-City Age.* Thousand Oaks, Cal.: Sage.

Savitch, H.V., & Vogel, R.K. (2000a). Paths to new regionalism. *State and Local Government Review* 32, 158–168.

Savitch, H.V., & Vogel, R.K. (2000b). Metropolitan consolidation versus Metropolitan Governance in Louisville. *State and Local Government Review* 32, 198–212.

Savitch, H.V., & Vogel, R.K. (2004). Suburbs without a city: Power and city-county consolidation. *Urban Affairs Review* 39: 758-790.

Savitch, H.V., & Vogel, R.K. (2005). Local government in the United States: Executive centered politics. In: B. Denters & L. E. Rose (eds.), *Comparing Local Governance*. New York: Palgrave.

Self, P. (1999). *Rolling Back the Market: Economic Dogma and Political Choice*. New York: St. Martin's Press.

Sharpe, L.J. (1995). The future of metropolitan government. In: L.J. Sharpe (ed.), *The Government of World Cities*. New York: John Wiley & Sons., pp. 11-31.

Siegel, F. (1997). *The Future Once Happened Here: New York, D.C., L.A. and, the Fate of America's Big Cities*. New York: Free Press.

Stone, C.N. (1989). *Regime Politics*. Lawrence, Kansas: University Press of Kansas.

Stren, R. (2003). *Decentralization and Development: Rhetoric or Reality?* Paper presented at the Canadian Political Science Association, Halifax, Nova Scotia, May.

Vogel, R.K. (1992). *Urban Political Economy*. Gainesville, FL: University Press of Florida.

Vogel, R.K., & Nezelkewicz, N. (2002). Metropolitan planning organizations and the new regionalism: The case of Louisville. *Publius: the Journal of Federalism* 32, 107–129.

Wallis, A. (1994a). Evolving structures and challenges of metropolitan regions. *National Civic Review*, Winter-Spring, 40-53.

Wallis, A. (1994b). Inventing regionalism: The first two waves. *National Civic Review,* Spring-Summer, 159–175.

Wallis, A. (1994c). The third wave: Current trends in regional governance. *National Civic Review*, Summer-Fall, 290-310.

Wallis, A. (1994d). Inventing regionalism: A two-phase approach, *National Civic Review,* Fall-Winter, 447–468.

White, J.W. (1998). Old wine, cracked bottle?: Tokyo, Paris, and the global city hypothesis. *Urban Affairs Review* 33, 451–478.

Yates, D. (1977). *The Ungovernable City*. Cambridge: MIT Press.

JUNG-HO KIM AND PATRICK J. SMITH

Consolidating Local Governments and Metropolitan Governance in Korea

Introduction

From an historical perspective, Korean local administration and the present structure of local government were fashioned at the time of the late Lee Dynasty and the early rule of Japanese imperialism. In the latter part of the Lee Dynasty (1392-1910), local administrative units were altered. In 1895, for example, the nation was divided into 23 Bus and 331 Kuns. In 1896, the nation was again divided into 13 Dos (upper-level local governments), 1 Mok, 7 Bus and 341 Kuns (counties). In 1914, under the Japanese, they were reorganized into 13 Dos, 12 Bus, 220 Kuns and 2,521 Myuns (villages) (see Korean Association for Local Government Studies, 1999, for some discussion of these terms/forms of local administration). The local administrative structure in 1930 reflected practices of local autonomy imposed by the Japanese. However, this system was not intended to enhance citizen participation in a wide-range of local public affairs, but was intended to appease and soften Korean antagonistic sentiment toward Japanese colonial rule. Local autonomy was highly centralized and bureaucratic.

During the period of American Military Administration (1945-1948), efforts were made to set up a democratic system of local administration.[1] The South Korea Constitution, adopted on July 17, 1948, provided for a system of local government to be established by subsequent legal enactments (Constitution, Ch.VIII, Article 117 [2]). In 1949, the Local Autonomy Act was passed; it substantially established the current system of local governments in South Korea. At that time, the local government units were Seoul Special City, Do (province), and lower level local governments: City, Eup (township), and Myun

---

1   An important element in the development of local autonomy in Korea was the establishment of the Seoul Special City Charter, which provided for citizen participation in local administration.

(village).[2] The democratic local administration system was, however, ended by the military revolution in 1961. The Provisional Measure Act for Local Autonomy initiated by the Military Revolution Commission changed local governments, Eup and Myun, into a different local government form - the Kun (county). In 1988, the Sixth Republic made significant revisions to the Local Autonomy Act – seeking a revival of local autonomy.[3] Over time, there also have been other changes in the local government system in the country, not by a comprehensive scheme of reform, but by ad hoc measures relating to individual reorganizations in specific city-regions. The structure of local government, in particular, has varied with the political and social situation of the time. For example, restructuring local governments has become increasingly critical in responding to the demands of globalization since the early 1990s (Kim, 2000).

As of 2005, there are five units of local government in Korea: metropolis (Gwangyouk-Shi including Seoul Special City), province (Do), city (Shi), county (Kun), district (Ku).[4] The units are classified by a demographic definition with economic, social, and physical conditions. Their structure is a two-tier system (see Fig. 1). The first tier is area-wide local governments (metropolis, province),[5] the second tier is basic local governments (city, county, district).[6] Each local government has its own functions – generally similar in nature – that are exercised with some degree of independence, although the central government has supervisory powers over these units. In Korea, all

---

2   The upper-level local governments (Seoul Special City, Do) were under the direct control of the national government, while the lower-level local governments (City, Eup, Myun) were under the direct control of an upper-level local government (Do).

3   In this revision the upper-level local governments included Seoul Special City, Area-Wide City, Do (province); the lower-level local governments included City, Kun (county), Ku (autonomous district).

4   Only the city (urban-rural complex city) and the county have townships as parts of them. Township in Korea is just an administrative unit, not a unit of local government. Townships especially have a symbiotic relationship with the rural areas surrounding them. They are an important intermediate place between urban and rural areas. Thus, only an urban-rural complex city of cities has townships.

5   A city of over one million inhabitants can be a metropolis by being acknowledged as a large city which has different characteristics from any other small and medium sized city. However, metropolis and province have the same status of power and role.

6   Only metropolis has districts that have the same status as city or county. There are cases where a city of over half a million people, not a metropolis, can have districts just as administrative units, not as local government units.

governments below the national level are constitutionally subservient to the national authority. Area-wide local governments (metropolis, province) include many basic local governments (city, county, district) and supervise them in financial and administrative terms. There are also specific forms of local government responsibilities for each type. For example, the metropolis has responsibility for area-wide functions, such as transportation, and the city has responsibility for local welfare. The population distribution in units of local government has been changed by urbanization that leads to a concentration of population in urban areas. This shift was employment-driven, motivated also by a desire for better access to education.

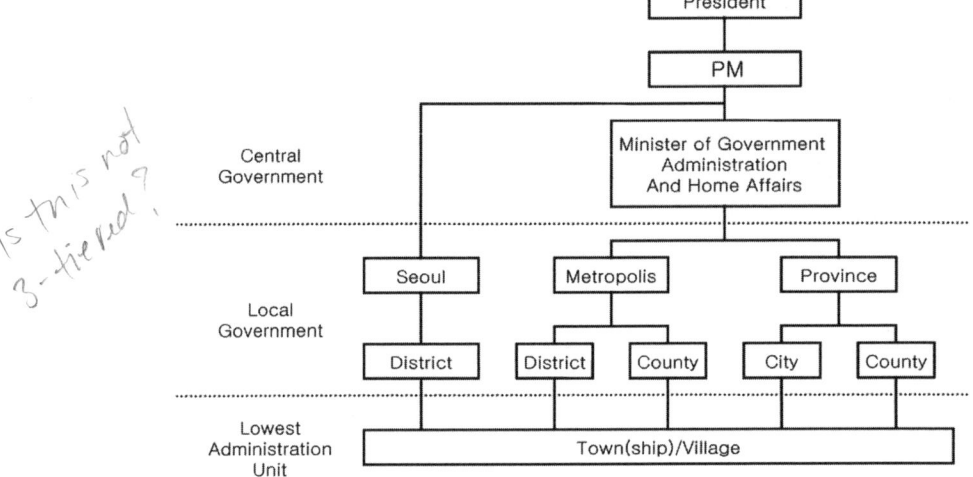

Figure 1. Local government system

Consolidating local governments

In reforming local government fragmentation, consolidating local governments is one general and comprehensive approach, which falls within the centrist category[7] for governmental reorganization.[8]

---

7   In the ways in which the political system of local units should be organized the centrists favor political consolidation as the most effective means of achieving efficiency, eliminating service inequalities, and managing growth and development (Bollens & Schmandt, 1982:302).

8   Reorganization is defined as a reformulation of formal institutions, structures, rules and

Beginning in the late 1950s, and through the next decade, a number of local governments in America, including Nashville (1962), Jacksonville (1967), and Indianapolis (1969), reorganized through consolidation – arguing it would bring greater efficiency. This was more a goal than an actual reality. The process undertaken usually consisted of the merger of a county government with the principal city or all the municipalities within its borders (Bollens & Schmandt, 1982: 311). This meant the regionalization of local government services by reducing the number of local governments. Some have argued that too many governments make effective governance impossible. Uniting local governments into one strong local government is seen as a vehicle for dealing effectively with area-wide problems. In general, the consolidation argument suggests expansion of administrative efficiency, feasibility of balanced development, enlargement of residents' life conveniences, enhancement of autonomy for local government, internalization of externalities, efficient execution of area-wide administration, coping with conflicts by the sectional egoisms among municipalities and the need for strong united leadership as reasons for considering such amalgamation (Lim, 1995; Cho, 1996; Dolan, 1990; Park, 2000; Choi, 2000).

One of the significant reorganizations of local governments has been consolidation which concentrates on the new political configurations considered necessary to promote local economic interests in a competitive, globalized world. Elsewhere in this volume, Stewart notes this "global city" motivation of UK Prime Minister Tony Blair in his reorganization of Greater London. Since 1995, the Korean central government has forced four metropolis-county consolidations and 49 city-county consolidations to attain efficiency and equity between local governments. These consolidations, however, have not been considered a panacea. There have been both expected and unexpected problems. It is useful for policy analysts and other local governments to see some of the lessons and policy implications of these changes, to review how they were realized and what results they generated.

---

practices that govern geographic areas and control their operations. Reorganization may involve changes in the hierarchical setting of organizations, it may include changes in the scope of operations, and it may encompass changes in functions carried out by institutions (Savitch, 1994).

There are three primary objectives of this study of local consolidations in Korea:

- how these consolidations developed historically;
- a review of the results and remaining challenges;
- an assessment of lessons and policy implications from this consolidation experience.

Urbanization and local government fragmentation

The rapid process of urbanization in Korea has been one of the most significant vehicles for the transformation of national society over the past several decades. Since the 1970s, when economic development was propelled by industrialization, the Korean population has been increasingly concentrated in metropolises and cities. The proportion of the national population in urban areas of 20,000 or more had increased to 89% in 2000 from 28% in 1960 (Korean Ministry of Government Administration and Home Affairs, 2001a). This is especially the case in metropolises like Seoul and Pusan which led the urbanization push. During this period, economic development in Korea was propelled by these large urban centers. Their population had increased steeply together with their economic development. One of the characteristics of urbanization in Korea was metropolis-initiated urbanization. Population growth between 1960 and 2000 in the seven metropolises increased about 3.2 fold, and also their proportion in the national population increased to 49.7% in 2000 from 21.8% in 1960 (Korean Ministry of Government Administration and Home Affairs, 2001a).

This urbanization has brought about local government fragmentation. Cities of a million or more, and townships of 50,000 or more, have been promoted to the status of metropolis[9] and city respectively by the Local Autonomy Act.[10] The number of metropolises and cities increased from one metropolis and 20 cities in 1950 to seven metropolises and 72 cities at the start of the 21st century respectively. Although there were many causes, six metropolises and

9   Metropolis was originally incorporated as a result of specific legislation relating only to it.
10   The Local Autonomy Act was promulgated in 1949. The introduction of local autonomy in its modern sense has been derived from the passing of this Act.

54 cities were separated from provinces or counties to which they had been attached since the Korean government and constitution were established in 1948 (see Tables 1&2), leaving the affected provinces or counties as rump areas.[11]

Table 1. Metropolis-Province Separations

Year	Number of Cases
1946	1 (Seoul)[12]
1963	1 (Pusan)
1981	2 (Daegu, Incheon)
1986	1 (Gwangju)
1989	1 (Daejeon)
1997	1 (Ulsan)

Source: Korean Ministry of Government Administration and Home Affairs (2001b)

Table 2. City-County Separations

Year	Number of Cases
1955	6
1956	2
1963	4
1973	3
1978	1
1980	4
1981	10
1986	12
1989	12

Source: Korean Ministry of Government Administration and Home Affairs (2001b)

In addition to urbanization, there were other reasons why these separations of local governments occurred in South Korea. One of the major causes was the national political system itself and political

---

11 The administrative and financial abilities of the rump provinces and counties had been reduced by the separation of central cities or townships that were due to raising a city or a township to the status of a metropolis or a city.

12 Korea was put under the American Military Administration from 1945 to 1948. The American Military Administration separated Seoul, called Kyungsung-bu, from Kyonggi province in 1946.

behavior: a strong form of centralization and some history of authoritarianism. Almost all such separations/alterations were carried out as a result of political decisions of the national government, including its profits and losses, administrative convenience, and national government initiative without considering rational studies, physical, economic, cultural, psychological situations, and citizen participation or convenience (Kim, 1993, 116–119; Yu, 1994; Park, 2000). They were targets of political bargaining and used as campaign promises by local or national politicians. On the other hand, the residents of cities or townships hoped their unit of local government would indeed be promoted to metropolis or city because of the independence from political control by higher level government (for example, province or county) this changed status would entail.

There was also another reason which should not be overlooked as a catalyst: that is, growth pole policy,[13] the regional development policy in Korea in the 1970s and early 1980s. The urban-biased nature of Korea's industrial policy helped directly or indirectly in the matter of local government separations, through its emphasis on economic growth.

Responses to the problems of city-county separation

City-county separation brought about a number of problems when it was undertaken: social disharmony, discordance between area life and administrative controls, unfavourable fiscal conditions in the rump areas left behind, the irrationality of geographic and spatial structure in these rump areas, difficulties for comprehensive development in the region, inequality among local governments – especially between city and county in the provision of public facilities and services, increases in administrative costs, lower investment efficiencies for regional

13 Rondinelli has succinctly captured the main aspects of the growth pole concept in the following terms: "The growth pole concept of spatial development suggests that by investing heavily in capital-intensive industries in the largest urban centers, governments in developing countries can stimulate economic growth that will spread outward to generate regional development." The growth pole concept can thus be seen to be overtly concerned with where development takes place, and explicitly within it is the idea that emphasis will be placed on urban initiatives with the expectation that these will in turn generate rural development on both a regional and local scale.

development, and making county administration subordinate to city administration (Choi and Yoon, 1993; Oum & Hwang, 1995, 25; Lim, 1995; Cho, 1996; Park, 2000).

There were three main forces which affected consolidations of local governments in Korea:

the first was the disparity between city and county. The 'growth pole policy' adopted in the second master plan (1982-1991) to solve this disparity did not produce the benefits promised: the expected 'trickle-down' benefits (Rondinelli, 1985, 4) failed to materialize; indeed, they were replaced by adverse 'backwash' effects which led to actual increases in the disparities (Lipton, 1988, 43; Cho & Kim, 1999).[14] That city-county separations actually deepened the disparities between city and county (see, for example, Table 3), meant that this keynote of national economic development added to social and political problems. Thus, it became a key factor affecting further city-county consolidations (Cho & Kim, 1999).

Table 3. Comparisons of Developments between City and County – before Consolidation: 1994, Korea.

	City	County
Ratio of Road Pavement (%)	92.5	82.6
Diffusion Ratio of Water Supply (%)	90.1	25.8
Diffusion Ratio of Sewerage (%)	53.6	43.3
Social Welfare (facilities number/10,000persons)	0.21	0.18
Medical Facilities (persons/a sickbed)	188	979
Per Capita GRP(million won)	4.02	2.89

Source: Oum and Hwang (1995:127).

Third, changes in the social and economic environments more generally affected the structure of local governments in Korea. In particular, economic changes in Korea made an impression on the structure of local governments. Changes caused by the era of globalization and economic openness with the inauguration of the

14   Reasons for the failure of the growth pole policy can be offered, including the setting of planning horizons of too short a duration, the lack of sustained commitment on the part of decision-makers, sudden changes in underlying conditions during the implementation phase, etc. (Parr, 1999). Parr suggested a number of more general reasons for it: the growth pole policy was inappropriate, infeasible, unrealistic, and its logic was violated.

WTO (World Trade Organization) system (1995) and the settlement of the UR (Uruguay Round) negotiations (1986) (Cohn, 2002)[15] required more world competitiveness of national or local governments. This was especially the case with the openness of agricultural products from 1997 by the UR negotiation; as a result, county governments composed largely of rural areas and agriculturally-based were faced with serious challenges to their economic competitiveness (Lim, 1995; Pai, Lee & Choe, 2000). This was also a problem in countries like Canada, where agriculture is an important economic component too (Cohn, 1990).

In this context, the national government of Korea found it increasingly necessary to introduce city-county consolidations. Discussions on consolidating were formalized by national or local politicians, the mass media and other elements of civil society.[16] Increasingly, the emerging policy consensus - by politicians, scholars and public officials – was that local governments should be consolidated.[17] There was general agreement, at least among all but a vocal opposition from some county residents, that city-county consolidation was an alternative to solve problems in Korea's urban areas.[18] So, though the issue of consolidation in North America was generally regarded as too difficult to handle (Rothblatt & Sancton, 1993), consolidation in Korea was designed by the national government and there was about 70% support for it of residents in cities and counties. The national government initiated this era of consolidation and directed the subsequent re-organizations. Therefore, 49 consolidated cities have been created through the process (shown in Table 4) since 1995 by "The Act on the Establishment of Urban-Rural Complex Typed Cities" (see Table 5).

---

15 On the development of international trade institutions such as the WTO see Cohn (2002).

16 The national government initiated the city-county consolidation. This consolidation in the beginning was a national government-initiated policy without the will of residents in cities and counties being considered. So, the national government utilized mass media and public officials in cities and counties to get residents' consent.

17 There were many opponents, who were residents, especially in counties. A poll in 1994 showed that about 30% of residents in cities and counties opposed their consolidations.

18 In general, urban area needs more lands to fill its scarcity and encroaches on its nearby rural areas.

Table 4. Process of Consolidation[19]

Stage	Contents
1	Residents' poll for consolidation and opinion survey of basic local councils, proposal of consolidation to area-wide local government
2	Opinion survey of area-wide local council, establishment of the basic plan for consolidation, proposal of consolidation to national government
3	National government's preparation and suggestion of legislative bill, decision of the National Assembly and proclamation
4	Operating plan development and application by the national government

Table 5. City-County Consolidations

Year	Number of Cases
1995	39
1996	5
1997	2
1998	1
2001	2
total = 49	

One of the characteristics of the consolidated cities is that they have large geographic areas for their population sizes (see Table 6). The total area of 32,372km^2 represents 32.6% of the national area of Korea; their average size is 719.4km^2 which surpasses the area of Seoul (605.5km^2) city. The total population of the consolidated cities is about 9.96 million persons, equal to 22.4 % of Korea's population. The average population is 221.4 thousand persons, which would belong to the category of a middle-sized Korean city (see Table 7).

---

19   The process of the city-county consolidation was prescribed by the Act on the Establishment of Urban-Rural Complex Typed Cities. Thus, it was equally applied to all cases.

Table 6. Distribution by Area Size of Consolidated Cities

Area Size (km²)	Number of Cities
1,000 or more	8
900 – 1,000	5
800 – 900	2
700 – 800	3
600 – 700	8
500 – 600	7
400 – 500	9
300 – 400	4
300 or less	3

Source: Korean Ministry of Government Administration and Home Affairs
(2001a)

Table 7. Distribution by Population Size of Consolidated Cities

Population Size (thousand persons)	Number of Cities
100 or less	2
100 – 200	28
200 – 300	11
300 – 400	5
400 – 500	2
500 or more	1

Source: Korean Ministry of Government Administration and Home Affairs
(2001a)

Challenges to city-county consolidation

There are several challenges to city-county consolidation in Korea:
the disparity between urban (city) and rural(county) areas;
the decreased citizen participation (especially in rural areas);
the problem of efficiency.

One of the greatest challenges facing city-county consolidated local
governments in Korea is the disparity between urban (city) and rural
(county) areas. Empirical studies have proved that consolidation failed

to create equitable or balanced development between urban and rural areas (Cho, 1996; Choe, 2001; Choi, 2000; Pai, Lee & Choe, 2000). While in the period from 1994 to 1998, the proportion of rural population in city-county consolidated local governments decreased from 44.3% to 39.8%, the proportion of urban population grew from 55.7% to 60.2% (Choe, 2001). This lower rural percentage was due to poorer development, which contributed to rural-urban migration that was reasonably connected with the distribution of urban service facilities between the two areas. A higher urban percentage in the proportion of service facilities encourages the rural population to move into urban settings; after consolidation, the proportion of service facilities in urban area grew from 64% to 72.3% (Choe, 2001). Before this consolidation, per capita expenditures in rural areas for social and economic developments were much higher than in urban ones; after consolidation, the rural areas were relatively disadvantaged in the investment for social and economic development (Pai, Lee & Choe, 2000).

Consolidation in Korea resulted in more differentiation in terms of urban vs. rural development because of the backwash effects which concentrated development benefits on urban areas. The development of traffic networks helped facilitate these backwash effects (Kim, 1996). In fact, many residents in rural areas, as Lipton (1988) pointed out, believe that the underdevelopment of rural areas owes much to the urban-biased nature of current economic development policy. They are anxious about urban-biased development based on an economic logic which ensures that economic investment effects are generated more in urban areas than in rural areas (Choi, 2000). Despite this finding, there has not been any adjustment in the national development policy.

Another challenge is decreased citizen participation (especially in rural areas). There are those who argue that larger government by consolidation will be more remote from the citizen and will discourage active citizen participation (Carver, 1973; Hong, 1997; Kernaghan & Siegel, 1987; Lim, 1994; Lyons & Lowery, 1989). According to one Korean case (Choi, 2000), citizen participation and citizen accessibility to public administration were exacerbated by city-county consolidation.[20] The distance – real and apparent – between

---

20   In a case research (Choi, 2000) using a questionnaire, for example, only 12% of respondents

consolidated government and its citizens is further than in the case of city-county separation – especially for citizens in rural areas (Choi, 2000). Rural political powers are also weaker than for citizens in urban areas because of population differentials. Urban classes have been able to win most of the rounds of struggle with rural classes.[21] In the process of establishing a consolidated city, a systematic skewing of the administrative processes involved favoring some (generally urban) interests and disadvantaging others (in rural settings). To be successful, this inequity ratio has to be improved.

The final challenge is the problem of efficiency. There was a proposition that city-county consolidation would bring about greater efficiency. As shown elsewhere in this volume – as with Golden and Slack in Metropolitan Toronto – the same policy promise has been made in other countries such as Canada. The proposition was proven to be erroneous in many research cases in Korea as well as in Canada (Cho & Kim, 1999; Choi, 2000; Kim, 2000). The failure to deal with the challenges raised by non-fulfillment of the efficiency policy promise may undermine the political system as well as the economy (Keller & Perry, 1991).

Consolidations: a summary

City-county consolidations in Korea have to be supplemented in terms of participation and development. First, a new idea and framework of participation is needed. That means more involvement of those affected by public services in defining and discovering needs and in helping to formulate remedies and carrying them out. Involvement in a service by the people who benefit from it has a danger that the result may be

---

answered that "the citizen participation and citizen accessibility to public administration have been improved by city-county consolidation."

21   There were objections to consolidation by what we call "local politics" like this. For example, in the United States, racial minorities in the 1970s and 1980s used urban government, the only level which they could hope to control, as a means of advancement and came to resist consolidation, which would reduce their voting power, and in the UK, Labour opposed the creation of the Greater London Council in 1963, seeing it as a mechanism to break their urban power base by the merger with the suburbs (Keating, 1995: 122). And it did. When Labour gained control again of the Greater London Council in the late 1970s, Margaret Thatcher abolished it.

selfish and sectional. This danger of selfishness could be overcome by a new body – such as the neighborhood council – an idea which comes largely from the American experience. The American neighborhood council idea is based on citizen participation and a decentralization of authority. In England, such neighborhood councils are an additional means of representation – particularly of minority and interest groups, or, for example, rural citizens – and a valuable sounding board of opinion. Like parish councils for rural areas (including rural boroughs), the neighborhood council could be helpful in ensuring more equitable democratic participation (on various forms of local democratic reform, see Stewart, 2003).

For real local democracy and autonomy, it is necessary to allocate the functions of consolidated cities based on a bottom-up strategy that seeks to place the emphasis on the provision of the basic needs of each sub-area's inhabitants. Consolidated governments must strategically ameliorate a sharing of the resource base between urban and rural areas in an effort to make it beneficial to rural areas if they are to avoid the pitfalls of unequal development – both economic and political. The most a consolidated city can hope to achieve is to establish a rational land use system as a new development plan system in an attempt to temper the negative effects, which would otherwise lead to further disordered sprawl and as a result deepen the unbalanced development between urban and rural areas. Its key elements are development control, management schemes in levels of comprehensiveness, flexibility and harmony between urban and rural areas and fostering more local democracy.

Metropolitan Governance Reconsidered in Korea

In the 1970s, when the industrialization of Korea was set about in earnest, the population of metropolises rose from about 3.6 million to about 14 million. These became important political, administrative and economic centers in Korea. Although there were differences according to the size of the city, continuous increases in population produced sprawl in the metropolises. Furthermore, increases in affluence, automobile use, highway expansion and plentiful quantities of land established opportunities for the metropolises' sprawl. By the year

2000, their collective population had reached about 23 million (see Table 8).[22] It accounted for more than half (53%) of the country's population. The metropolises' roles and importance escalated from the primary city to its surrounding region as well, and brought considerable investments in infrastructures, so that at present they dominate the urban sectors as well as the rural sectors in Korea. With a population of over 10 million, in particular, Seoul as Korea's capital city, emerged as a focus for Asia and the world.

Table 8. Metropolis Population: 2000, Korea

	Population	
National	44,116,305	(100.0)
Seoul	10,321,449	(23.4)
Pusan	3,831,454	(8.7)
Daegu	2,517,203	(5.7)
Incheon	2,524,251	(5.7)
Gwangju	1,359,646	(3.1)
Daejeon	1,368,287	(3.1)
Ulsan	1,027,280	(2.3)

Source: Korean Ministry of Government Administration and Home Affairs (2001a)

The continuous expansion of Korea's metropolises brought about sprawl in their surrounding areas. The metropolis and its adjacent areas perform specialized functions depending upon one another to carry out their respective functions. For example, the adjacent areas with many factories look to the metropolis for a wide range of business and commercial services provided by both public and private bodies. In return, the metropolis is dependent for a large part on its adjacent areas for the shelter of its work-force. Metropolises and their surrounding areas are more interdependent and interactive than ever. Furthermore, the development of traffic and telecommunication, good transport networks, a highly mobile population, and interlocking land uses accelerated this interdependency and interactivity between the two areas. The distinctions between the metropolis and its adjacent areas

---

22 By the 1980s four new metropolises were established (Daugu, Incheon, Gwangju, Daejeon) and one more – in Ulsan – was established in 1997 (see Table 1).

are becoming more blurred. The suburbs, like the areas surrounding its central city, have come to share problems with the central city (Gappert & Knight, 1982; Rosentraub & Nunn, 1994). As a result, problems with reorganizing service provision, local/regional governance, and intergovernmental relations have become increasingly obvious and pressing (Smith, 1995). Therefore, it has been argued, the relationships should be seen not as separate issues, but rather as integrated linkages and flows between the metropolis and its adjacent areas. This reorientation of attention provided a basis for metropolitan areas to be formed. That is, the fundamental interdependence suggested by these interconnections makes the need for metropolitan reforms more pressing in fast-growing metropolitan areas.[23] In Jacobs's terms, the metropolis-centered areas form one coherent city region (Jacobs, 1984) – and such city- regions are the engines of national economies.

A metropolitan area is a large identifiable area of continuous urbanization, often consisting of several administrative jurisdictions.[24] Although metropolises and their surrounding areas often have different administrative boundaries they are the same sphere for a host of activities including economy, society and culture. That is, the central city of the metropolis and the suburban zone around it have to be perceived as belonging to one (even if a sometimes vaguely delimited) urban system which has metropolis-centered spatial and functional integrations (Sin, *et al.*, 1992:70; Lee, *et al.*, 1988: 88).[25] The metropolitan area often has fragmented local governments, which seem

---

23   The establishment criteria of metropolitan areas differ according to scholars and nations. For example, there are SMSA (Standard Metropolitan Statistical Areas) and MSA (Metropolitan Standard Area) in the USA, Standard Metropolitan Labour Areas in the United Kingdom, Census Metropolitan Areas in Canada, and so on. In general the establishment criteria of a metropolitan area are the linkages (physical, economic, technological, service delivery, population, political and administrative) between a central city (metropolis) and its surrounding areas, as well as the urbanism of surrounding areas.

24   Demographers often classify cities with populations of more than 1 million people as a metropolis, and in common usage the term is widely employed to symbolize social, economic and political status. A metropolitan area is composed generally of the metropolis and its surrounding area.

25   For example, a Census Metropolitan Area in Canada is defined as a very large urban area (known as the urban core) together with adjacent urban and rural areas (known as urban and rural fringes) that have a high degree of social and economic integration with the urban core (Statistics Canada, 1996: 181; and 2001).

to be both the cause and the effect of sprawl (Razin & Rosentraub, 2000).

Table 9. Local Governments and Population in the Metropolitan Areas of Korea

Metro Area	Local Governments	Population (2000)
Seoul	Seoul (metropolis), Incheon (metropolis), Gyunggi (province)	20,965,413
Pusan	Pusan (metropolis), Ulsan (metropolis), Yangsan (city), Kimhae (city), Milyang (city), Geoje (city), Tongyoung (city), Masan·Changwon·Jinhae (cities)[26]	6,901,322
Daegu	Daegu (metropolis), Kyungsan (city), Cheongdo (county), Goryung (county), Youngcheon (city), Gunwi (county), Chilgok (county), Seongju (county)	2,939,093
Gwangju	Gwangju (metropolis), Naju (city), Jangseong (county), Hwasoon (county), Damyang (county), Hampyung (county)	1,564,588
Daejeon	Daejeon (metropolis), Gongju (city), Nonsan (city), Okcheon (county), Kumsan (county), Yungi (county), Cheongwon (county)	1,832,169

The spatial sphere of metropolitan areas in Korea differs according to researchers or establishment criteria. The Korean government does not have formal criteria as in North America (Kwon, 2001). This present research limits the spatial sphere of metropolitan areas in Korea to a metropolis and only its adjacent – and inter-linked – cities or counties, excepting Seoul (Capital) metropolitan area[27] (see Table 9 and Fig. 2). Although Korea has seven metropolises, this research

---

26   They are the conurbanized area, located near Pusan. Thus, many researches separate the conurbanized area, Masan-Changwon-Jinhae(cities), from Pusan metropolitan area.

27   The strong impacts of Seoul on its adjacent areas have led to close interactions with other areas within Kyunggi-do. Thus, Seoul (Capital) metropolitan area includes Seoul (metropolis), Incheon (metropolis), and Kyunggi-do (province), regardless of any criteria (Kwon, 2001).

suggests five metropolitan areas.[28] The population of the metropolitan areas in Korea has reached over 34 million, more than 77% of the national population. This has created what could be termed the emergence of an era of metropolitan Korea.

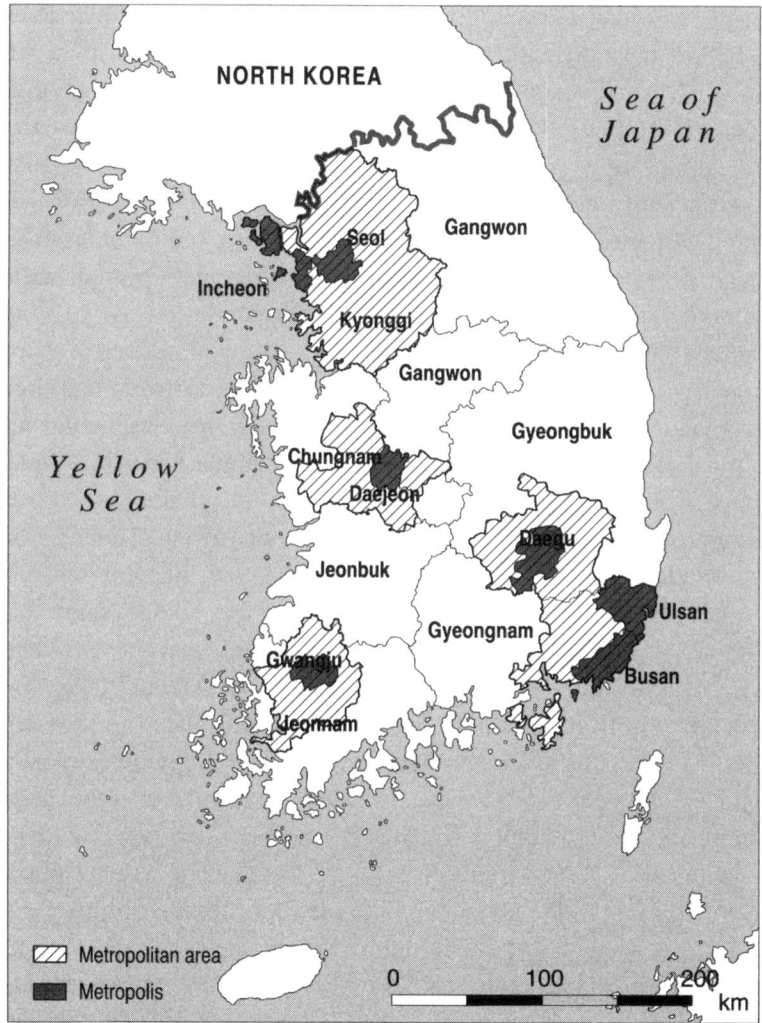

Figure 2: Metropolises and metropolitan areas in Korea

---

28   Korean Ministry of Construction and Transportation established six metropolitan areas –
     Seoul, Busan, Daegu, Daejeon, Gwangju, Masan-Changwon-Jinhac – to arrange a greenbelt
     in the year 2000 (Kwon, 2001).

Metropolitan-area problems and governance

Metropolitan areas represent most of the resources of Korea. They are centers of commerce and industry, fashion, culture and thought. Metropolitan areas are also wealthier and more populated than any other area in Korea. However, metropolitan areas are in trouble. These urban centers have difficulties that are referred to as "metropolitan-area problems"[29] (Altshuler *et al.*, 1999: 13), and failure to deal with them may undermine the political system and the economy of Korea as a whole. Among the key causes of metropolitan-area problems are diseconomies of scale and fragmentation. The one stems from the formation of metropolitan areas as a single system, the other from the mismatch between function and structure within metropolitan areas. Metropolitan-area problems can be classified by these causes.

First are the problems of *diseconomies of scale.* Physically and functionally, the rising flood of people in Korea's metropolitan areas has overwhelmed existing health, safety, sanitary, environmental and educational facilities and services. For example, in the highly urbanized centers, there is crime, air quality challenges, traffic congestion, unemployment, poverty, as well as conflicting and sometimes chaotic use of land. These city-regions are also burdened by high taxes and inflationary prices. Unlike many other small and medium-sized cities, metropolises have serious specific problems mainly because they are center cities in metropolitan areas. For example, they have increasingly experienced costs related to problems such as massive traffic congestion, lengthening commutes, poor air quality and loss of open space. Extensive sprawl and suburban developments have helped create a further scarcity of land; subsequently, this forced industry to move to adjacent areas (cities or counties); as a result, the tax base of the metropolises has shrunk. They have also faced increased expenditures on services for the incoming population from adjacent areas (cities or counties).

Moreover, because of economic globalization, technological change and interdependencies between the metropolis and its adjacent areas, government efforts to deal with transportation, pollution and land use

---

29 Metropolitan-area problems are defined as problems affecting the entire metropolitan area or significant parts of it, as well as problems caused by the characteristics of metropolitan areas.

problems in isolation will be ineffective. In this setting, the term "government" is no longer appropriate to describe the way populations and territories are organized and administered (OECD, 2001: 11). As Smith and Oberlander note – and Savitch and Vogel – *government* has in such circumstances often been superceded by *governance* (see elsewhere, this volume). Because of their metropolitan-wide character, the solution of these problems requires the development of comprehensive policies that pull together many of the disparate parts of the overall metropolitan area.

Second are the problems of *fragmentation*. In metropolises and their suburbs alike, citizens are beset by complexities that disturb their everyday lives because of a multiplicity of different governmental units in both areas; this is what is usually labelled as governmental fragmentation (Dente, 1990).[30] It is often argued that fragmented local governments in metropolitan areas are more inefficient for more capital-intensive services, since they cannot take advantage of decreased costs associated with economies of scale. The resulting fragmented system of local government in metropolitan areas has frequently been pointed to as a contributor to the unequal opportunity and disparity, and the costs threaten the future well-being of society (Altshuler *et al.*, 1999: 3–12).

Governments (or governance) in metropolitan areas must develop relevant substantive activities or processes designed to deal with a host of diverse and elusive metropolitan problems and implement them effectively. Individuals, groups within the community, and in different geographic areas, each seeing the world from their own perspective, tend to place different values and priorities upon the functions performed by public agencies. The divergence of views produces competition and conflicts among interests that should be resolved through the political process. The conventional machinery of public administration is thus confronted with social, physical, functional, and economic crises demanding new, often large-scale, unconventional responses. This is metropolitan governance. Metropolitan governance refers to the activities or processes for solving metropolitan problems rather than formal institutional definitions. Although governance is

30 Metropolitan areas that are more fragmented in jurisdictional terms tend to be more complexly organized in other ways (Parks & Oakerson, 1989).

generally taken to include the institutions of government,[31] it is essentially about activities or processes rather than institutional structures, by which we, as Osborne and Gaebler (1992, 24) have pointed out, collectively solve our problems and meet society's needs (Leach and Percy-Smith, 2001, 2–5). Metropolitan governance is the governance of a wider area – for example, a metropolis and its extended areas. So it is distinguished from the governance of individual, incorporated cities (Sancton, 2002). Metropolitan governance is the ability to produce coherent decisions, develop effective policies, and implement programs to solve metropolitan problems.[32] Metropolitan governance – where it works well – promotes cooperation and lessens differences in perception and action between a metropolis and its surrounding area.

Approaches to metropolitan governance and cases in Korea's metropolitan areas

The key concepts for metropolitan governance are boundaries, functions, special purpose bodies and tiers (Sancton, 2002). Savitch and Vogel (1996) suggest three types on a continuum, ranging from what they term *"avoidance and conflict"* non-cooperation models, such as New York, Los Angeles and St. Louis, through *"mutual adjustment"* – or partial cooperative approaches – as in Washington, DC., Louisville and Pittsburgh, to the most comprehensive form of regional cooperation – something approximating actual *"metropolitan government"* – as demonstrated by the experiences of Miami/Dade County, Minneapolis-St.Paul, Jacksonville and Portland, Oregon. Each represents different responses to regional pressures: metropolitan government (single tier, two tier), mutual adjustment (interlocal

---

31   The Committee on Improving the Future of US Cities Through Improved Metropolitan Area Governance defined metropolitan governance broadly to include governmental institutions within metropolitan areas, processes (the way in which groups participate, decisions are made, resources are allocated, and activities undertaken in metropolitan areas), and policies that influence the metropolitan area (Altshuler et al., 1999, 14).

32   Yates (1977) regarded the definition of governability as the capability of "producing coherent decisions, developing effective policies, and implementing .... programs", Dente (1990) made a similar point, suggesting ways to avoid problems of metropolitan governance.

agreements, public-private partnerships), and avoidance and/or conflict.

In general, there are three approaches to metropolitan governance (Bollens & Schmandt, 1982; Kim, 1992):

- consolidationist/amalgamation (one-tier)
- public choice (mutual adjustment, intergovernmental cooperation)
- two-tier system

First, the consolidationist approach takes the form of a single-tier unification. Consolidationists regard changing the boundaries under a one-tier system as a solution to metropolitan problems and the best way to achieve efficiencies.[33] Proponents point to the ability of the one-tier system to allocate public financial resources on the basis of needs of the different parts of the metropolitan area, thus eliminating great disparities between resources and needs that prevail when there are many local units. In contrast to these claims, opponents of the consolidationist approach most frequently argue in terms of loss of local control, decreased citizen access to public officials, and reduced attention to local services.[34] The consolidationist approach has involved three techniques: absorption of nearby unincorporated territory (annexation); merger of two municipalities (municipal consolidation or amalgamation); or merger of some or all of the municipal governments in a county with the county government (city-county consolidation).

An important characteristic of the structure of Korean governments before the mid-1990s was the strong concentration of power in the national government. Using this strong power, the national government unilaterally planned and implemented the reorganization of local government boundaries in metropolitan areas (Kim, 1993). The central government in Korea used the consolidationist approach as the most common method for the reorganization of local government boundaries

---

33 The logic of consolidation is based on economies of scale. However, it is losing its powers of persuasion because of recent assessments of technical progress which imply a decreasing importance of scale and agglomeration economies (Camagni & Pompili, 1990).

34 Consolidation makes decentralization more difficult, which formulates local governments near to their citizens and harmonizes public policies with public preferences (Bennett, 1990, 32).

to solve metropolitan problems. Some were successful – such as area-wide planning; other problems – such as continuing disparities between urban and rural areas – remained.

Annexation is a spatial policy pursued by local governments to promote urban development and to guide processes of urbanization. Annexation occurs when an incorporated place takes only a portion of the total area from another incorporated place (jurisdiction). Annexations in Korea occurred frequently without much difficulty, especially because of the role of the national government. Annexations of a small area adjacent to an existing metropolis provided it with room for growth. Small and medium sized cities need such annexations to develop into a metropolis and to meet the demands of land to accept the growing population and its related facilities. Annexations in Korea were due not to the necessity of the governments surrounding metropolises, but to the necessity of metropolises.[35] All metropolises in Korea used a number of annexations for the present status of their boundary configurations (see Table 10). Unlike other countries, annexation procedures in Korea require only an administrative determination by the national government without popular (by vote), legislative or judicial determination. The national government determines each case of boundary extension through a presidential decree.

Complicated political processes for annexation are not necessary. Within the Korean political and administrative context, it has been a simple task to restructure local government boundaries. Annexation in Korea was the prevalent form of local government reorganization. For example, Seoul's area has been expanded to 606.5 km^2 in 2001 from 328.2 km^2 in 1963 through three annexations, and Pusan with four annexations grew to 542.4 km^2 in 1994 from 343.3 km^2 in 1963. With the continuous population increase of metropolises they needed further annexations. In the end, some of them consolidated with their adjacent counties (see Table 11). Annexation was a simple and partial way to solve metropolitan problems, but it was not an effective solution to them.

---

35   In Canada, as many municipalities surrounding metropolises – Montreal and Toronto, for example – sank into bankruptcy (in some cases by design) because of excessively optimistic investment in expensive infrastructure, they were annexed by the metropolises (Sancton, 2000).

Table 10. Metropolis Annexations

	Cases
Seoul	3
Pusan	4
Daegu	3
Incheon	4
Gwangju	2
Daejeon	3
Ulsan	1

Source: Korean Ministry of Government Administration and Home Affairs
(2001b)

Metropolises hoped to amalgamate the adjacent areas, especially counties which had plenty of land, less political power, and limited impact of amalgamation on surroundings. In contrast, the dependence of counties on their neighboring metropolises was so serious that their development goals could not be achieved in isolation from neighboring metropolises. Five metropolises reorganized to consolidate, broaden, or strengthen the authority of metropolitan government. This occurred in Gwangju in 1988, and in Pusan, Daegu, Incheon and Ulsan in 1995 (see Table 11). For Gwangju's case in 1988, there were agreements amongst the three local-regional governments that allowed the national government to start with a consolidation not associated with conflict. The other – later – consolidations involved local conflict between the two governments.

Table 11. Metropolis-County Consolidations

	Metropolis-County
1988	Gwangju-Songjung (city)-Gwangsan
1995	Pusan-Gijang
1995	Daegu-Dalseong
1995	Incheon-Kanghwa, Ongjin
1995	Ulsan-Ulju

Source: Korean Ministry of Government Administration and Home Affairs
(2001b)

Second, the public choice approach is a process of mutual adjustment or cooperation. It basically supports the multiplicity of government and a multinucleated system in the metropolitan area. It is a partnership of municipalities and a consensual model. Advocates of public choice do accept the general proposition that small municipalities are indeed efficient and they respond more effectively to citizen concerns than do larger governments, seeing a metropolitan area as a vast public market in which citizens choose between contending public providers (Bish, 2001; Ostrom, Tiebout & Warren, 1961; Parks & Oakerson, 1989; Teaford, 1979). Robert Bish has labelled their alternative – local government amalgamations – as discredited 19th century ideas alive in the 21st century. (Bish, 2001). It can take the form of interlocal agreements or cooperation within a metropolitan area (Bollens & Schmandt, 1982; Rothblatt & Sancton, 1993) or, alternatively, public-private partnerships among business, government(s), and citizens in a metropolitan area (Peirce et al., 1993). In most cases, these arrangements do not yield formal institutions of metropolitan government but are carried out by existing agencies or networks of actors. One Canadian example of such a less-than-formal governmental arrangement is in the Greater Vancouver Regional District. As discussed elsewhere in this volume – by Smith and Oberlander – the regional district is indeed largely governance without government.[36]

The public choice approach includes several forms, including the following: interlocal agreement, transfer of functions, council of governments, public-private partnerships and area-wide city planning. This approach in Korea has received increased advocacy and use. As Table 12 indicates, all metropolises in Korea have councils of governments. Despite the popularity of the council mechanism, councils of governments are somewhat ineffective. They have no power to make – or at least to enforce - any policy to solve metropolitan problems and implement it. Since 1995, after a new president was elected in 1993, local autonomy in Korea was generally enhanced; there have been 78 cooperations among metropolitan governments – through interlocal agreements, via transfer of functions, for example – in fields such as water supply, sewage disposal, solid waste disposal, regional development and administrative functions (see Table 13). Although the cases of cooperation in Korea have tended to

---

36   Regional Districts are agencies responsible for the provision and/or administration of numerous services to local residents on the metropolitan area basis. In Greater Vancouver that is an amalgam of 21 municipalities and one electoral area.

increase gradually, they are regarded as incapable of producing sufficiently comprehensive results.

Table 12. Metropolitan Councils of Governments

	Governments
1988	Seoul, Incheon, Gyunggi(province), Gwangwon(province), Chungcheong(province)
1971	Pusan, Gyungnamdo(province)
1989	Daegu, Gyungbukdo(province)
1989	Gwangju, , Cheonnamdo(province)
1995	Daejeon, Chungbukdo(province), Chungnamdo(province)

Source: Korean Ministry of Government Administration and Home Affairs
(2001)

Table 13. Intergovernmental Cooperation Cases: 1995-2001

	Number of Cases
Metropolis-Province	74
Metropolis-City or County	4

Source: Korean Ministry of Government Administration and Home Affairs
(2001)

Third is the two-tier system. Under this system area-wide functions are allotted to area-wide governments while local functions remain with local units, thus creating a metropolitan-local system. This is a municipal federal/confederal model/two-tier system. It is a compromise or middle position between the extremes of more drastic consolidationist and more moderate public choice arrangements for attacking metropolitan problems (Kim, 1992; Sancton, 2002).

There are two types: a full two-tier system *by government* (federation), which features the establishment of a new area-wide government, and two-tier system *by instrumentality*, which has a new area-wide authority (district) or county (comprehensive urban county plan) of the restricted (one or a few) functions transferred from municipalities in the metropolitan area. The case of metropolitan Toronto, discussed elsewhere in this volume, highlights the first form. There were two cases of the two-tier system in Korea: they were single or multi-purpose, for example, school districts and associations. The

Local Autonomy Act stipulates the establishment and management of the associations which has considerable autonomy. These are special local governments: in terms of function, they might be single-purpose special districts. For example, in 1991, an association for the management of the reclaimed land in a Seoul metropolitan area – Seoul (metropolis), Incheon (metropolis), and Gyunggi (province) – was established. However, in 2000 it was abolished and changed into the nationally-owned corporation.

Conclusions

With the continued growth of intergovernmental needs and problems in metropolitan areas, the necessity of effective metropolitan governance in Korea has greatly increased in an effort to meet the challenges of adequate services and facilities. As a result of the addition of a chapter on area-wide city planning to the City Planning Act, it will be possible to manage land uses within a metropolitan area. However, the metropolitan-wide assessment of needs and resources and the establishment of sectoral and area priorities have seldom been undertaken on an ongoing basis. Although there are many methods in Korea, either metropolitan regions have not been mandated to undertake these specific tasks or their structure has not been designed to enable them to develop a metropolitan perspective.

A metropolitan policy continues to be lacking, and there is little coordination of spatial and socioeconomic planning for the metropolitan areas. As political and socioeconomic situations in Korea are considered, a method of metropolitan governance to get greater harmony between democracy and efficiency is needed. There is an example in Canada. The Regional District model in British Columbia is such a consensual model. It is a partnership of local municipalities/ districts/electoral areas that is responsible for the provision and/or administration of numerous services to local residents on a region-wide basis. Greater Vancouver's experience with its regional governance is illustrative here. It is a clear alternative to metropolitan restructuring being pursued in Korea – and elsewhere. The Greater Vancouver experience suggests that this more consensual model is not a peculiar event in one BC regional district either (Smith & Oberlander, 1998, and the Smith/Oberlander case in this volume). Its application to restructuring urban centers in Korea might prove fruitful.

References

Altshuler, A., Morrill, W., Wolman, H., & Mitchell, F. (eds.) (1999). *Governance and opportunity in Metropolitan America.* Washington, D.C.: National Academy Press.

Bennett, R.J. (1990). *Decentralization, local governments, and markets.* New York: Oxford University Press.

Bish, R. (2001). *Local Government Amalgamations: Discredited Nineteenth-Century Ideals Alive in the Twenty-First,* Toronto: C.D. Howe Institute Commentary: The Urban Papers, no.150, March.

Bollens, J.C., & Schmandt, H.J. (1982). *The metropolis.* New York: Harper and Row.

Camagni, R., & Pompili, T. (1990). Competence, power and waves of urban development: an Italian example. In: P. Nijkamp (ed.), *Sustainability of urban systems: A cross-national evolutionary analysis of urban innovation.* Avebury: Aldershot, pp. 37–86.

Carver, J. (1973). Responsiveness and consolidation: A case study. *Urban Affairs Quarterly* 9, 211–249.

Cho, B-H., & Kim, D.-W. (1999). The scale of local government and its productivity. *Korean Public Administration Quarterly* 11(2), 345–361.

Cho, S-J. (1996). *The analysis of operation performance of city-county complex typed City.* Korea Research Institute for Local Administration, vol. 96-1.

Choe, J-S. (2001). A study on evaluation of city-county consolidation policy. *Korean Policy Studies Review* 10(1), 55–82.

Choi, R-I. (2000). A study on the effectiveness of city-county consolidation: The case of Yeosu City. *Journal of Korean Association for Local Government Studies* 12(3), 169–188.

Choi, Y.-B., & Yoon, W.-G. (1993). Establishing city-county administration area in terms of city-county consolidation. *The Korea Local Administration Review* 8(2), 87–104.

Cohn, T.H. (1990). *The International Politics of AgriculturalTrade.* Vancouver: University of British Columbia Press.

Cohn, T.H. (2002).*Governing Global Trade: International Institutions in Conflict and Convergence,* Aldershot: Ashgate.

Dente, B. (1990). Metropolitan governance reconsidered, or how to avoid errors of the third type. In Research Committee on the Structure and Organization of Government of the International Political Science Association, *Governance: An International Journal of Policy and Administration* 3(1), 55–74.

Dolan, D.A. (1990). Local government fragmentation: Does it drive up the cost of government? *Urban Affairs Quarterly* 26, 28–45.

Gappert, G., & Knight, R.V. (1982). Urban management and the future. In: G. Gappert & R.V. Knight (eds.), *Cities in the 21st Century.* Beverly Hills: Sage, pp. 335–348.

Hong, J-H. (1997). An evaluation of local government restructuring by city-county consolidation. *Korean Society and Public Administration* 8(2), 59–90.

Jacobs, J. (1984). *Cities and the Wealth of Nations: Principles of Economic Life.* New York: Random House

Keating, M. (1995). Size, efficiency and democracy: consolidation, fragmentation and public choice. In: D. Judge, G. Stoker, & H. Wobnan (eds.), *Theories of urban politics.* London: Sage, pp. 117–134.

Keller, L.F., & Perry, D.C. (1991). The structures of government. In: R.D. Bingham (ed.), *Managing local government: Public administration in practice.* Newbury Park, Cal.: Sage, pp. 31–58.

Kernaghan, K., & Siegel, D. (1987). Structures and Politics of Local Government Administration. In: K. Kernaghan & D. Siegel, *Public Administration In Canada: A Text.* Toronto: Nelson, pp. 587-612.

Kim, I-S. (1992). A study on the redesign of Seoul metropolitan governance system. *Korean Public Administration Review* 25(4), 329–352.

Kim, J-H. (2000). A study on the effect of city-county consolidation on efficiency changes of local governments. *Korean Policy Studies Review* 9(2), 47–66.

Kim, S-K. (1996). Urban planning system of city-county consolidated cities. *The Korea Local Administration Review* 11(1), 117–141.

Kim, W. (1993). *Urban Administration.* Seoul: Pakyoungsa.

Korean Association for Local Government Studies (1999). *Theories of Korean local autonomy,* Seoul: Samyoungsa.

Korean Ministry of Government Administration and Home Affairs (2001a). *Municipal Yearbook of Korea.*

Korean Ministry of Government Administration and Home Affairs (2001b. *General review of local administrative districts.*

Kwon, Y-W. (2001). The delineation of the Seoul metropolitan region in Korea. *Journal of the Korean Planners Association* 36(7), 197–219.

Leach, R., & Percy-Smith, J. (2001). *Local governance in Britain.* New York: Palgrave.

Lee, J-H. *et al.* (1988). *A study on the governance of metropolitan area.* Seoul: Korean Research Institute for Local Administration.

Lim, C-H. (1995). The evolutionary process and future problems of city-county consolidation. In: Korea Land Corporation. *Land Research* 6(5), 6–26.

Lim, S-I. (1994). Administrative and financial problems of city-county consolidated city. *Urban Affairs* 29, 44–59.

Lipton, M. (1988). Why poor people stay poor: urban bias in world development. In: J. Gugler (ed.), *The urbanization of the Third World.* New York: Oxford University Press, pp. 40–51.

Lyons, W.E., & Lowery, D. (1989). Governmental fragmentation versus consolidation: Five public-choice myths about how to create informed, involved, and happy citizens. *Public Administration Review* 49(6), 533–543.

OECD (2001). *Cities for citizens: Improving metropolitan governance,* France: OECD Publications.

Osborne, D., & Gaebler, T. (1992). *Reinventing government.* Reading: Addison Wesley.

Ostrom, V., Tiebout, C.C., & Warren, R. (1961). The Organization of Government in Metropolitan Areas: A Theoretical Inquiry. *American Political Science Review* 55, 831-842.

Oum, K-C., & Hwang, S.-S. (1995). *A study on the directions of development planning and investment policy for the city-county unified cities.* Korea Research Institute for Human Settlements 95–15.

Pai, I-M., Lee, M.-S., & Choe, J.S. (2000). The performance evaluation of city-county consolidations: Focused on the financial effect. *Korean Policy Studies Review* 9(1), 139–161.

Park, J-G. (2000). Can the industrial merger theory explain the structure/process of local government consolidation? *Korean Public Administration Review* 34(4), 303–322.

Parks, R.B., & Oakerson, R.J. (1989). Metropolitan organization and governance. *Urban Affairs Quarterly* 25(1), 18-29.

Parr, J.B. (1999). Growth-pole strategies in regional economic planning: A retrospective view. *Urban Studies* 36(8), 1247–1268.

Peirce, N.R., Johnson, C.W., & Hall, J.S. (1993). *Citystates: How urban American can prosper in a competitive world*. Washington, DC: Seven Locks.

Razin, E., &Rosentraub, M. (2000). Are fragmentation and sprawl interlinked? North American evidence. *Urban Affairs Review* 35(1), 821-836.

Rondinelli, D.A. (1985). *Applied methods of regional analysis: The spatial dimensions of development policy*. Boulder: Westview.

Rosentraub, M. S., & Nunn, S. (1994). City and suburbs: linkages, benefits, and shared responsibilities. Indianapolis: Center for Urban Policy and the Environment.

Rothblatt, D.N., & Sancton, A. (eds.) (1993). *Metropolitan governance: American/Canadian intergovernmental perspectives*. Berkeley: Institute of Governmental Studies Press.

Sancton, A. (2000). The municipal role in the governance of Canadian cities. In: T. Bunting & P. Filion (eds.), *Canadian cities in transition*. Ontario: Oxford University Press, pp. 425–442.

Sancton, A. (2002). Metropolitan and regional governance. In: E.P. Fowler & D. Siegel (eds.), *Urban policy issues: Canadian perspectives*. Ontario: Oxford University Press, pp. 54–68.

Savitch, H.V. (1994). Reorganization in three cities: Explaining the disparity between intended actions and unanticipated consequences. *Urban Affairs Quarterly* 29, 565–595.

Savitch, H.V., & Vogel, R.K. (eds.) (1996). *Regional Politics: America In A Post-City Age*. Thousand Oaks, Cal.: Sage.

Schultze, W.A. (1985). *Urban politics: A political economy approach*. New Jersey: Prentice-Hall.

Sin, J-C. *et al.* (1992). *A study on the establishment and management of metropolitan area*. Seoul: Korean Research Institute for Human Settlement.

Smith, P.J. (1995). Governing metropolitan change: Public policy and governance in Canada's city regions. In: J. Lightbody (ed.), *Canadian Metropolitics: Governing Our Cities*. Toronto: Copp Clark, pp. 161–192.

Smith, P.J., & Oberlander, H.P. (1998). Restructuring metropolitan governance: Greater Vancouver – British Columbia reforms. In: D.N. Rothblatt & A. Sancton (eds.), *Metropolitan governance revisited: American/Canadian intergovernmental perspectives*. Berkeley: Institute of Governmental Studies Press, pp. 371–405.

Statistics Canada (1996). *1996 census dictionary*. Cat. No. 92-351-XPE.

Statistics Canada, *Canadian Census, 2001*. Ottawa: Supply and Services Canada, 2002.

Stewart, K. (2003). *Think Democracy: Option for Local Democratic Reform in Vancouver*. Vancouver: Institute of Governance Studies, Simon Fraser University.

Teaford, J.C. (1979). *City and Suburb: The Political Fragmentation of Metropolitan America – 1850-1970*, Baltimore: John Hopkins University Press.

Yates, D. (1977). *The Ungovernable City: The Politics of Urban Problems and Policy Making*. Cambridge, Mass.: MIT Press.

Yu, B-U. (1994). A fundamental discussion for reforming local government structure: Key research issues in si-kun consolidation. *Korean Public Administration Review* 28(2), 525–541.

ERAN RAZIN

Initiatives to Reform Metropolitan Governance in Israel:
a Sisyphean Task?

Introduction

Israel's local government system has not been consciously reformed
for over half a century. It is basically a single-tier system, composed of
cities, smaller urban local councils and rural regional councils (the
latter having lower-tier village committees), with no form of
metropolitan or regional government. Although numerous amendments
were made in the 1934 municipal ordinance and the 1941 local
councils ordinance, the legal basis of the system still largely dates back
to the British Mandate that preceded the establishment of Israel in
1948. Incremental changes in the local government map included the
establishment of new local authorities, annexation of land to existing
local authorities and transfer of land from one local authority to
another. A marked change in local government finance that occurred in
the mid- 1980s, was largely unintentional and not part of a conscious
reform. The only major intentional change made in the local
government system was the move from council-elected mayors to
directly elected ones in cities and local councils in 1975 and later also
in regional councils (Razin, 2004).

   Thus, Israeli local government has shown a remarkable resistance to
far-reaching reforms. Proposals that were raised periodically and a
perpetual discourse of reform produced little change. This paper first
describes briefly attributes of Israel's four metropolitan areas and then
sums up the agenda for reform in each of these metropolitan areas,
demonstrating the discourse for metropolitan reform between the 1960s
and 1990s. It then discusses how the severe political and economic
crisis of the early 2000s has influenced the agenda, perhaps opening a
window of opportunity to implement changes that were not feasible in
previous decades.

Israel's metropolitan areas

Definitions

Four metropolitan areas can be defined in Israel in the early 2000s: Tel Aviv, Haifa, Jerusalem and Beer Sheva. Only three of them are formally defined by Israel's Central Bureau of Statistics (CBS) (Figure 1). The metropolitan area of Jerusalem has no formal statistical definition because much of it is in the West Bank, beyond the formal boundaries of the State of Israel. The delineation of the four metropolitan areas presented in Figure 2 accepts the formal statistical definitions for the Tel Aviv and Haifa metropolitan areas. It provides an informal definition for the Jerusalem metropolitan area and suggests a narrower definition for the Beer Sheva metro, excluding vast tracts of extremely sparsely populated desert and rural areas that probably do not have functional ties with Beer Sheva of a magnitude that justifies inclusion.

Tel Aviv

The Tel Aviv metropolis is Israel's economic and cultural heart. It is approaching three million inhabitants and is predominantly Jewish (Table 1). The demarcation of this metropolitan area, made by the CBS prior to each of the censuses of population and housing held between 1961 and 1995, shows remarkable expansion (Figure 3). However, the expansion of the metropolis according to these definitions is an overestimation of its actual expansion, because it reflects the diminishing weight given to the continuity of built-up area criteria and the growing weight awarded to functional linkages. Nevertheless, most substantial spatial expansion and population growth did take place, and in the 1990s this spatial expansion also reflected the diminishing distinction between urban and rural space, as rural settlements have become fully integrated in metropolitan activity patterns.

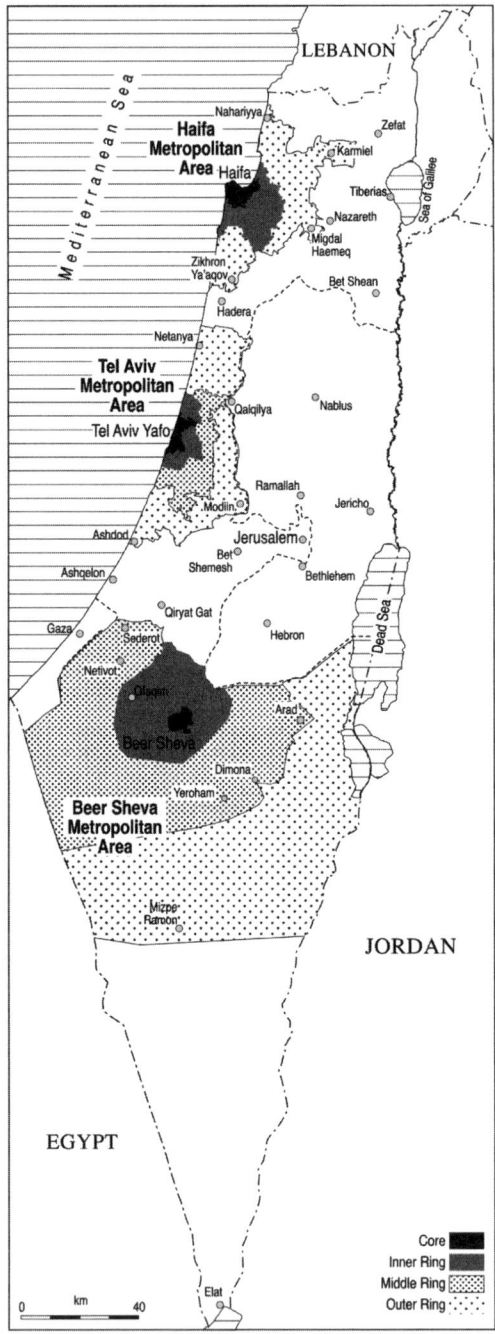

Figure 1: The three metropolitan areas in Israel according to the definition of
Israel's Central Bureau of Statistics, 2002

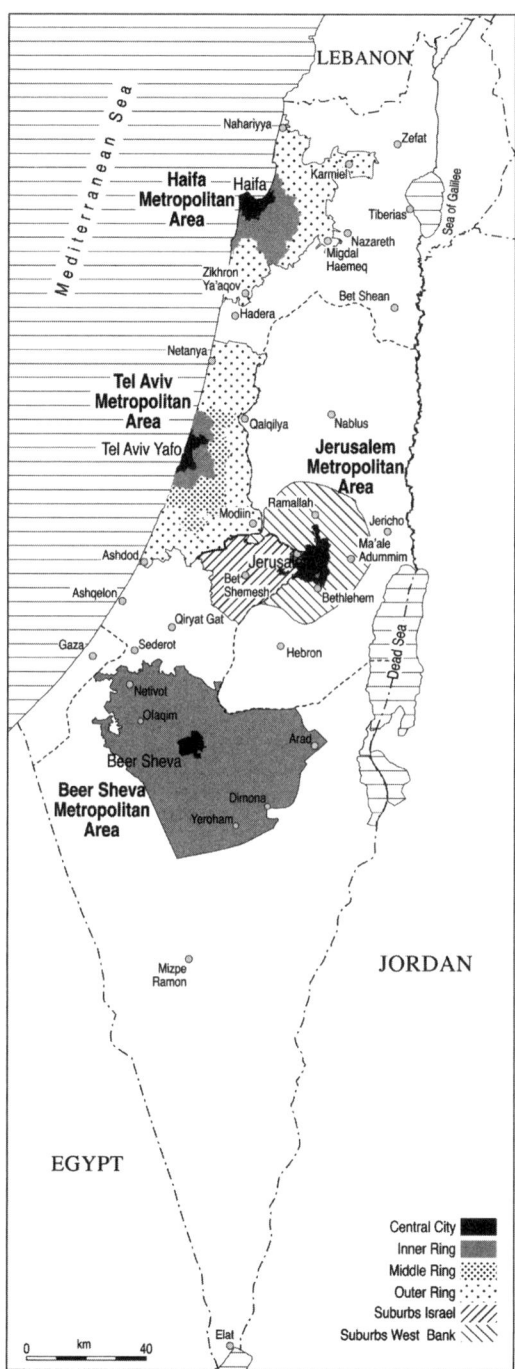

Figure 2: Israel's four metropolitan areas – author's definition, 2002

Table 1: Population in Israel's four metropolitan areas, 2002

	Tel Aviv metro	Haifa metro	Jerusalem metro[1]	Beer Sheva metro[2]
Population – total (thousands)	2889.8	971.3	906.4	457.6
Jews	2626.1	653.8	662.0	303.0
Arabs (inc. Druze)	138.0	264.8	229.8	127.1
Others	125.7	52.7	14.6	27.5

1. The Jerusalem metropolitan area includes two, perhaps three, distinct parts. The first consists of areas within the State of Israel (including annexed East Jerusalem). The second consists of Jewish settlements in the West Bank that functionally form part of the metropolis. The third consists of Palestinian localities formally controlled by the Palestinian National Authority that geographically form an integral part of the metropolis, but in recent years functionally have very limited ties with the Israeli metropolis. The above statistics thus refer only to the first two parts. It can be estimated that Palestinian localities include about 500,000 inhabitants.
2. The definition of the Beer Sheva metropolis used in this paper is narrower than that defined by the CBS in 2000 that includes vast empty or sparsely populated rural areas.

Taking into account the spatial expansion of the Tel Aviv metropolis, it can be assumed that the share of this metropolis in Israel's total population has been fairly stable at around 44–45 percent. Economically it is even more dominant; thus any strong form of metropolitan government encompassing the whole metropolis could have become an extremely powerful political agent challenging the powers of central government ministries.

The Tel Aviv metropolis is characterized by the highest levels of economic well-being in Israel. A prominent feature of its social geography is a north-south divide – the north tends to be wealthier than the south. This distinction is evident within the city of Tel Aviv, but extends also to the suburbs. However, despite of this divide, suburban Tel Aviv is heterogeneous in each of its parts and forms a complex mosaic (Gonen, 1995).

With an average local authority size of above 40,000 inhabitants (Table 2), local government in the Tel Aviv metropolis is more fragmented than most Canadian metropolitan areas, but not extremely fragmented from an international comparative perspective and less fragmented than local government in the rest of Israel. Still, more than one third of the local authorities in the Tel Aviv metropolitan area have less than 10,000 inhabitants. Close to 60% of the metropolitan population lives in cities that have more than 100,000 inhabitants, but the central city – Tel Aviv – includes only 360,000 inhabitants – 12.5% of the metropolitan population.

Table 2: Israel's four metropolitan areas, basic local government statistics, 2002

	Tel Aviv metro	Haifa metro	Jerusalem metro	Beer Sheva metro[1]
No. of localities	258	132	114	71
No. of local authorities	69	47	14	21
Cities	28	13	4	6
Local councils	28	28	7	10
Regional councils	13	6	3	4
Local industrial councils	0	0	0	1
Average population of local authorities	41,628	21,477	64,743	21,210
% local auth. up to 5000 inhabitants	20.3	12.8	21.4	5.0
% local auth. up to 10,000 inhabitants	37.7	48.9	35.7	55.0
% local auth. Over 100,000 inhabitants	13.0	2.1	7.1	5.0
% population in loc. Auth. <5,000	1.6	1.7	1.0	1.1
% population in loc. Auth. <10,000	4.1	14.7	2.3	17.1
% population in loc.auth. >100,000	57.9	26.8	75.1	42.8

1. A significant population of Bedouin lives outside the jurisdictional area of any local authority.

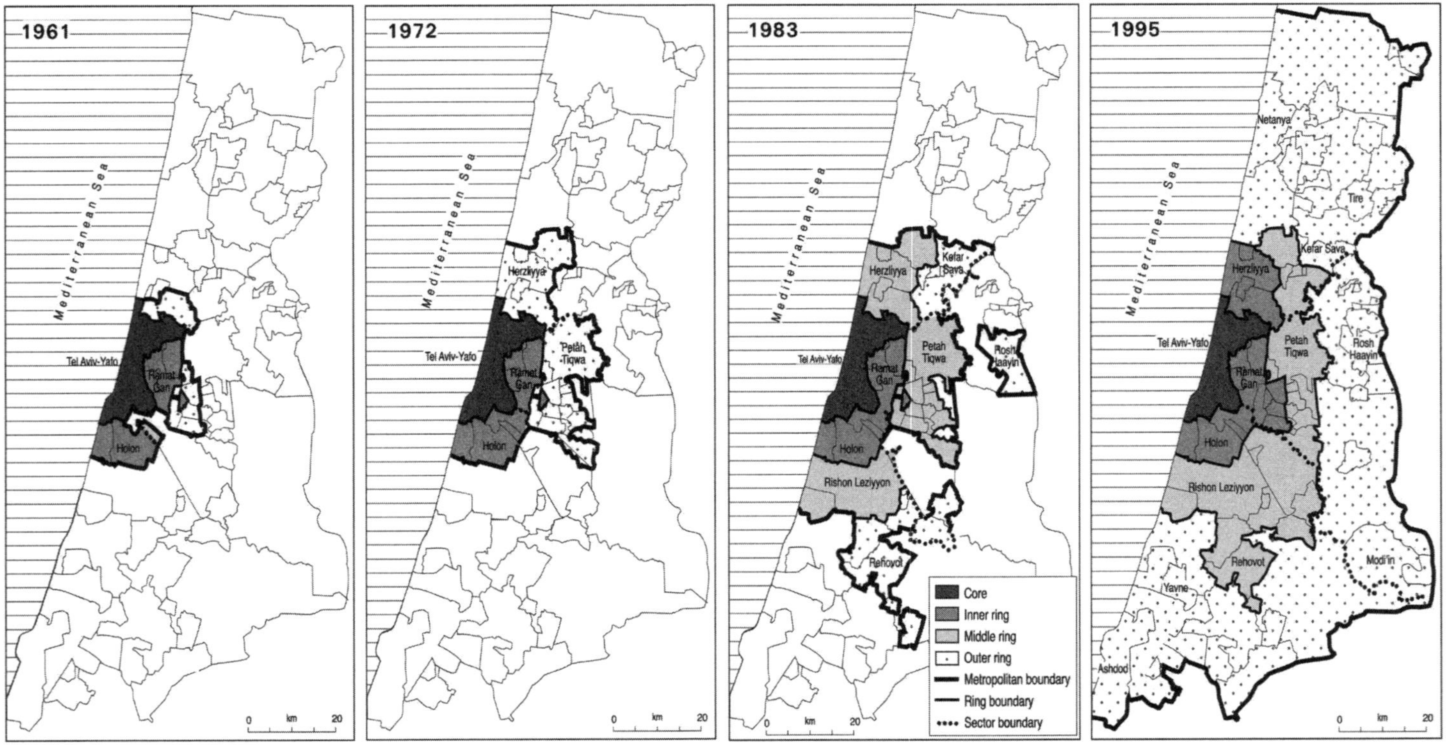
1961
1972
1983
1995
Mediterranean Sea
Tel Aviv-Yafo
Ramat Gan
Holon
Herzliyya
Petah Tiqwa
Kefar Sava
Rosh Haayin
Rishon Leziyyon
Rehovot
Netanya
Tire
Modi'in
Yavne
Ashdod
Core
Inner ring
Middle ring
Outer ring
Metropolitan boundary
Ring boundary
Sector boundary
0 km 20

Figure 3: Expansion of the Tel Aviv metropolitan area according to formal definitions of Israel's Central Bureau of Statistics, 1961–1995

Haifa

Haifa is Israel's second largest metropolitan area (Table 1), serving as the hub of northern Israel and as one of Israel's two major ports. The relative importance of Haifa has gradually declined since the establishment of the State in 1948. It lost its status as Israel's largest port, some of its heavy industry moved to more peripheral locations where capital incentives have been available, and the Tel Aviv metropolis even somewhat eclipsed Haifa as a major business center for the Galilee. However, a cluster of high-technology enterprises and other industries has retained the economic vitality of this metropolis.

Topography is a major attribute that influences the spatial structure of the Haifa metropolis. The central city of Haifa, predominantly Jewish since 1948, is largely middle class, with the more affluent population residing on the Mount Carmel ridge. The inner suburbs are largely lower-middle class, consisting of Jewish cities in the Haifa Bay, two Druze towns (amalgamated in 2003) on top of Mount Carmel, and a single Jewish town at the southwestern entrance to Haifa. The outer suburbs – considered as part of this metropolis only since the 1990s – are a complex mix of Jewish cities and towns, Jewish exurban settlements, Jewish rural settlements and Arab localities of all types. It is mostly middle to lower class, except for Jewish exurban and some rural settlements.

The boundaries of the Haifa metropolis are hard to define. A large Arab hinterland exists in the central Galilee, just beyond its metropolitan boundaries (except for its northern part, included within metropolitan boundaries along with the Jewish city of Karmiel). It is unclear whether the central Galilee will form in the future a separate metropolitan area, centered perhaps in Nazareth or whether the Haifa metropolis will absorb this region. As of the mid-1990s, internal links within the central Galilee and external links with Haifa did not justify either of the two definitions.

The Haifa metropolis is much more municipally fragmented than the Tel Aviv metropolis, largely because of the small size of most local authorities in its outer ring. The city of Haifa is the only one in the metropolis with a population of over 50,000. However, its 271,000 inhabitants form only 27% of the metropolitan population.

Jerusalem

The Jerusalem metropolitan area (Figure 4) has a dominant central city – the largest in Israel – with close to 700,000 inhabitants, 66% Jewish and 33% Arab. Most spatial deconcentration processes until the 1980s took place within Jerusalem, whose jurisdictional boundaries were greatly expanded after the 1967 war to include Arab East Jerusalem, some Arab suburbs and open space where large Jewish neighborhoods were subsequently built. Suburbanization beyond the municipal boundaries of the central city accelerated only since the 1980s.

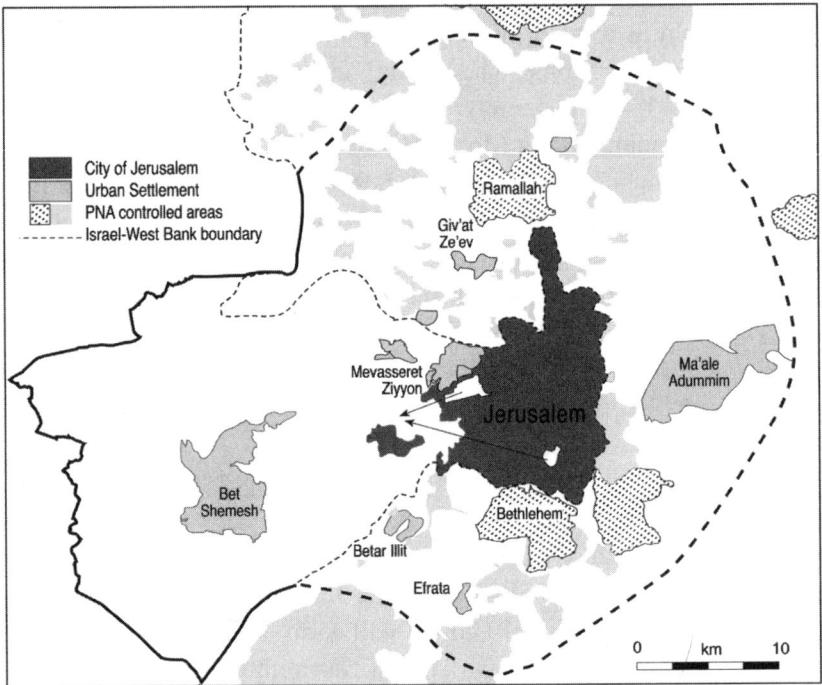

Figure 4: The Jerusalem metropolitan area

Within the official boundaries of Israel the Jerusalem metropolis roughly includes the Jerusalem District. Nevertheless, much of the suburbanization flows since the 1980s have been to adjacent Jewish settlements in the West Bank. The population of these settlements was roughly equal to that of the Jerusalem District (not including Jerusalem) in 2002, but both suburban parts included only 25% of the total metropolitan population (not including cities and localities that form part of the Palestinian National Authority).

Jerusalem has traditionally served as a central city for the Palestinian West Bank. About 500,000 Palestinian Arabs live in localities that can be considered as part of the Jerusalem metropolis included in the Palestinian National Authority since 1994. Access for residents from these localities to Jerusalem has become increasingly difficult since the commencement of the first Intifada in 1987, and their ties with the Israeli metropolis of Jerusalem are rather limited.

Spatial structure of the Jerusalem metropolis is shaped by its unique geopolitical situation and the major cleavages between Israelis and Palestinians and between ultra-orthodox Jews and secular/non-ultra-orthodox Jews. Pre-1967 western Jerusalem is a mix of middle class, lower to middle class, secular, religious and ultra-religious Jewish neighborhoods. Eastern Jerusalem, annexed by Israel in 1967, actually surrounds western Jerusalem to the north, east and south and is now a mix of Arab neighborhoods of diverse character and large Jewish neighborhoods. The western suburbs of Jerusalem (within Israel's boundaries) largely consisted until the 1980s of below middle class rural population and two poor immigrant towns. However, substantial suburbanization and exurbanization of the middle class has taken place in the last two decades. Extensive suburbanization of diverse populations has taken place also in Jewish settlements in the West Bank: several cities and towns and numerous Jewish villages. The ultra-religious population of Jerusalem also suburbanized substantially into specific fast-growing localities.

Deteriorating Jewish-Arab relations profoundly influenced the spatial structure of the Palestinian part of the Jerusalem metropolis. Jerusalem lost much of its central city functions, practically transferred to Ramallah due to travel barriers between Jerusalem and the West Bank and because Ramallah has become the major seat of government of the Palestinian National Authority. The advantageous position of Palestinians living under Israeli control in Jerusalem and fears of Palestinians to lose Jerusalem residency benefits, such as social security, has constrained suburbanization of Palestinians from Jerusalem to suburbs in the West Bank. It even encouraged a trend of counter migration of Palestinians who had previously left Jerusalem to nearby West Bank localities.

The Jerusalem metropolis (excluding the PNA) is the least fragmented metropolitan area and 75% of its population still resides in its central city (Table 2). Despite increasing suburbanization and the complex problems within the city of Jerusalem, no suburban city has managed so far to become a competing node in size, employment concentration and economic-well being. It seems that the more substantial economic competition to Jerusalem comes from the adjacent Tel Aviv metropolitan area, rather than from Jerusalem's suburbs.

Beer Sheva

The Beer Sheva metropolis has been acknowledged as such only since the 1990s. It is located in Israel's southern periphery, largely in a semi-arid and arid environment. The population of the Beer Sheva metropolis grew considerably during the 1990s. The metropolis absorbed a large number of new immigrants from the former USSR, mainly attracted by inexpensive housing available in this region. The Bedouin-Arab population has also grown rapidly and constitutes, at present, about 28% of the metropolitan population (Table 1).

The Beer Sheva metropolis is both the poorest in Israel and rather polarized. A large proportion of its population consists of lower-middle class and lower class Jewish immigrants and descendents of immigrants from Arab countries, who reside in the city of Beer Sheva, in low status development towns and in some rural settlements. Fast-growing poor Arab-Bedouin population is spread in several planned towns around Beer Sheva, characterized by lowest socioeconomic status, and in numerous informal settlements that do not form part of any local authority. The relatively small middle class population increasingly concentrates in few exurban settlements around Beer Sheva, characterized by the highest socioeconomic status.

Despite rapid demographic growth, Beer Sheva is not a typical metropolitan area. The city of Beer Sheva functions as a dominant regional service center, but there is no substantial concentration of built-up area around the central city. Suburbanization is rather limited except for three exurban settlements. Otherwise, localities in this region do not attract substantial population flows from Beer Sheva, and those coming from elsewhere are usually not attracted to the region because of particular employment opportunities offered in its central city. The metropolitan area includes some major out-of-town regional employment centers – mainly heavy chemical industries, mineral-extracting plants and the Nuclear Research Center – but these do not represent a typical process of employment deconcentration.

The discourse of metropolitan reform between the 1960s and the 1990s

Early centralization and the lack of interest in reform
Metropolitan reforms were not on the public agenda before the 1960s in the new small and rather centralized State of Israel. Emphasis in the early phases of state-building was on the development of central state institutions. The country's population was rather small, reaching two million only in 1958. Metropolitan areas were modest in size and hardly recognized as such. Public attention mainly focused on the absorption of new immigrants in Israel's peripheral regions, and on the establishment of new local authorities for new urban and rural localities, rather than on the restructuring of Israel's core areas in the name of principles such as efficiency, development or equality. A weak and fragmented local government could have even served to assure practical control by central government ministries of functions performed by local authorities.

Metropolitan reforms first appeared on the public agenda during the 1960s, when the "entrepreneurial" phase of state-building gave way to more mature and formal forms of public decision-making. Rapid economic growth was accompanied by expansion of welfare state mechanisms, thus steps associated with the welfare state elsewhere, such as metropolitan reforms carried out in Canada and Britain and other Western European and North American countries, inspired similar proposals in Israel.

The Tel Aviv metropolis – does Israel's world city deserve a world city type reform?
Tel Aviv has apparently been the most suitable Israeli metropolitan area for experimentation with wide-scale reforms that resemble those implemented in major metropolitan areas in North America and Europe. Not only has it been Israel's largest and closest to the

definition of a world city, it has also been Israel's most "ordinary" metropolitan area that fits textbook generalizations on structure and development of metropolitan areas. The main attempt to implement a comprehensive metropolitan reform in Israel took place in the early 1970s and indeed involved the inner part of the Tel Aviv metropolis. The initiative was influenced by the era of welfare state metropolitan reforms in Western Europe and North America. However, the proposed reform was not implemented and little happened since then. The economically and politically powerful cities of the Tel Aviv metropolis have been able to block various proposals to impose changes that consisted mainly of amalgamations of specific suburban local authorities.

The earliest proposal, made by a Ministry of Interior commission in 1965, was to establish a multi-purpose municipal union in the Tel Aviv metropolis. Municipal unions have been the only legal form of municipal cooperation in Israel. Based on a 1955 legislation, such unions are usually formed to perform a specific function, such as sewerage, fire control or environmental quality. They are rather weak, unable to levy taxes and dependent on the transfer of funds from the cooperating municipalities; hence they comprise only a miniscule share of local government expenditures. The initiative did not get far, but led in 1970 to a more far-reaching proposal to establish a strong upper-tier municipality for the inner part of the Tel Aviv metropolis.

A commission headed by C. Ben Shachar was appointed by the government to assess the proposal. Its report (Israeli Institute for Urban Research and Information, 1973) referred to the cities of Tel Aviv, Ramat Gan, Givatayim, Bene Beraq, Holon and Bat Yam. The report identified the problems of municipal fragmentation, such as lack of coordination, lack of a broad vision of growth patterns and disparities between central cities and suburbs. The evaluation of alternatives in the report revealed that all criteria supported the establishment of a two-tier municipal structure with a strong upper-tier metropolitan municipality. A metropolitan municipality would enable a more efficient allocation of resources and enjoy economies of scale in providing services. It is a just solution in terms of income distribution, and better reflects local preferences. A metropolitan municipality strengthens the power position of the metropolis. It would attract quality personnel and enjoy additional fiscal and organizational advantages. In summary, according to the Ben Shachar report, all criteria support the establishment of a strong metropolitan municipality, and not even one (!) criterion was found to point, for example, to a decentralized alternative of separate municipal unions as a preferred alternative. The report recommended, therefore, to establish an upper-tier metropolitan municipality, whose council and chairman would be appointed by the lower-tier elected municipalities. The report proposed to grant extensive authority and to transfer a broad range of functions to the metropolitan municipality.

The report's recommendations were not implemented, although they enjoyed, at least officially, the support of the government and of the mayors. The change in the political map of the metropolis after the local elections of December 1973 was the direct cause for the burial of the report. The new mayor of Tel Aviv – Shlomo Lahat – did not support the initiative, and the Labor-controlled central government was reluctant to give a new power base to cities that were now largely controlled by the Likud party.

Furthermore, it was argued (Razin, 1996) that the Ben Shachar report, while based on a comprehensive analysis, did not fully reflect the complexity of the issue and the tradeoff inherent in each option. Disadvantages and risks in establishing a metropolitan municipality were not mentioned, and only political constraints were identified as factors that could justify limitations on the magnitude of functions transferred to the metropolitan municipality. Despite the wealth of data collected and evaluated by the commission, it seems that its recommendations were largely based on the common wisdom that prevailed in the era of large metropolitan reforms in the Western world at the time.

No serious attempt at a comprehensive metropolitan reform was made since then. In 1976, a proposal for amalgamating local authorities in the Ono area east of Tel Aviv – the most fragmented part of the Tel Aviv metropolis – was outlined by a professional commission appointed by the Ministry of Interior. The need to reduce social polarization in the area through amalgamation, the establishment of a regional planning board and a multi-purpose municipal union, were particularly emphasized. The recommendations, however, were not implemented, since they were opposed by the planning administration of the Ministry of Interior itself, due to their anticipated negative impact on macro-spatial goals of population dispersal and preservation of agricultural land.

The Ono initiative was probably the last attempt to create a welfare state type reform (Razin, 1996). The report of the Zanbar Commission (State Commission on Local Government Issues, 1981) – the most comprehensive (failed) attempt to reform Israel's local government – did not include recommendations to alter the structure of local government in metropolitan areas.

Even modest attempts to change municipal boundaries in the Tel Aviv metropolitan areas faced immense difficulties, compared to other areas of the country, because of the substantial political power of local authorities in this region and because of the high land values, thus the high stakes involved. A boundary commission that dealt again with fragmented area around Qiryat Ono, proposed in 1990 a modest rationalization. In 1933, another commission proposed to amalgamate the cities of Lod and Ramla. The recommendations of neither commissions were implemented.

Municipal amalgamation was back on the agenda in 1995 when the government of Israel appointed a professional commission, headed by A. Shachar, to examine the feasibility of municipal amalgamations, in order to save resources and improve quality of services. The commission recommended several amalgamations within the Tel Aviv metropolitan area, the major one being a large-scale amalgamation of seven municipalities and portions of two additional municipalities in the Ono area (Ministry of Interior, 1998). Except for steps undertaken to amalgamate one tiny municipality of about 1,000 inhabitants, none of the recommendations were implemented. The rapid turnover in the Ministry of Interior during the 1990s further reduced prospects for implementation of such a report. The Minister appointing a commission could hardly be expected to be the Minister who received its recommendation, and this latter Minister could hardly be expected to remain in office long enough to reach a decision and to consistently followup on its implementation.

One should not overestimate the impact of municipal fragmentation on the functioning of the Tel Aviv metropolis. As Israel is a rather small and centralized country, central government ministries do aim to perform some of the coordination, service and development functions usually awarded metropolitan municipalities, although one can raise doubts on the effectiveness and responsiveness of this action.

The Police is fully controlled by the central government in Israel, and the government is deeply involved in domains such as education, public transportation, housing, welfare and housing (Sharkansky, 1997). Land use planning, transportation and regional infrastructure are coordinated to some extent by central government agencies. For example, during the 1990s the Planning Administration at the Ministry of Interior prepared development plans for each of Israel's metropolitan areas. A strategic metropolitan development plan for the Tel Aviv region was prepared for the Ministry of Interior in 1996–1997. As a non-statutory plan this document has limited influence, but it forms a basis for an updated statutory land use plan for the Tel Aviv district. The Tel Aviv and Central district plans approximately cover the Tel Aviv metropolitan area and serve as the basic tool of the Planning Administration of the Ministry of Interior to coordinate land use development in the metropolis.

Some inter-municipal cooperation does take place in parts of the Tel Aviv metropolis in the form of municipal unions. Most substantial is the Dan Municipal Union for Sewerage. Fifteen local authorities, including all large cities in the core and inner ring of the metropolitan area, are members of this union and additional ones use its services for a fee. Other municipal unions are involved with sewerage, environmental control, etc., but most are weak and all depend on member local authorities for their finance. In general, the Tel Aviv metropolitan area has been composed of politically and economically strong local authorities that cooperate only on rare occasions, sometimes when facing a common threat (such as the expansion of the Ben Gurion International Airport). More profound tensions evolved in recent years, particularly between large cities in the outer rings and adjacent rural regional councils. The latter compete rather successfully on commercial and industrial land uses, being able to offer lower land cost, lower local taxes and, for retail enterprises, an easier possibility to open their outlets on the Jewish Sabbath.

In sum, no welfare state metropolitan reform intended to promote coordination and equality has ever taken place in Tel Aviv. The globalization discourse, justifying metropolitan reform in the name of competitiveness in a global economy, did not have a significant influence in Tel Aviv either. Thus, the metropolitan area has retained its fragmented patterns, mitigated by central government action, and by the fact that most large cities in the metropolis, including the city of Tel Aviv, are still fiscally sound compared to small suburban and exurban municipalities. The city of Tel Aviv actually benefits from its small share in the metropolitan population. This small share enables this city to maintain a high ratio of business per residential land uses, despite the suburbanization of businesses, thus assuring so far its financial strength.

The Haifa metropolis – coordinated planning and development?
Metropolitan government has not been high on the agenda also in Haifa. An attempt to establish a meaningful multi-purpose municipal union for Haifa and its neighboring municipalities did not get much further than in the Tel Aviv area. The public discourse since then has focused on two issues:

1. Relations between the city of Haifa and its neighbors, particularly frequent complaints of adjacent municipalities on the political dominance of Haifa. Many of these complaints concerned the legacy of Aba Hushi – Haifa's powerful mayor during 1950–1969. It was claimed that Aba Hushi tended to develop and operate the metropolitan area for the benefit of Haifa. According to these claims, the large neighborhood of Qiryat Haim in the Haifa Bay area was annexed to Haifa in 1950 in order to strengthen the electoral power of the Labor Party in the city, and to assure that the large industrial zone located between Haifa and Qiryat Haim would be included within Haifa's jurisdictional area. Haifa also annexed substantial land from adjacent Nesher, much of it to develop the campuses of Haifa's two institutions of higher learning – The Technion (Israel Institute of Technology) and Haifa University. Consequently, tensions between Haifa and Nesher over municipal boundaries prevail to the present.

2. The debate over the wisdom in amalgamating the Haifa Bay municipalities (Qerayot). These localities form a continuous built up area on the low-lands of the bay to the north of Haifa and include the cities of Qiryat Motzkin, Qiryat Yam and Qiryat Bialik, as well as

Qiryat Haim, which is part of Haifa, and perhaps also the municipality of Qiryat Atta to the east.

A merger of Qiryat Motzkin, Qiryat Yam and Qiryat Bialik was suggested in the 1970s as a precondition for awarding the three local councils a city status. However, each of the three received city status separately in 1976. Only the land use planning function was merged through the establishment of a joint local planning committee that replaced the three separate planning committees. Whereas this planning committee has generally functioned satisfactorily since then, some argue that it has not particularly engaged in coordinating planning and development. Rather, the three municipalities tend to focus on matters within their jurisdictional areas and to avoid intervening in decisions that concern their neighbors.

Amalgamating the Haifa Bay cities was recommended again in 1998 by the municipal amalgamation commission (Ministry of Interior, 1998). This time, the proposed amalgamation included all four cities, including Qiryat Atta, but not the transfer of Qiryat Haim from Haifa to the amalgamated city. Proposed large-scale urban development on agricultural land between Qiryat Bialik and Qiryat Atta was regarded as a new rationale for this large-scale amalgamation that would have created a city eventually becoming larger than Haifa. The recommendations, however, were not implemented.

The outer ring of the Haifa metropolitan area is increasingly being integrated in the metropolis in functional terms. However, in terms of administration and regional identities it is regarded more as part of the Galilee, with its own unique problems, rather than as a region that requires metropolitan solutions in the context of the Haifa metropolitan area.

The Jerusalem region – a metropolitan solution to a binational metropolis?

Immediately following the 1967 war, Israel annexed an expanded area of East Jerusalem into the jurisdictional area of Jerusalem (and into the State of Israel), an area that practically included much of Jewish and Arab suburbanization in the following 15 years.

The public debate over the municipal structure of the Jerusalem metropolitan area mainly concerned annexation. Whereas the 1967 annexation of area from the formerly Jordanian controlled West Bank was a one-time affair, options for expansion toward the Judaean Mountains to the west have been periodically on the agenda. Requests of the city of Jerusalem to expand westward have usually been justified by the need to enhance the city's position as Israel's capital and to sustain a large Jewish majority within its municipal boundaries. These requests have been opposed by residents of suburbs and rural settlements (such as Mevasseret Ziyyon, Motza Illit and Ora) that were either included in Jerusalem's annexation requests, or were to become enclaves surrounded by the jurisdictional area of Jerusalem. The requests have also been opposed by the environmental lobby, whose interest was to protect the prime open space of the Judaean Mountains.

Proposals for the establishment of a metropolitan municipality or a loose metropolitan framework for cooperation were raised in the context of political solutions to the management of this binational metropolitan area. The whole notion of the Jerusalem metropolitan area has been sensitive, because delineation of its boundaries determines the ratio of Arab versus Jewish population, and could also be interpreted as a statement that concerns the future of Arab and Jewish localities (settlements) in the West Bank. Indeed, a metropolitan plan prepared for Jerusalem in 1993 was shelved without even being published.

A proposal to establish an upper-tier municipality for the Jerusalem metropolitan area (not including Palestinian localities) was outlined by Hasson (1997). This proposal emphasized the relations between the Israeli and the Palestinian parts of the metropolis, in the context of the Oslo peace process. Various alternatives outlined suggested Israeli and Palestinian upper-tier metropolitan municipalities that would work with some level of coordination. The major issue discussed was the relationship between the city of Jerusalem and Jewish suburban settlements in the West Bank. Alternatives referred to possible solutions for settling the Israeli-Palestinian conflict in Jerusalem and the management of the complex metropolitan area in the context of two separate states.

In 1998, the city of Jerusalem submitted to the Minister of Interior a request for large-scale annexation to its west. The request was to annex land through special legislation, bypassing the ordinary time-consuming procedure of a boundary commission. As usual, it provoked opposition of suburbs fearing either annexation or being engulfed by

Jerusalem, and of the environmental lobby fearing excessive urban development in the Judaean Mountains. In light of this opposition the city modified its request. It now included only open space, whereas existing suburbs only would be incorporated into an upper-tier metropolitan municipality.

The proposed metropolitan municipality was to become responsible for land use planning, economic development, regional infrastructure, transportation policy, tourism promotion, regional institutions, environmental quality and representation of the metropolitan area. It would have obtained functions transferred from the lower-tier local authorities and from district offices of central government ministries. The idea of an upper-tier municipality was adopted also by the strategic plan prepared by the city of Jerusalem (Jerusalem Municipality, 2003).

In 1999, the Minister of Interior appointed a boundary commission to examine Jerusalem's annexation request. The 2002 recommendations of this commission supported a large-scale expansion of Jerusalem's jurisdictional area. However, at the time of writing (October, 2004), the Minister of Interior has not decided whether to accept these recommendations. The proposals to establish some sort of an upper-tier metropolitan municipality did not trigger any serious debate or action. It seems that meaningful discussion of new forms of metropolitan governance will return to the agenda if and when the political issue of managing the Jerusalem region in the context of a two-state solution will be on the Israeli-Palestinian negotiation table.

Prospects for various forms of metropolitan government face obstacles associated with the dominance of the city of Jerusalem over it suburbs. Suburban local authorities fear that they will become subordinate to the interests and political power of the capital city. The legal impossibility to establish municipalities that include parts in both Israel and the West Bank, and the present control of the Jerusalem municipality by ultra-religious parties also reduce the feasibility of such a structure. The city of Jerusalem is characterized by complex problems associated with the relationships among its three major population groups: non-ultra-orthodox Jews [= liberal Jews], ultra-orthodox Jews, and Arabs. The two latter groups are also very weak economically. Annexations or the establishment of metropolitan government in which Jerusalem predominates could export the problems of Jerusalem to its suburbs.

Beer Sheva – regional government as a tool to consolidate political power in the periphery?

The whole notion of the Beer Sheva metropolitan area is rather recent. A non-statutory metropolitan plan for the region was first prepared for the Planning Administration of the Ministry of Interior in the mid-1990s. The Central Bureau of Statistics first attempted to define the metropolitan area in 2002. However, calls for the establishment of some form of regional government are not new to the Northern Negev, where Beer Sheva is located. Yehuda Gradus, of the Ben-Gurion University of the Negev, argued as early as the 1980s that regional government can serve as a tool to consolidate political power of this weak peripheral region. According to Gradus, the Negev lacks effective representation in the Knesset (Israel's legislature), because in an election method of proportional representation, members of Knesset represent national parties and are not accountable to a particular voting district. A regional government could be an alternative channel of forming effective political leadership that would lead regional development, mobilizing both internal and external resources.

Despite the ongoing calls for such a step, implementation has never been seriously considered. In the case of the Negev, it has not even been the political strength of mayors that blocked such an initiative. Mayors in this region have been much weaker than in the Tel Aviv metropolitan area, and regional government could have probably been imposed on them if the central government had the will to do so. Rather, a general lack of interest in regional government by the central government and the public is apparently the main explanation for the minimal impact of such proposals.

The establishment of upper-tier regional governments is unlikely in Israel. In the past, the government could have been expected to refrain from any step that clearly constitutes a new power base potentially challenging its authority. At present, neo-conservative ideologies that emphasize cost savings and trimming the public sector are the more marked barrier. Cost efficiencies associated with the realization of economies of scale in upper-tier regional governments are dubious, because of duplication of tasks and high fixed administrative costs of such entities. Jewish-Arab tensions could present another hurdle for the establishment of regional governments in Israel's peripheral regions where large Arab minorities reside.

Is small beautiful or costly?

Amalgamations have increasingly been on the local government reform agenda in the second half of the 1990s. The professional commission for the amalgamation of local authorities, appointed in 1995, submitted its recommendations in 1998 (Ministry of Interior, 1998). These did not include a metropolitan component, but, as mentioned before, two of the major proposed amalgamations were in the Tel Aviv metropolitan area (the Ono area) and the Haifa metropolitan area (the Qerayot of the Haifa Bay). As usual, implementation was minimal. Within metropolitan areas, the only step undertaken was the appointment of a boundary commission to examine the possibility to annex the tiny local council of Ramot HaShavim to an adjacent city or regional council. However, the rationale that supports reduction in the number of local authorities has gained momentum, despite strong opposition of stakeholders – elected politicians and employees of small local authorities – and protests that mainly emphasized the role of small local authorities in retaining local identities. The more meaningful step implemented in these years consisted of legislation initiated by the Ministry of Finance that determined a minimal size for the establishment of a new local authority (3,000 and later on 5,000 inhabitants). This step, combined with the increasingly negative attitude toward municipal fragmentation, has practically made it extremely difficult to establish new local authorities since 1998.

Israel's local government system is not as fragmented as frequently portrayed (Razin, 2004). In 2003 it included 266 local authorities, reduced to 252 through an amalgamation reform in 2004 and up again to 255 a few months later (Table 3), when one of the amalgamated local authorities was split again into its former parts. The problem of Israel's local government system thus does not necessarily stem from excessive municipal fragmentation, but from the lack of sufficient mechanisms that mitigate problems associated with fragmentation.

Table 3: Local authorities in Israel by type and population group, 1951–2004

		City	Local council	Regional council	Local industrial council	Total
1951	Total	20	64	42	0	126
	Jewish authorities	18	53	42	..	113
	Arab authorities	2	11	0	..	13
1961	Total	25	107	50	0	182
	Jewish authorities	23	78	50	..	151
	Arab authorities	2	29	0	..	31
1971	Total	29	117	48	0	194
	Jewish authorities	27	71	47	..	145
	Arab authorities	2	46	1	..	49
1981	Total	37	125	54	0	216
	Jewish (n.i. territories)	35	67	47	..	149
	Jewish – territories	0	5	6	..	11
	Arab authorities	2	53	1	..	56
1991	Total	47	140	54	2	243
	Jewish (n.i. territories)	41	64	45	..	150
	Jewish – territories	1	12	7	..	20
	Arab authorities	5	64	2	..	71
2001	Total	69	141	54	2	266
	Jewish (n.i. territories)	56	56	45	..	157
	Jewish – territories	3	14	7	..	24
	Arab authorities	10	71	2	..	83
1.2004	*Total*	*72*	*124*	*54*	*2*	*252*
(amalgamation	*Jewish (n.i. territories)*	*56*	*49*	*45*	*..*	*150*
Reform)	*Jewish - territories*	*3*	*14*	*7*	*..*	*24*
	Arab authorities	*13*	*61*	*2*	*..*	*76*
5.2004	*Total*	*71*	*128*	*54*	*2*	*255*
	Jewish (n.i. territories)	*56*	*49*	*45*	*..*	*150*
	Jewish - territories	*3*	*14*	*7*	*..*	*24*
	Arab authorities	*12*	*65*	*2*	*..*	*79*

Source: Central Bureau of Statistics.

Jewish local authorities – including mixed local authorities with a Jewish majority.

Despite growing average size, around 60% of Israel's local authorities still had less than 10,000 inhabitants in the 1990s (Table 4), arguably suffering from lack of economies of scale. Small local authorities were shown to constitute a burden on the central government's budget, characterized by high expenditures per capita that were compensated by large central government grants (Table 5). True, the city of Tel Aviv has been characterized by high expenditures per capita as well. However, this was a result of an exceptionally high concentration of business land uses that has enabled Tel Aviv to maintain a high level of expenditures per capita, much of these expenditures arguably serving the businesses themselves, as well as metropolitan functions performed in this central city of the metropolis.

Table 4: Israel – local authorities and population in local authorities by population size, 1951–1999 (in percentages)

Year	Up to 2,500 residents	Up to 10,000 residents[1]	Over 100,000 residents	total
% of local authorities				
1960	29.6	81.0	1.7	100
1961	29.1	80.8	1.6	100
1965	25.4	75.1	2.2	100
1970	22.9	72.4	2.1	100
1975	19.6	68.8	3.5	100
1980	18.1	65.7	3.8	100
1985	19.9	66.4	4.9	100
1986	21.1	66.2	4.8	100
1990	18.8	62.3	4.6	100
1993	15.5	59.8	4.8	100
1996	13.1	61.2	4.6	100
1998	11.0	57.8	4.6	100
1999	11.0	57.4	4.6	100
% of population in local authorities				
1961	3.4	25.5	35.2	100
1965	2.7	21.3	35.6	100
1970	1.9	18.3	34.5	100
1975	1.6	17.0	41.0	100
1980	1.3	15.3	41.4	100
1985	1.5	15.5	46.8	100
1986	1.7	15.5	46.6	100
1990	1.5	13.7	45.9	100
1993	1.1	12.7	45.9	100
1996	1.0	13.8	44.4	100
1998	0.8	13.0	43.8	100
1999	0.8	12.8	43.2	100

Source: Central Bureau of Statistics.

1. Including local authorities of up to 2,500 residents.

Table 5: Grants and expenditures per capita of local authorities in Israel by population size, 2000

Population size	No. of local authorities	General grant per capita	Total grants per capita, regular budget	Expenditures per capita, regular budget	Expenditures per capita, development budget
Up to 2,000	16	5.75	2.84	1.90	2.75
2,001–5,000	61	3.40	2.05	1.46	1.93
5,001–10,000	74	2.81	1.79	1.13	1.51
10,001–15,000	30	1.67	1.29	1.00	1.20
15,001–20,000	17	2.27	1.74	1.12	1.10
20,001–30,000	24	1.53	1.37	1.02	1.14
30,001–40,000	14	0.86	0.93	0.98	0.90
40,001–50,000	6	0.82	0.96	0.96	0.78
50,001–100,000	9	0.35	0.73	0.93	0.91
Over 100,000	12	0.23	0.64	0.95	0.79

Source: Based on data of: Ministry of Interior, Department of Local Government Auditing (2001) *Report Audited Financial Data, Local Authorities 2000*, Jerusalem.

The table includes unweighted means for each population size group. Indicators per capita: 1.00=the figure for all local authorities.

Crisis and the agenda for reform in the early 2000s

Crisis as a trigger for reform

Israeli local government, and perhaps Israel's public sector as a whole, has been characterized by exceptionally high barriers for reform (Razin, 2004). Apparently, close links between local and national politics in Israel have hampered reforms, which are easier to implement in countries such as Canada, where local politics have not been an arena in which national parties directly play. In a multiparty coalition government structure, such as in Israel, reforms are particularly risky, because they can lead to conflicts within the central government, and not only between the party in power and its opposition. Ethno-religious heterogeneity also formed a significant obstacle for the implementation of territorial reforms, and political decentralization and social fragmentation since the 1970s have made reforms even more difficult to implement. Instability of the Israeli government between 1984 and 2001 and prolonged battles in the High

Court of Justice over nearly every controversial central government action have formed impediments that reduced the propensity of broad steps of reform.

Israel plunged into deep recession in 2001–2003, associated with renewed Israeli-Palestinian violence, and exacerbated by a global economic downturn. Declining revenues have led to a financial crisis that compelled many local authorities to engage in survival strategies. In some cases, self-generated revenues have declined – particularly development fees and property taxes paid by businesses hard-hit by recession, such as in tourism related activities and in terror-stricken downtowns. However, the major problem was the large cuts in central transfers that had unprecedented impact on the local authorities that depend most on these grants: financially weak local authorities that are characterized by low socioeconomic status, small size and lack of businesses and facilities that pay non-residential property tax.

A crisis of local democracy has accompanied the financial crisis. Voter turnout declined to an unprecedented extent (about 40% on average) in the October 2003 local elections. Consequently, municipal councils have become fragmented to an unprecedented extent. Even in the city of Tel Aviv, the mayor's party received only 11.4% of the votes (4 out of 31 seats). The clear outcome of the low voter turnout was an often-disproportional representation of small and organized pressure groups. In extreme cases, nearly every elected member represented a different party, hence forming a stable coalition could prove expensive, and particularly difficult in a period of meager resources.

The crisis situation has created a window of opportunity for the implementation of reforms promoted unsuccessfully for years by the Ministry of Finance, overcoming what used to be considered as most formidable obstacles for reform. Promoting a public climate of severe crisis, in which local authorities were portrayed as bloated, inefficient and corrupt organizations, has been conducive for radical reforms.

Moreover, the January 2003 elections to the Knesset enabled the formation of Israel's most stable coalition government, perhaps since the 1970s. Thus, for more than a year, between early 2003 and mid-2004, the Ministry of Finance was rather free to pursue wide-scale changes in local government with the support of the Ministry of Interior and with little opposition from other government ministers. A stable majority in the Knesset also meant that members of Knesset representing particular stakeholders had minimal power to derail central government initiatives – a very different reality than that of the previous 20 years.

The direction of reform: following the neo-conservative path
Government policies in 2003–2004 largely followed lean government neo-conservative ideologies. These have emphasized downsizing the bloated and inefficient public sector, reducing public expenditures and subsidies associated with welfare state mechanisms, encouraging privatization and competition. The Minister of Finance – Benjamin Netanyahu – has been a strong supporter of American neo-conservatism, and his views have apparently been not far from those of the Ministry's bureaucracy. Nevertheless, given Israel's legacy of centralization, which is far from American political traditions, implementation seemed to have followed much more the Thatcherian legacy of privatization and reduction of the public sector. In line with this legacy, reform tended to be in the direction of renewed centralization in the name of efficiency, in which the powers to supervise privatized or semi-privatized local services are frequently awarded to central government agencies rather than to failed local governments. Local government is considered in these approaches as a part of the public sector that should be reduced and bypassed through privatization, rather than as a local actor that assumes responsibilities that the central government no longer wishes to perform.

The Ministry of Finance proceeded with several steps that concerned local government in 2003–2004. One step was a compulsory reduction in the cap on the number of paid deputy mayors. A second step was an unprecedented amalgamation of municipalities through legislation. Both steps were only partly implemented, due to political pressures, particularly of Likud Party local activists, on Likud members of Knesset. For a time it seemed that the anti-amalgamation lobby would fully succeed in the burial of a revised proposal for 34 amalgamations, based on the recommendations of special hearing commissions. However, intense last moment pressures of the Prime Minister's Office and the Minister of Finance, utilizing the atmosphere of crisis and urgent need for change, has led to the passage of a reduced amalgamation law in July 2003. This law included 12 amalgamations that concerned 27 municipalities, mainly small ones of several thousand inhabitants each, and an option to proceed with more amalgamations in the future. One of these amalgamations – of four Druze local authorities in the Galilee – was reversed in 2004, reducing the number of municipalities involved in the amalgamation initiative to 23 in 11 amalgamations.

Two additional, more fundamental, steps undertaken by Ministry of Finance included amendments to the local government laws passed concurrently with the approval of the 2004 budget, and a large cut in central government transfers to local authorities. Amendments attached to the 2004 budget proposal defined unprecedented steps towards recentralization. These authorize the Minister of Interior to appoint an external tax collector to local authorities that perform poorly, or to appoint an external controller who will practically be in charge of the municipality's finance, expropriating powers from the elected mayor. The amendments also grant extended powers to the Minister to terminate the term of mayors or dissolve councils of local authorities that suffer from financial mismanagement as defined by specific criteria. They also stipulate that the loyalty of representatives of local authorities in municipal unions and special municipal corporations (owned by the municipality) would be to the union and corporation, rather than to the local authority they represent. Such measures substantially reduce the political autonomy of local government, constrain the ability of mayors to allocate funds according to their priorities and increase the influence of the Ministers of Interior and Finance on local decisions.

The drastic cut in central government transfers could lead to the most profound change in local government finance in Israel since 1985. Following a local government strike in early 2004, the dramatic cuts were somewhat reduced. However, sums were not returned to the general grant allocated according to a rather transparent formula. Rather, they were diverted to recovery programs in which the Ministries of Interior and Finance have a wide room for discretion – steps can be imposed on local authorities that depend on these programs.

Implications for metropolitan governance
The substantial steps undertaken in 2003–2004 do not have a

metropolitan component. The usual metropolitan agenda, with its equity, sustainability, local economic growth and coordination components, has not been a priority. The focus on efficiency and cost-savings has not been linked to metropolitan solutions. A new level of government is certainly not in line with downsizing the public sector. The explicit instructions given by the Minister of Interior to the hearing committees engaged with the amalgamation proposals was to refer solely to cost savings and perhaps to good governance practices that lead to cost savings. Coordinated development and equity were not accepted as justifications for amalgamation. In fact, the Minister of Interior has rejected proposed amalgamations that bring together upper-middle class localities with much weaker municipalities, because the damage to the character and well-being of the former localities has been assumed to outweigh possible benefits to weaker municipalities.

Nonetheless, the changes described above could have profound implications for metropolitan governance in three major respects. The first concerns amalgamation of local authorities. Amalgamations concerned, so far, a few small and politically weak local authorities. Large-scale amalgamations were not implemented within metropolitan areas, but several exurban settlements were amalgamated in the Tel Aviv and Haifa metropolitan areas. Nevertheless, substantial pressure is being exerted on small middle-class local authorities that were not amalgamated in the first wave. These are not compensated anymore for lack of economies of scale by the equalization grant of the Ministry of Interior. Moreover, no recovery programs were approved in the first half of 2004 to local authorities of less than 4,000 inhabitants. This financial pressure exerted on small municipalities, if sustained long enough, could reduce prospects for further fragmentation in metropolitan fringe areas, making the municipal segregation of small exurban settlements less beneficial.

The second implication concerns widening fiscal disparities among local authorities within metropolitan areas, and even more between central metropolitan areas and peripheral regions. The large reduction in grants in 2003–2004 has widened dramatically the gap between local authorities that do not depend on central government grants, and those that depend on them because of insufficient non-residential tax base and low socioeconomic status. The former even benefited from steps such as a permission to increase the local property tax and an imposed reduction in the salaries of employees in the public service. The latter local authorities, on the other hand, have come to the verge of collapse.

This situation has brought equality issues back into the agenda. In 2004, the Ministry of Interior appointed a commission to examine possibilities for redistribution of non-residential property taxes through sharing at least some of this tax base. It is unclear if this step represents a genuine move to reduce fiscal disparities at the regional, metropolitan or national level, or whether it is basically a move to further erode local government revenues. In this latter scenario, a new pool of "surplus" resources of non-residential property tax, mainly coming from cities with high concentration of businesses such as Tel Aviv, would be used to ease the fiscal crisis of peripheral local authorities. However, by doing so, weakening the now fiscally sound cities, it would reduce pressures on the Ministry of Finance to roll back some of the cuts in the general equalization grant. Some also fear that such a step would lead to an erosion in the non-residential property tax rates, under pressures of the business sector. The step can also have a detrimental effect on the willingness of local authorities to approve plans for business land uses and to compete over the location of industries, retail centers and offices. Implementation of such tax base sharing mechanisms is uncertain, but the increased disparities can be expected to emerge on the metropolitan agenda much more than ever in Israel, as the central government practically ceases to take responsibility for the provision of local services of a certain level in each locality. In fact, a general strike in September 2004 compelled the government to transfer funds for salaries of employees of weak local authorities that had not paid their employees for months. Some retreat from the large cuts in the general grant is also likely.

A third implication concerns the possible evolution of privatized or semi-privatized organizations in charge of various local service and development functions. These include, for example, water and sewerage systems, joint industrial and business parks, and perhaps even regional education boards. Such a step could reduce the autonomy of local authorities, if these bodies are isolated from the local government budgets and from the direct control of the mayor and council; supervision largely given to central government ministries. Nevertheless, this process does present a potential for development of single-function metropolitan organizations, which has been very limited so far due to the limited willingness of local authorities to cooperate.

Conclusions

The review of the changing agenda for metropolitan reforms in Israel reveals the insubstantial influence of this agenda, particularly the weak case for upper-tier metropolitan government in the Israeli context. United States-type metropolitan problems – fiscal crisis of central cities and central city-suburbs disparities – are not issues that produce pressures for reform in Israel. Partisan-electoral considerations are also not a significant factor in debates over local government reform in Israel's metropolitan areas. Improved competitiveness in a global economy – a common theme in the agenda for metropolitan reform in advanced economies – has generally been absent from the Israeli discourse as well, perhaps because the entire State of Israel has been perceived as the relevant geographical scale for competition in the world economy.

The more powerful motive for reform in the early 2000s was cost efficiencies. Steps aimed at cost savings, backed by neo-conservative ideologies that perceive the public sector as bloated, inefficient, frequently corrupt and an impediment to economic growth, are only indirectly associated with a metropolitan agenda – amalgamations and greater inter-municipal cooperation being among the expected responses to pressures to reduce costs. Whereas government officials and economic commentators in the media have tended to emphasize the cost-saving potential in extensive amalgamations, local governments and some specialists have tended to emphasize the potential of improved mechanisms of metropolitan governance. These include extensive inter-municipal cooperation, partnerships of local governments, NGOs, the private sector and privatization.

The immediate impact of cost-cutting steps consisted, however, of widening fiscal disparities among local authorities. The growing disparities, particularly unprecedented crises in many peripheral local authorities have to some extent led to the reemergence of equality issues on the local government reform agenda.

In sum, promoting reform in metropolitan governance in Israel indeed seems to be a Sisyphean task. Issues of efficiency, effectiveness in service provision, coordination and equality have been raised periodically for nearly half a century as justification for reforms that either consist of the establishment of metropolitan governments, annexations and amalgamation or improved inter-jurisdictional cooperation mechanisms. Problems identified and proposed solutions remain fundamentally the same, and lack of implementation is also a rather permanent feature. The unprecedented steps taken in the early 2000s were triggered by a neo-conservative cost-cutting agenda that lacked a clear vision on future local and metropolitan governance. Thus, the gap between the local/metropolitan reform discourse and actual practice has remained as wide as ever.

However, one can argue that the lack of radical structural reform is not the real impediment to metropolitan governance in Israel. The fundamental issues concern deficiencies in governance culture at both the local and central government levels. Incremental changes of amalgamating small municipalities, promoting inter-municipal cooperation and establishing single-purpose local government units could be conducive in improving governance practices in some cases. However, the fundamental improvement needed may not be linked substantially to metropolitan solutions.

References

Gonen, A. (1995). *Between City and Suburb, Urban Residential Patterns and Processes in Israel*. Aldershot: Avebury.

Hasson, S. (1997). *The Municipal Organization of the Jerusalem Metropolitan Area: Conceptual Alternatives*. Jerusalem: The Jerusalem Institute for Israel Studies (Hebrew).

Israeli Institute for Urban Research and Information (1973). *Municipal Reform for the Gush Dan Cities*. Submitted to the Minister of Interior. Ramat Gan (Hebrew).

Jerusalem Municipality, Division of Research and Strategic Planning (2003). *Strategic Master Plan for Jerusalem in 2020, The Spatial-Municipal Dimension*. Jerusalem (Hebrew).

Ministry of Interior (Israel) (1998). *The Commission for the Amalgamation of Local Authorities, Final Report*. Jerusalem (Hebrew).

Razin, E. (1996). Municipal reform in the Tel Aviv metropolis: metropolitan government or metropolitan cooperation? *Environment and Planning C: Government and Policy* 14, 39–54.

Razin, E. (2004). Needs and impediments for local government reform: lessons from Israel. *Journal of Urban Affairs* 26, 623–640.

Sharkansky, I. (1997). Israel: Ametropolitan nation-state. *Cities, 14*, 363–369.

State Commission on Local Government Issues (1981). *Local Government in Israel – a Report*. Jerusalem.

Notes on Contributors

Caroline Andrew
Professor of Political Science in the School of Political Studies and past Dean, Faculty of Social Sciences at the University of Ottawa. Her research areas are municipal politics, urban development, women in local politics, social policy (municipal) and intergovernmental relations. Recent publications include *Urban Affairs: Back on the Policy Agenda*, co-edited with Katherine Graham and Susan Phillips. She is currently involved in the City for All Women Initiative, a participatory action research project with community-based women's groups and the City of Ottawa.
E-Mail Address: *candrew@uottawa.ca*

Anne Golden
Anne Golden became President and Chief Executive Officer of the Conference Board of Canada, Canada's premier applied research organization, in October 2001. Before joining the Conference Board, she served as President of the United Way of Greater Toronto for 14 years. Under her stewardship, the United Way was the country's largest annual local fundraiser and the largest non-governmental distributor of funds to the social services. Dr. Golden has received national recognition for her role in the public policy arena, especially for her work on homelessness. She Chaired the Greater Toronto Area Task Force, producing its Report for the Province of Ontario in 1996. In 1998, Toronto Mayor Mel Lastman appointed her to chair the Homelessness Action Task Force. Holder of a doctorate in history, Dr. Golden undertook her postgraduate studies at Columbia University, New York and the University of Toronto. She has taught at Newark College of Engineering, the University of Toronto and York University.
E-Mail Address: *golden@conferenceboard.ca*

Pierre Hamel
Professor of Sociology at the Université de Montréal. He has written extensively on social movements, urban politics and local democracy.

He is the author of *Action collective et démocratie locale* and has also co-edited several books, including two on social movements, *Urban Movements in a Globalising World* (2000) and *Globalization and Social Movements* (2001). He is currently completing a research project on Montreal's metropolitan governance.

E-Mail Address: *pierre.hamel@umontreal.ca*

Jung-Ho Kim

Professor at the Department of Public Administration, Sangju University, South Korea. Professor Kim has done research on comparative metropolitan government in North American and Asia, including during a sabbatical year at IGS, Simon Fraser University. He currently serves as Editor of *Korean Local Government Review*, the journal of the National Association of Korean Local Government Studies.

E-Mail Address: *jjhkim@sangju.ac.kr*

Christopher Leo

Professor, Department of Politics, University of Winnipeg and adjunct professor, Department of City Planning, University of Manitoba. He has been researching, teaching and writing about urban political and administrative problems for more than 20 years while holding faculty appointments at Queen's University, the University of Winnipeg and the University of Manitoba. His current research focuses on the politics of urban growth and urban development, as well as urban governance and the challenges facing cities in an era of global competition and a weakening national social safety net. He has done case studies of Winnipeg, Edmonton, Toronto, Vancouver and Portland, Oregon, as well as other research. He is the author of numerous articles and books, including *Land and Class in Kenya* and *The Politics of Urban Development*

E-Mail Address: *christopher.leo@shaw.ca*

H. Peter Oberlander, OC

Professor Emeritus and Founding Director, School of Community & Regional Planning, University of British Columbia; Adjunct Professor, Dept of Political Science / Senior Research Fellow, Institute of Governance Studies, Simon Fraser University. Dr. Oberlander was

Former Deputy Minister, Ministry of State for Urban Affairs, Government of Canada and First Exchange Professor in the Canadian Studies Program, Faculty of Social Sciences, the Hebrew University, Jerusalem (1979/80). He is author/editor of numerous publications, serves as senior organizer for the World Urban Forum in Vancouver, 2006, and has been named a Member (CM) and then Officer of the Order of Canada (OC) (for urban affairs).
E-Mail Address: *oberland@interchange.ubc.ca*

Mark Piel
Winner of the Institute of Public Administration of Canada, Manitoba Branch Undergraduate Essay Award, 1999-2000, he has authored/co-authored research at the Institute of Urban Studies, University of Winnipeg, the Canadian Political Science Association and in books such as *Municipal Reform in Canada* (with Chris Leo). He has completed an MA in Political Science at the University of Toronto and is currently studying law at Osgoode Hall Law School, Toronto.
E-Mail Address: *markpiel@hotmail.com*

Eran Razin
Associate Professor, Department of Geography, Director of the Institute of Urban and Regional Studies, the Hebrew University of Jerusalem. Specializes in local government and urban development research and policy. Recent studies on comparative local government, local government reforms, municipal boundary conflicts and local government finance were published in *Urban Studies, Space and Polity, Environment and Planning C, Urban Affairs Review, Political Geography, Geografiska Annaler, Journal of Urban Affairs.* He was one of the scientific coordinators in a European Commission – City of Tomorrow, 5th framework research project on spatial deconcentration of economic land use and quality of life in European metropolitan areas. He participates in the International Metropolitan Observatory group on comparative metropolitan politics.
E-Mail Address: *msrazin@mscc.huji.ac.il*

Hank Savitch
Brown and Williamson Distinguished Research Professor, School of Urban and Public Affairs, University of Louisville. Professor Savitch

has published nine books and more than 40 articles on various aspects of urban affairs, national urban policy and comparative urban development. Books include *Post Industrial Cities*, *Big Cities in Transition* (co-edited with John Thomas), *Regional Politics: America In A Post-City Age* (co-edited with Ron Vogel) and (with Paul Kantor), *Cities in the International Marketplace* (Princeton University Press)
E-Mail Address: *hvsavi01@louisville.edu* or *hank.savitch@louisville.edu*

Enid Slack
President, Enid Slack Consulting Inc.Toronto, since 1981. Dr. Slack is an economic consultant specializing in municipal, education, and intergovernmental finance. She received her PhD in economics from the University of Toronto and teaches a graduate course in urban public finance at U of T. Ms. Slack has served as Special Advisor to the Greater Toronto Area Task Force in 1995, a member of the Who Does What Panel in Ontario in 1996, was Co-Chair of the Learning Opportunities Grant Panel for the Ontario Minister of Education and Training in 1997, and Special Advisor to the Mayor's Task Force on Homelessness in 1998. She was a member of the City of Toronto's Business Reference Group on tax policy in 1999 and chairs the Intergovernmental Committee on Economic and Labour Force Development in Toronto (ICE Committee). Her clients in Canada and abroad include municipal, provincial, territorial and federal governments, government commissions, school boards, and private companies. Ms. Slack has co-authored three books on property taxes and urban public finance including *Urban Public Finance In Canada* (with R.M. Bird) and has published numerous articles on local government finance.

Patrick J. Smith
Professor, Department of Political Science and Director, Institute of Governance Studies, Simon Fraser University. He did his PhD in Government at the London School of Economics and has taught at the Open University (UK), University of Victoria, Acadia University, and Dalhousie University and since 1982 at SFU. He is the author/editor of *The Vision and the Game: Making the Canadian Constitution* (with L. Cohen and P. Warwick), *The Almanac of Canadian Politics*, (1991 and

1995) (with M. Eagles, J. Bickerton and A. Gagnon), *Ties That Bind: Voters and parties in Canada, (with J. Bickerton and A.Gagnon), Continuities and Discontinuities: The Political Economy of Social Welfare and Labour Market Policy in Canada (with A. Johnson and S. McBride and Urban Solutions to Global Problems: Vancouver-Canada-Habitat II* (with H.P. Oberlander and T. Hutton), as well as numerous articles/chapters in publications such as the *Canadian Journal of Political Science, Canadian Journal of Urban Research, International Political Science Review, Planning and Administration, BC Studies, International Journal of Canadian Studies* and *Policy Options.*

E-Mail Address: *psmith@sfu.ca*

Kennedy Stewart

Assistant Professor at Simon Fraser University's Graduate Public Policy Program. Kennedy completed his PhD in Government at the London School of Economics in 2003 and has taught at five University of London Colleges, including a term as Director of the Master's Degree in Public Policy and Public Management at Birkbeck College. Research interests include democracy, democratic theory, electoral and non-electoral public participation, electoral systems, urban governance and world cities. He has published in journals such as *The Canadian Journal of Urban Research, Korean Local Government Review*, and *State of the Federation*; written *Think Democracy,* completed government research reports and contributed to edited volumes such as *Municipal Reforms in Canada* (Oxford University Press) and *Policy Analysis in Canada: The State of the Art* (University of Toronto Press).

E-Mail Address: *kennedys@sfu.ca.*

Ronald K. Vogel

Professor of Political Science and Urban & Public Affairs and Director of the PhD Program in Urban and Public Affairs at the University of Louisville. His research focuses on metropolitan governance. Among his publications are *Political Change in the Metropolis* (seventh edition, 2003, with John J. Harrigan), *Handbook of Research on Urban Politics and Policy in the United States* (editor, 1997), *Regional Politics: America in a Post-City Age* (1996, co-editor with H.V. Savitch), and *Urban Political Economy* (1992). His articles have appeared in *Urban Affairs Review, the Journal of Urban Affairs, Publius,* and *State and Local Government Review.* He is currently working on a comparative study of metropolitan reforms and decentralization in Toronto and Tokyo. He co-directs a National Science Foundation Research Experiences for Undergraduates project analyzing the recent consolidation of Louisville and Jefferson County, Kentucky. He also heads the new Comparative Urban Politics related group in the American Political Science Association and serves on the advisory board of the "Multi-level Governance and Public Policy in Canadian Municipalities" project.

E-Mail Address: *ron.vogel@louisville.edu*